CW00516473

METRIC PATTERN CUTTING FOR CHILDREN'S WEAR

From 2–14 years

WINIFRED ALDRICH

COLLINS
8 Grafton Street, London W1

Collins Professional and Technical Books
William Collins Sons & Co. Ltd
8 Grafton Street, London W1X 3LA

First published in Great Britain by
Collins Professional and Technical Books 1985
Reprinted 1986, 1987

Distributed in the United States of America
by Sheridan House, Inc.

British Library Cataloguing in Publication Data
Aldrich, Winifred
Metric pattern cutting for children's wear.
1. Children's clothing—Pattern design
I. Title
646.4′072 TT640

ISBN 0–00–383115–9

Typesetting and origination by
CG Graphic Services, Aylesbury, Bucks
Printed and bound in Great Britain by
R. J. Acford, Chichester

Other books by the author

METRIC PATTERN CUTTING
A book on pattern cutting for women's wear

METRIC PATTERN CUTTING FOR MENSWEAR

CONTENTS

INTRODUCTION

In 1982 when I began to plan this book no recognised size chart was available on which one could base a system of pattern cutting for children's wear. The size chart offered by the British Standards Institution had been withdrawn because it was considered to be out of date and they did not expect to be able to offer a new one for at least two years. It was apparent that a book on pattern cutting for children's wear was required by schools and colleges, therefore I decided to begin a research project to measure children between two years and fourteen years.

A field study was undertaken, the measurements collected provided the necessary data required to produce size charts and to construct blocks. A total of 1,783 boys and girls were measured, account was taken of any differences which could have affected the study, for example, geographical areas, social class and ethnic grouping. The study was constructed to ensure that the children measured reflected the spread of children in the general population.

The results of the study were analysed and size charts were prepared based on the centilong system; the blocks constructed from the charts will fit a large proportion of children in each height interval.

It is hoped that the book will be useful to students who wish to specialise in the manufacture of children's wear and that it will encourage more students to become interested in this field of design. There is an increasing demand for original designs which recognise the shape of a child's body at a particular age and the practical demands of a child's life style. Many mothers now wish to design and make clothes for their children and these garments can be original yet inexpensive. The blocks can be used to draft designs for individual children; this is particularly useful when making patterns for children who are not standard size.

Many schools are encouraging their students to design their own patterns and a section on the developing figure has been included to assist teachers in senior schools in providing the correct blocks for the teen-age figure.

I hope that this book will contribute to the increasing interest in children's wear design.

Winifred Aldrich

Acknowledgements

I would like to thank:

Alec Aldrich for his assistance with the technical drawings;

Ann Rodgers for her constructive analysis of the book and her experimental work with the blocks with the students at Loughborough College of Art and Design;

Howard Long for his work on the computer which was required to analyse the statistical data;

Richard Miles the Editorial Director for his professional advice and his production of this book;

the National Children's Wear Association of Great Britain and Northern Ireland for their interest and advice;

the British Standards Institution for their information on size designation of children's wear. Material based on BS 3728:1982 is reproduced by permission of the British Standards Institution, 2 Park Street, London W1A 2BS, from whom complete copies of the document can be obtained.

I would also like to thank the staff of the play groups and schools listed below and the parents for consenting to the measurement of their children. Without their interest and co-operation I could not have written this book.

Quorn Nursery Group;
Dearnley Play Group;
Smithy Bridge Play Group;
Shelthorpe Play Group;
Woodhouse Eaves Baptist Play Group;
Loughborough Baptist Play Group;
St Paul's C. of E. School, Woodhouse Eaves;
New Parks House Primary School, Leicester;
New Parks House Junior School, Leicester;
Glenfield Hall County Junior and Infant School;
Hathern C. of E. Primary School;
Danemill County Primary School, Enderby;
New Parks Senior School, Leicester;
The Martin High School, Anstey;
Stonehill High School and Community College, Birstall;
The Bosworth College, Desford.

DESIGN FOR CHILDREN'S WEAR

Because children's wear is a neglected field of design in Britain, there are opportunities for students who have flair and imagination and who understand the problems which are integral to the design and production of children's wear.

French and Italian designers have a high reputation in this field. However they have been supported by a strong home market and continental parents have been willing to pay more than British parents for their children's clothes; the latter have not viewed children's wear in terms of fashion or design. This factor is beginning to change and a new generation of parents and children is more aware of design and is generating a demand for children's wear that has quality and style.

The over-riding problem is how to produce this type of product without the costs becoming unrealistic. Children's garments appear to be expensive in relation to adults' garments, but a child's dress can take longer to make up than an adult's (the intricate parts require more handling during the making-up process). A child's every-day garment has to be made up in a fabric that will stand up to punishing wear and repeated launderings; the seams have to be strong and the trimmings and fastenings secure. The large chain stores demand high standards from their suppliers and these standards add to costs. British manufacturers have to make goods which compete with imports from developing countries where labour costs are low. They are responding to the challenge and are investing in new technology to reduce costs. This new technology requires a high initial investment, particularly for small companies, which means that the new machinery has to be fully utilised; designers have to be aware of all its potential as well as its limitations. Many manufacturers now include designers in their production and development meetings as they recognise that designers have to become part of the production team. The size of the company and the market they are selling to will affect the limits within which a designer has to work; a designer is an artist working within a discipline imposed by outside factors. This need not be inhibiting as working within set limits can generate original and experimental techniques which are also cost effective.

Any student wishing to design clothes for children must be aware of the changing shape of the child as it grows and the changing proportions of different parts of its body. Garments which flatter a four-year-old with a tummy bulge will look immature on a 'leggy eight-year-old'. The proportions and lengths of children's garments are crucial. Students should study children of different ages, they should experiment with shapes that are innovative but practical and use techniques that allow for the child's growth. This requires a sound knowledge of pattern cutting and the techniques of making up. Many British designers have remained conventional in their cut of children's clothes. Continental designers however have been developing attractive new shapes with interesting design detail based on the kimono block and new trouser shapes. These garments are easy to make up in mass production and are therefore cost effective.

The designer must also understand the life style of children at different ages. Young children share the general life style of their parents which has become more relaxed, less formal, and often includes an active interest in sports, this has increased the demand for children's casual clothes. While a girl may have a 'best dress', most of a child's every-day clothes have to cover a range of activities. There remains a demand for school uniforms and school-type garments and also a small but steady demand for traditional tailored clothes, however, manufacturers are finding it increasingly difficult to produce them at competitive prices.

The most difficult market to design for is the sub-teen group. Boys' attitudes are rigid; they wish to be part of a group and not stand out from the crowd. Fashions often start at street level with simple ideas that are exploited and manufacturers have to respond quickly; for example, jeans, shirts and sweaters will not be bought in a season unless they display a badge decoration. These fashions often disappear as quickly as they appear and can leave unwanted stocks in shops and manufacturers' stock rooms. Girls in this age group are becoming fashion-conscious yet their figures are not mature enough to carry adult styles and many boutique owners can recount stories of sales lost through arguments between mothers and daughters. Some British manufacturers are gaining success in this area. They are paying attention to current fashion colours and fabric texture and they are also recognising the general shape of current fashion but they are modifying it to fit the immature figure and give the garment independent style. Adult fashion does have some influence on children's wear design, for example, the success of co-ordinated fashion ranges in some of the new fashion groups has been recognised by the chain stores who are now trying to develop more co-ordinated ranges in their children's wear departments.

Children's wear offers special opportunities to designers to experiment with colour, decoration and design detail. Buyers state that the continental competition offers two advantages; first, they have 'hanger appeal' and secondly their delivery is very reliable. They state that the colours and the imaginative detail on continental clothes seduce grandparents, who buy a large proportion of children's wear, and parents into paying higher prices when they see them hanging next to garments in basic colours and of traditional cut. Manufacturers are becoming aware of the importance of design, the need to deliver goods on time and to keep a consistent quality. The designer can make an important contribution to a firm's efficiency; the speed at which he/she is able to respond to market changes and to adapt ranges to tight schedules will affect the company's ability to compete in this difficult but rewarding field of design.

The Growth of Children and Adolescents

Designers of children's clothes should be aware of the way that a child's body shape changes as it grows and they should also be able to recognise the shape of a child at a particular stage. Well designed children's clothes take account of the child's continually changing shape.

GENERAL FEATURES

The speed at which a child grows decreases steadily from birth onwards until puberty when the rate of growth accelerates (this acceleration is known as the 'adolescent spurt' or 'growth spurt'). Until the growth spurt occurs there appears to be little difference between boys and girls in the speed at which they grow.

The decrease in the rate of growth varies from approximately 8cm per year at three years to 5cm per year at ten years. Manufacturers have decided to accept a 6cm height interval as a base for a coding scheme, as this approximates to the average growth per year over this period. However it must be noted that the range of heights in children in any particular age group is larger than the amount of growth that occurs in any one year, therefore a child's age is only a very crude guide or 'designation' of his/her expected stature. It is better to link other body measurements, to height rather than age, and one must recognise that age on clothing labels is only a secondary description. During puberty, age ceases to have even a descriptive value as variations in height linked to heredity are further distorted by the variability of the onset of puberty and the growth spurt.

In early childhood there is little difference between the sexes. Significant differences begin to appear at about seven which means that by this age it is necessary to offer a size chart for each sex. Puberty brings dramatic differences between boys and girls, the onset of puberty occurring eighteen months to two years earlier in the girl.

Children of the same height can have variable arm and leg measurements and these differences become more apparent as the limb length increases.

Children in the North of England, Scotland and Northern Ireland have been found to be slightly smaller than average. This may be due in part to the greater numbers of working-class children in these areas. Significant differences can be found between children of classes 1 and 2 (managerial and professional occupations) and classes 4 and 5 (semi-skilled and unskilled occupations). Children from classes 1 and 2 appear to be taller (2cm–5cm) but not heavier than classes 4 and 5.

CHILDREN FROM BIRTH TO AGE SEVEN

The most apparent characteristic of a small child's shape is the size of its head; by the age of three the child's head has almost completed its growth. A small child has a head one fifth of its height while the adult's head is only one eighth. The head size of a child must be taken into account when designing openings on the bodice for the head to pass through.

From about the age of two, the average child loses fat until about the age of eight. This 'slimming down' process is very apparent and it is generally spoken of in terms of the child 'losing his baby fat'.

Boys are often a little thinner than girls at this stage, but as the differences in measurements are small, a common size chart can be used. The most significant difference occurs on the hip/seat measurement and some manufacturers of boys' wear take account of this.

Toddlers have very little waist shaping and their stance gives them a hollow back and protruding stomach. These features decrease as the child grows and loses fat.

CHILDREN FROM AGE EIGHT TO PUBERTY

By the age of eight the posture of the child has straightened. From eight years to puberty the average child has a greater relative increase in body girth to height. Despite this increase, a girl's waist develops more shape. At this period the legs of children of both sexes grow faster than the trunk.

Although the speed at which a boy and a girl grows is similar until puberty, the average girl is slightly shorter than the average boy and slightly heavier. During this period, figure differences become more apparent, the most significant being the wider shoulders of the boy and the smaller waist and larger hips of the girl (the latter features are increasingly apparent as the girl enters puberty earlier than the boy).

BOYS AND PUBERTY

The average boy starts his growth spurt at about the age of thirteen and grows rapidly until the age of fifteen, then more slowly until he is seventeen, but as the timing of the spurt varies, height and age have little correlation at this time. Age, therefore has little relevance on size charts at this stage. Boys often become thinner during this growth spurt but they begin to gain muscle.

Before puberty, leg length grows faster than trunk length, but during the period of peak growth the trunk grows faster than the limbs, the rate of growth of the shoulders is at a maximum and the rate of growth of the head accelerates slightly. Boys have two more years of growth than girls and therefore attain a greater final height.

GIRLS AND PUBERTY

Girls begin to grow quickly at about the age of eleven or twelve; however their growth spurt is shorter in duration than that of boys and proceeds at a slower rate. Because girls enter puberty earlier, a proportion of eleven to thirteen-year-old girls are taller than boys of the same age. Girls continue to get fatter during their growth spurt, but this is in the trunk rather than the limbs and a girl's hip size shows a particular increase.

The bust development of a girl is the most dramatic change in her shape. The early stages of development result in little bust prominence and it is only when the bust begins to develop a structural shape that a girl will require to have blocks which have bust darts. The age at which these different development stages of maturity are reached can differ widely, which means that children between ten and fourteen of similar height and weight can have very different bust measurements. Girls who have developing figures require a specific size chart and block construction as children's blocks are inadequate and women's blocks are too mature.

At this stage in a girl's development the relationship between height and age is now too variable to be recorded as yearly increments.

1 THE BASIC PRINCIPLES

Tools and Equipment for Making Patterns

A student should aim to acquire a good set of equipment. However, some items are very expensive. The items marked with an asterisk denote those that are not essential immediately.

Working surface A flat working surface is required. However, a tracing wheel will mark any polished or laminated top, therefore some protection must be given to this type of surface.

Paper Strong brown paper or white pattern paper is used for patterns. Parchment or thin card should be used for blocks that are used frequently.

Pencils Use hard pencils for drafting patterns (2H). Coloured pencils are useful for outlining complicated areas.

Fibre pens These are required for writing clear instructions on patterns.

Rubber

Metric ruler and metre stick

Curved rules These are used for drawing long curves.

Metric tape measure

Set square A large set square with a 45° angle is very useful; metric grading squares can be obtained.

Compass The compass is used for constructing patterns which are based on a circle.

Tracing wheel

Shears Use separate shears for cutting cloth and paper as cutting paper will blunt the blades.

Sellotape

Pins

One-quarter and one-fifth scale squares These are essential for students to record pattern blocks and adaptations in their notebooks.

Stanley knife

Tailors chalk This is used for marking out the final pattern onto the cloth and for marking alterations on the garment when it is being fitted.

Toile fabrics Calico is used for making toiles for designs in woven fabrics. Make sure the weight of the calico is as close to the weight of the cloth as possible. Knitted fabric must be used for making toiles for designs in jersey fabrics; the toile fabric should have the same stretch quality.

**Calculator* The calculator is now a common tool in all areas of skill as it eliminates the hard work of calculating proportions and it is accurate. If a calculator is not available use the table of aliquot parts on page 11.

**French curves* Plastic shapes and curves are available in a range of sizes and they are useful for drawing good curves. A flexicurve which allows a shape to be manipulated is also available.

**Pattern notcher* This is a tool which marks balance points by snipping out a section of pattern paper.

**Pattern punch*

**Pattern hooks*

**Pattern weights* These keep pieces of pattern in position on the paper or cloth.

**Model Stands* Although not essential for a beginner, they are invaluable to the serious student for developing designs.

The equipment can be obtained at:
R. D. Franks Ltd, Kent House, Market Place, London W1N 8EJ.
E. Alexander & Co. (International) Ltd, Unit 9, Central Park Estate, Trafford Park, Manchester M17 1PG.
Morplan, 56 Great Tichfield Street, London W1P 8DX.

Aliquot Parts

If a calculator is not available for working out fractional parts, the following table can be used.

(Figures in columns marked with an asterisk are calculated to one decimal place.)

CHEST, WAIST AND HIP SEAT (cm)

	*1/16	*1/12	*1/6	1/4	1/2
52	3.3	4.3	8.7	13	26
53	3.3	4.4	8.8	13.25	26.5
54	3.4	4.5	9	13.5	27
55	3.4	4.6	9.2	13.75	27.5
56	3.5	4.7	9.3	14	28
57	3.6	4.8	9.5	14.25	28.5
58	3.6	4.8	9.7	14.5	29
59	3.7	4.9	9.8	14.75	29.5
60	3.8	5	10	15	30
61	3.8	5.1	10.2	15.25	30.5
62	3.9	5.2	10.3	15.5	31
63	3.9	5.3	10.5	15.75	31.5
64	4	5.3	10.7	16	32
65	4.1	5.4	10.8	16.25	32.5
66	4.1	5.5	11	16.5	33
67	4.2	5.6	11.2	16.75	33.5
68	4.3	5.7	11.3	17	34
69	4.3	5.8	11.5	17.25	34.5
70	4.4	5.8	11.7	17.5	35
71	4.4	5.9	11.8	17.75	35.5
72	4.5	6	12	18	36
73	4.6	6.1	12.2	18.25	36.5
74	4.6	6.2	12.3	18.5	37
75	4.7	6.3	12.5	18.75	37.5
76	4.8	6.3	12.7	19	38
77	4.8	6.4	12.8	19.25	38.5
78	4.9	6.5	13	19.5	39
79	4.9	6.6	13.2	19.75	39.5
80	5	6.7	13.3	20	40
81	5.1	6.8	13.5	20.25	40.5
82	5.1	6.8	13.7	20.5	41
83	5.2	6.9	13.8	20.75	41.5
84	5.3	7	14	21	42
85	5.3	7.1	14.2	21.25	42.5
86	5.4	7.2	14.3	21.5	43
87	5.4	7.3	14.5	21.75	43.5
88	5.5	7.3	14.7	22	44
89	5.6	7.4	14.8	22.25	44.5
90	5.6	7.5	15	22.5	45
91	5.7	7.6	15.2	22.75	45.5
92	5.8	7.7	15.3	23	46
93	5.8	7.8	15.5	23.25	46.5

NECK SIZE (cm)

	*1/8	*1/5
26.4	3.3	5.3
27	3.4	5.4
27.6	3.5	5.5
28.2	3.5	5.6
28.8	3.6	5.8
29.4	3.7	5.9
30	3.8	6
31	3.9	6.2
32	4	6.4
33	4.1	6.6
34	4.3	6.8
35	4.4	7
36	4.5	7.2
37	4.6	7.4

Methods of Measuring Body Dimensions

Body measurements are taken over light underclothes with the child barefoot. The natural waistline should be identified with a piece of tape or elastic.

A: Height The child's height and other vertical measurements are taken with the child standing erect with the feet together. The height measurement is taken from the head crown to the soles of the feet.
B: Chest/bust The maximum girth measurement under the armpits with the tape passing over the shoulder blades and across the chest or bust.
C: Waist The measurement of the natural waist girth measurement with the child's abdomen relaxed.
C′: Low waist The measurement taken 3–4cm below the natural waistline (used for jeans and low waisted trousers).
D: Hip/seat The horizontal measurement taken round the fullest part of the seat.
E: Across back The measurement taken across the back from armscye to armscye mid-way between the cervical and the base of the armscye.
F: Neck size The girth measured around the base of the neck touching the cervical and the top of the front collar bone.
G–H: Shoulder The measurement taken from the base of the side neck to the shoulder edge.
I: Upper arm The girth measured around the upper arm mid-way between the shoulder and the elbow. The measurement is taken with the arm bent.
J: Wrist The girth measured at the base of the arm over the wrist bone.
K–L: Scye depth The measurement from the cervical to a line which touches the base of the armscye (armscye line).
K–M: Neck to waist The measurement taken from the cervical to the waistline.
M–N: Waist to hip The measurement taken from the waistline to the hip/seat line.
K–O: Cervical height The measurement taken from the cervical to the soles of the feet.
M–P: Waist to knee The measurement taken from the centre back waistline to the crease at the back of the knee.
Q–R: Body rise The measurement is taken on a seated figure from the side waistline to the top of the stool. This measurement can also be calculated by measuring M–O (waist height) and subtracting S–O (inside leg) from M–O.
S–O: Inside leg The measurement taken from the crutch to the soles of the feet.
H–T: Sleeve length The measurement from the shoulder edge to the wrist bone.
U: Head circumference The horizontal girth of the head.
V: Vertical trunk The measurement taken from the centre of one shoulder, down the back, under the crutch returning over the abdomen and chest to the original shoulder position.

EXTRA MEASUREMENTS (GARMENTS)
Extra measurements are standard measurements of specific parts of basic garments. They are offered as a guide to be used when drafting basic blocks. They are:

Cuff size, two-piece sleeve
Cuff size, shirts
Trouser bottom width
Jeans bottom width.

Drafting the Blocks for Individual Figures

The blocks can be drafted for individual figures by substituting the personal measurements of a figure for the standard ones shown in the standard size charts on pages 18, 19 and 129. Successful blocks can only be drafted if the personal measurements are taken accurately in the correct position on the body. The description of the measurements listed above should be read carefully before measuring the figure.

All the body measurements listed should be taken except the scye depth and the waist to hip. These measurements are difficult to take accurately, therefore they should be taken from the standard size charts (pages 18, 19 and 129) using the child's height as a reference.

The dart size for blocks for girls with developing figures should be taken from the size chart on page 129 after reference to the notes on the development of the bust.

When the figure has been measured the individual measurements should be checked against a list of standard measurements for the height group of the child. If significant differences are apparent, the figure should be re-measured and checked to see if it is in fact wider or narrower than the average figure.

Body measurements

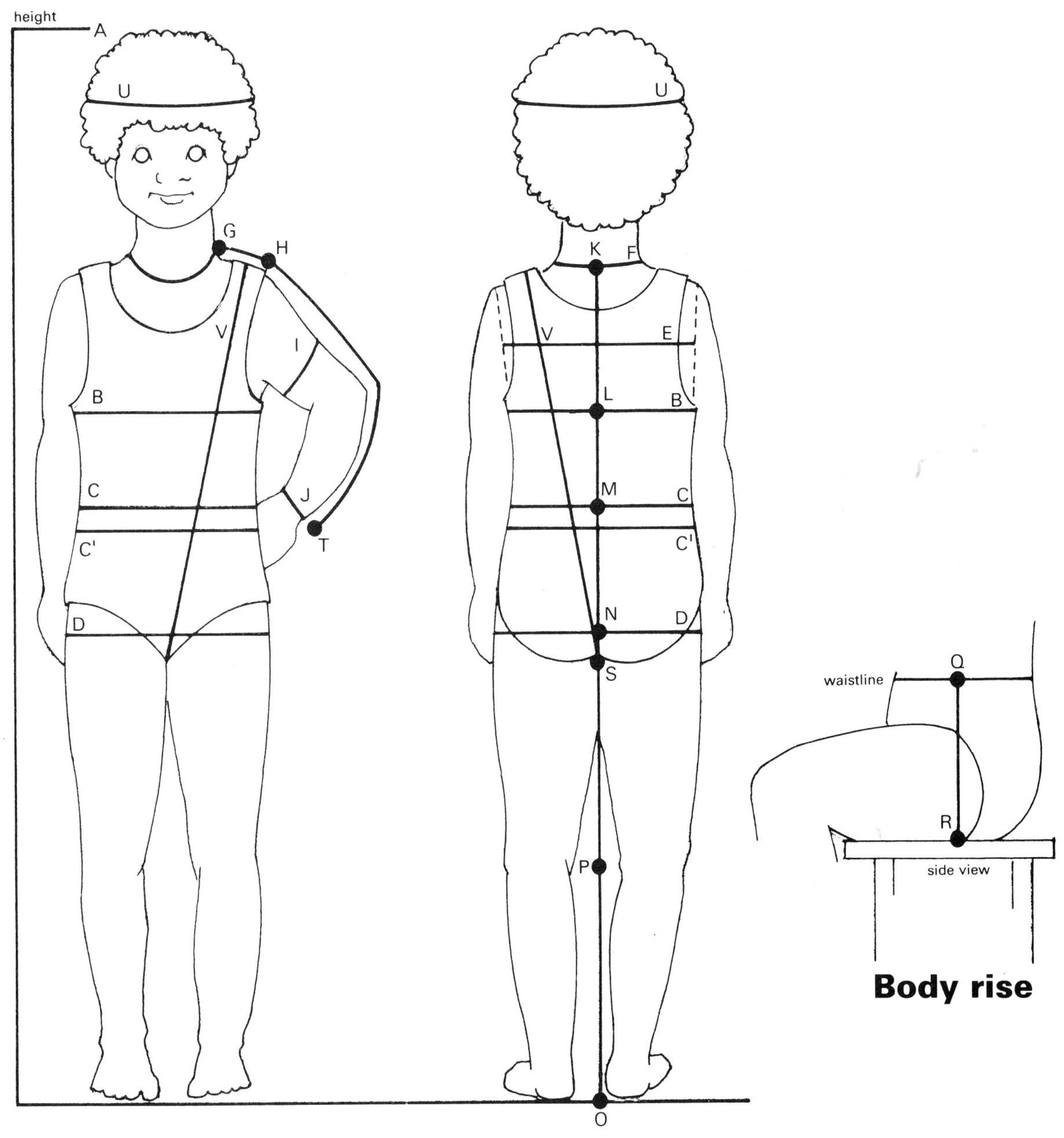

Body rise

Metric Sizing and Size Charts

The sizing of children's garments available in shops which are not a part of the multiple chain stores is somewhat chaotic. A move has been made by the British Standards Institution to designate size by the height dimension and this is being accepted by an increasing number of small manufacturers. Some manufacturers are using this system for children up to the age of eleven but see it as less useful for older children where the correlations of girth and limb length to height become more variable. For this group they prefer to mark the garments with chest or bust, waist, hip and inside leg measurements.

Students wishing to work in the field of children's wear should become familiar with the new British Standard on size designation as it is expected to influence the sizing of children's garments in the future.

SIZE DESIGNATION

In 1982 the British Standards Institution published their specification for Size Designation of Children's and Infants' Wear, BS 3728:1982. Their work on size designation takes into account international sizing agreements and this move towards a common system of labelling is an aid to exporters and of great value to the consumer.

The British Standard (BS 3728) deals with the size designation of clothing and is not concerned with sizing systems and size charts.

The primary aim of this British Standard is the establishment of a size designation system which indicates the body size of the child or infant that a garment is intended to fit. Provided that the shape of the child or infant's body has been accurately determined, this system will facilitate the choice of garments that fit.

The size designation system is based on body and not garment dimensions. Choice of garment measurements is normally left to the designer and the manufacturer, who are concerned with style, cut and other fashion elements and must make due allowance for garments normally worn beneath a specific garment.

CONTROL DIMENSIONS

Control dimensions are the dimensions of the body given on labels to enable consumers to buy clothes that fit.

The basic control measurement for all infants' and children's garments is height. The height interval used for labelling purposes should be 6cm based on a specified fixed point, e.g. 98cm, 104cm, 110cm.

Infants (boys and girls up to 104cm) Height is the control dimension.

Girls (females who have not completed their growth) For all forms of outerwear, height will always be given. Other control measurements will be given depending on the area of the body the garment will cover and the type of garment; these are bust, waist and hip. Foundation garments will include bust and underbust girth.

Boys (males who have not completed their growth) For all forms of outerwear, height will always be given. Other control measurements given will be chest, waist and hips. Neck measurements will be given for uniform and formal shirts.

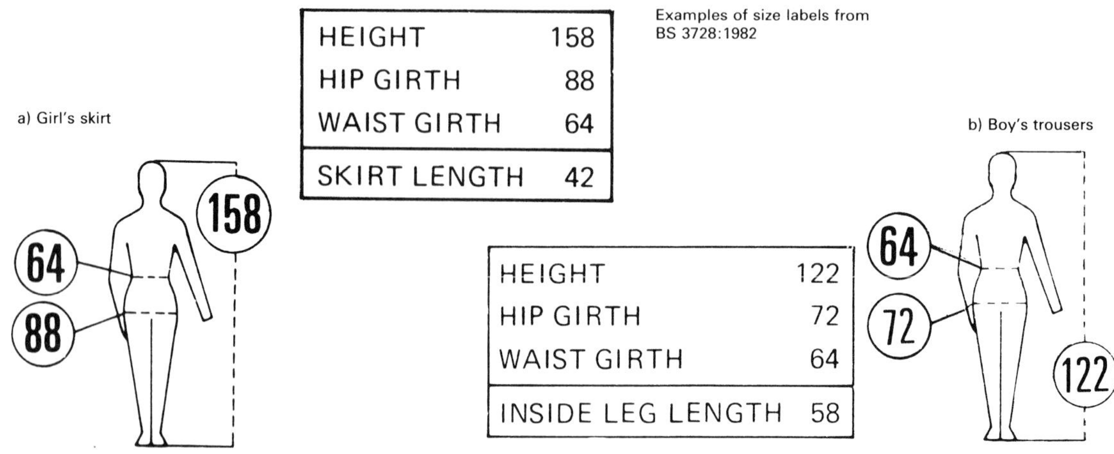

Examples of size labels from BS 3728:1982

a) Girl's skirt

b) Boy's trousers

LABELLING
The size designation on a label should have the control dimensions in centimetres of the intended wearer of the garment. Where possible a pictogram should be used. Where it is not possible to use a pictogram the control measurements should be given with the descriptive words such as bust girth, waist girth, etc.

Garment measurements are not included in the size designation, but where they are considered to be of value they can be added as additional information and indicated separately.
Additional information includes:
(a) extra body measurements, e.g. inside leg lengths are usually included on trouser labels;
(b) extra garment measurements;
(c) the approximate age of the child that the garment will fit.
Where size designation is supplemented by additional information this information should be separated from the size designation as shown in the diagrams.

It is recognised that age alone is an unreliable guide to fit as children's stature in relation to age is very variable. However its retention in addition to height, indicating the average child, is supported by the National Children's Wear Association as they state that many garments are purchased without the child being present.

The information offered in the section on Size Designation is published with the permission of the British Standards Institution (see page 4).

SIZE CHARTS
Important note It is advisable that students should read the section on the growth of children and adolescents (page 7) as this section offers explanations for the divisions of the size charts and blocks into separate groups.

The specification for size designation offered by the British Standards Institution does not offer a size chart. When considering the present revision the committee responsible chose not to retain the table of body measurements because the measurements were shown to be outdated. However a demand remains for a new size chart and many small manufacturers find it difficult to produce garments of an 'expected fit' without any basic reference. The British Standards Institution has recognised the need and they are at present working with the National Children's Wear Association to raise the money from industry and the government to have a large-scale measurement survey undertaken. The first part of this survey will concentrate on girls from six to sixteen years. It is expected to be 1985 before the study could be completed and a new size chart offered for these sizes. A survey of boys would follow shortly afterwards in the same sizes. Finally a survey of infants would be undertaken. Because of the delay the author undertook a smaller-scale survey on which the size charts offered in this book are based.

The main principle of the size designation system which will determine the structure of any size charts is the acceptance of the centilong system which bases children's sizing on height, the interval between sizes being 6cm based on specified fixed points, e.g. 98cm, 104cm, 110cm. These fixed points can be seen as sizes which give a reasonable fit to approximately 75% of children whose height falls 3cm each side of the fixed point. For example, given a size 110cm, the range will be from 107cm–112.9cm; a child who is 108.5cm in height will be seen as being in the size group 110cm height.

The changing shape of the growing child and the different figure changes of the sexes means that different size charts have to be offered for specific groups. The following size charts are offered in this book.
1. Size chart for boys and girls, 92cm–122cm height (approx. age 2–7 years);
2. Size chart for boys, 128cm–170cm height (approx. age 8–14 years);
3. Size chart for girls – undeveloped figures, 122cm–152cm height (approx. age 8–12 years);
4. Size chart for girls – developing figures, 146cm–164cm height (approx. age 11–14 years).

The Blocks

Instructions are given for blocks for a wide range of standard garments for children. The blocks include the basic amount of ease required for the function of the block, (e.g. a coat block has more ease than a dress block). Because the size range is large, 2–14 years, different blocks have to be used at different stages of growth. The student must check that he/she is constructing the correct block for the size. Note that size is designated by height.

Girls with developing figures require blocks that allow for the bust shape hence blocks with dart allowance (page 127) must be used.

The blocks are nett, they have no seam allowance, this must be added after the final pattern is constructed.

Glossary

Definitions of terms used when drafting patterns.
BACK PITCH/FRONT PITCH Points on body sections of the garment which match balance points on the sleeve, to ensure that the sleeve hangs correctly.
BALANCE MARKS Marks or notches that denote positions where seams are joined together.
BLOCK See page 34.
BUTTON STAND The distance between the button line and the front edge of the garment.
CIRCUMFERENCE See 'constructing a circle' below.
CRUTCH LINE The seam line, that joins the legs of trousers, passing between the legs.
DIMENSION A measurement; in clothing terms it is the measurement of a specific place on the body generally understood by most people, e.g. waist, hip.
EASE Extra allowance added to body measurements during block construction to allow for body movement and comfort.
ENCLOSED SEAMS Seams which have seam allowances hidden from view, e.g. inside a collar, facing or cuff.
FITTING LINES The lines along which a garment must be seamed when it is assembled.
FLY A flap to conceal buttons. Is also the term for the front fastening on men's trousers.
GIRTH A measurement around the body.
GRAIN LINE A line marked on a pattern. The pattern is placed on the fabric with the line parallel to the selvedge.
NETT A term which means that there is no seam allowance included in the pattern.
RADIUS See 'constructing a circle' below.
SCYE Armhole.
SEAT WEDGE The wedge that is opened on the back crutch line of trousers to increase the seat angle.
SLEEVE HEAD The section of the sleeve from scye depth line to top of sleeve.

The definitions for the following terms: STYLE LINE, ROLL LINE, STAND, FALL, BREAK POINT, BREAK LINE are given in the section on collars (page 54).

CONSTRUCTING A CIRCLE

Many patterns use circles as a base for their construction.

The circumference of a circle is the measurement around a circle.

The radius is a line from the centre of the circle to the outer edge.

To construct a circle the radius must be known. The circle can then be drawn with a compass or more primitively with a pencil and ruler.

In pattern cutting the waist or wrist measurement is known and one may be required to construct a circle whose circumference is exactly that measurement. The following calculation can be made to obtain the radius required to construct a circle.

Radius = circumference divided by 6.28

Working example Waistline measurement is 55cm. Construction of a circle is required whose circumference is 55cm.

Radius = 55 ÷ 6.28 = 8.76

Construct a circle as in diagram with a radius of 8.76cm; its circumference will be 55cm.

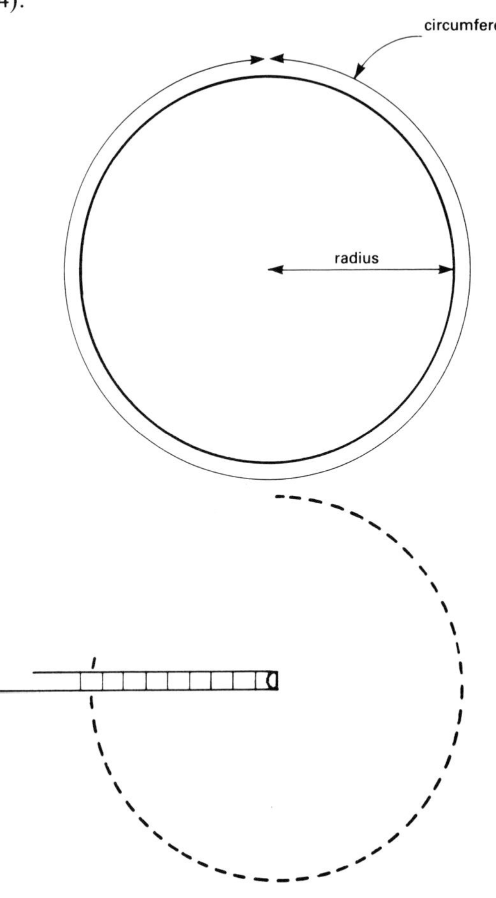

2 THE BASIC BODY BLOCKS AND SIZE CHARTS

Boys and girls, approximate age 2–7 years
Girls (undeveloped figures), approximate age 8–12 years
Boys, approximate age 8–14 years

Standard Body Measurements

Boys and girls, 92cm–122cm height: approximate age 2–7 years

Important note The standard measurements have been calculated from a measurement survey of children's body measurements. They have been calculated so that when they are used to construct the blocks, the blocks will fit approximately 75% of children in the height interval. The measurements on the chart have been marginally adjusted for easy size labelling and to give sensible grading intervals. However the balance over a range of sizes has been maintained.

A	HEIGHT	92	98	104	110	116	122
	APPROXIMATE AGE	2	3	4	5	6	7
B	CHEST	54	55	57	59	61	63
C	WAIST	53	54	55	56	58	59
D	HIP/SEAT	56	58	60	62	65	68
E	ACROSS BACK	22	22.8	23.6	24.4	25.2	26
F	NECK SIZE	26.4	27	27.6	28.2	28.8	29.4
G–H	SHOULDER	7	7.4	7.8	8.2	8.6	9
I	UPPER ARM	18	18.4	18.8	19.2	19.6	20
J	WRIST	13	13.2	13.4	13.6	13.8	14
K–L	SCYE DEPTH	12.6	13.2	13.8	14.4	15	15.6
K–M	NECK TO WAIST	22	23.2	24.4	25.6	26.8	28
M–N	WAIST TO HIP	11.4	12	12.6	13.2	13.8	14.4
K–O	CERVICAL HEIGHT	75.5	80.8	86.1	91.4	96.7	102
M–P	WAIST TO KNEE	31	33	35	37	39	41
Q–R	BODY RISE	16.5	17.3	18.1	18.9	19.7	20.5
S–O	INSIDE LEG	38	42	45	48	52	55
H–T	SLEEVE LENGTH	32	34.5	37	39.5	42	44.5
U	HEAD CIRCUMFERENCE	51	51.6	52.2	52.8	53.4	54
V	VERTICAL TRUNK	97	101	105	109	113	117
Extra measurements (garments)							
	CUFF SIZE, TWO-PIECE SLEEVE	10	10.2	10.4	10.6	10.8	11
	CUFF SIZE, SHIRTS	15.4	15.6	15.8	16	16.2	16.4
	TROUSER BOTTOM WIDTH	15.5	16	16.5	17	17.5	18
	JEANS BOTTOM WIDTH	13.5	14	14.5	15	15.5	16

Boys from the age of four start to develop larger waists and smaller hips than girls. The size chart above should be used for garments for both sexes. Manufacturers of boys' wear only may wish to use the waist and hip measurements shown below.

Measurements for boys' wear only							
C	BOYS' WAIST	53	54	55	57	59	60
D	BOYS' HIP/SEAT	56	58	60	62	64	66

Standard Body Measurements

Girls (undeveloped figures) 128cm–152cm height: approx. age 8–12 years
Boys, 128cm–170cm height: approx. age 8–14 years

		GIRLS					BOYS							
A	HEIGHT	128	134	140	146	152	128	134	140	146	152	158	164	170
	APPROXIMATE AGE	8	9	10	11	12	8	9	10	11	12	13 – – –	– – –	–14
B	CHEST	66	69	72	75	78	67	70	73	76	79	82	86	90
C	WAIST	60	61	62	63	64	61	63	65	67	69	71	73	75
C′	LOW WAIST						64	66	68	70	72	74	76	78
D	HIP/SEAT	71	74	78	81	84	70	73	76	79	82	85	89	93
E	ACROSS BACK	27.4	28.6	29.8	31	32.2	28	29.2	30.4	31.6	32.8	34	35.6	37.2
F	NECK SIZE	30	31	32	33	34	30	31	32	33	34	35	36	37
G–H	SHOULDER	9.5	10	10.5	11	11.5	10	10.5	11	11.5	12	12.5	13.1	13.7
I	UPPER ARM	20.8	21.6	22.4	23.2	24	20.8	21.6	22.4	23.2	24	24.8	25.8	26.8
J	WRIST	14	14.4	14.8	15.2	15.6	14.2	14.6	15	15.4	15.8	16.2	16.6	17
K–L	SCYE DEPTH	16.2	16.8	17.4	18	18.6	16.6	17.4	18.2	19	19.8	20.8	21.6	22.4
K–M	NECK TO WAIST	29.2	30.4	31.6	32.8	34	29.8	31.2	32.6	34	35.4	36.8	38.4	40
M–N	WAIST TO HIP	15	15.6	16.2	16.8	17.4	15	15.6	16.2	16.8	17.4	18	18.8	19.6
K–O	CERVICAL HEIGHT	107.4	112.8	118.2	123.6	129	107.4	112.8	118.2	123.6	129	134.4	139.8	145.2
M–P	WAIST TO KNEE	44	46	48	50	52								
Q–R	BODY RISE	21.6	22.4	23.2	24	24.8	21.2	22	22.8	23.6	24.4	25.2	26.2	27.2
S–O	INSIDE LEG	58	61	65	68	71	58	61	65	68	71	74	77	80
H–T	SLEEVE LENGTH	47	49	52	54	56	47	49	52	54	56	58	61	63
U	HEAD CIRCUMFERENCE	54	54.4	54.8	55.2	55.6	55	55.4	55.8	56.2	56.6	57	57.4	57.8
Extra measurements (garments)														
CUFF SIZE, TWO-PIECE SLEEVE		11.5	12	12.5	13	13.5	11.5	12	12.5	13	13.5	13.8	14	14.2
CUFF SIZE, SHIRTS		17	17.5	18	18.5	19	17.5	18	18.5	19	20	20.5	21	21.5
TROUSER BOTTOM WIDTH		18.5	19	19.5	20	20.5	18.5	19	19.5	20	20.5	21	21.5	22
JEANS BOTTOM WIDTH		16.5	17	17.5	18	18.5	16.5	17	17.5	18	18.5	18.8	19	19.2

The Bodice Block

For boys and girls, sizes 92cm–122cm height
For girls (undeveloped figures), sizes 128cm–152cm height

MEASUREMENTS REQUIRED TO DRAFT THE BLOCK

(e.g. size 110cm height)

Refer to the size charts (pages 18 and 19) for standard measurements.

Chest	59cm
Across back	24.4cm
Neck size	28.2cm
Shoulder	8.2cm
Neck to waist	25.6cm
Scye depth	14.4cm

Body sections

Square both ways from 0.

0 – 1 Neck to waist plus 1.25cm; square across.

0 – 2 ½ chest:
sizes 92cm–122cm height plus 4cm
128cm–152cm height plus 4.5cm;
square down to 3
(e.g. 110cm height: (59 ÷ 2) + 4 = 53.5cm.)

0 – 4 1.25cm.

4 – 5 Scye depth plus 1cm; square across to 6.

4 – 7 ½ measurement 4–5; square out.

4 – 8 ¼ scye depth minus 2cm; square out.

0 – 9 ⅕ neck size minus 0.2cm; draw in neck curve.

5 –10 ½ across back plus 0.5cm; square up; mark point 11.

9 –12 Shoulder measurement:
sizes 92cm–122cm height plus 0.3cm ease
128cm–134cm height plus 0.5cm ease.

Draw back shoulder line to touch line from 8.

2 –13 ⅕ neck size minus 0.5cm.

2 –14 ⅕ neck size minus 0.2cm; draw in neck curve.

12–15 0.5cm; square across.

13–16 Shoulder measurement; draw front shoulder line to touch the line from 15.

14–17 ½ measurement 6–14:
sizes 92cm–122cm height plus 1cm
128cm–152cm height plus 1.5cm;
square across.

6 –18 The measurement 5–10:
sizes 92cm–122cm height minus 1cm
128cm–152cm height minus 0.75cm;
square up to 19.

18–20 ½ measurement 10–18 plus 0.5cm; square down to 21.

Draw in armscye shape as shown; measurement of curve:
Sizes 92cm–122cm height from 10 2cm; from 18 1.75cm
128cm–152cm height from 10 2.25cm; from 18 2cm.

3 –22 Sizes 92cm–122cm height 1.5cm
128cm–152cm height 1cm.

Join 22– 1 with a curve.

Sleeve

Draft a one-piece sleeve (page 30) or two-piece sleeve (page 32) to fit armscye measurement.

Shaping the Bodice Block

For some designs the bodice may require some shape. Waist shaping without darts is used for sizes up to 100cm height and often up to 122cm height. Many dress designs have no waist shaping or only side seam shaping: they are then elasticated or belted to provide a fit for a wide range of children.

The standard ease allowed on the waistline of a shaped dress is 6cm.

Skirts on waisted dresses are usually gathered, tucked or pleated; the controlling measurement for this type of skirt is the waist measurement of the completed bodice pattern.

BODICE SHAPING WITHOUT DARTS

Always used for sizes up to 110cm height and often used for sizes up to 122cm height.

Mark points 1, 20, 22 on bodice block.

1–A ¼ waist plus 1.25cm.

22–B ¼ waist plus 1.75 cm.

Draw in curved side seams 20–A and 20–B.

Adjust the line of the waistline at A and B to ensure that the lines 20–A and 20–B are the same length.

BODICE SHAPING WITH DARTS

Mark points 1, 5, 6, 10, 18, 20, 22 on bodice block.

5–A ½ measurement 5–10; square down to B.

6–C ½ measurement 6–18; square down to D.

A–E and C–F 2cm.

1–G ¼ waist:
sizes 116cm–122cm height plus 1.75cm
128cm–134cm height plus 2.25cm
140cm–152cm height plus 2.75 cm.

22–H ¼ waist:
sizes 116cm–122cm height plus 2.25cm
128cm–134cm height plus 2.75cm
140cm–152cm height plus 3.75cm.

Draw in curved side seams 20–G and 20–H.

Construct back and front darts on lines E–B and F–D:
sizes 116cm–122cm height both darts 0.5cm
128cm–134cm height both darts 1cm
140cm–152cm height back dart 1.5cm
front dart 2cm.

Adjust the line at waistline to ensure that the lines 20–G and 20–H and the dart lines are the same length.

The bodice block

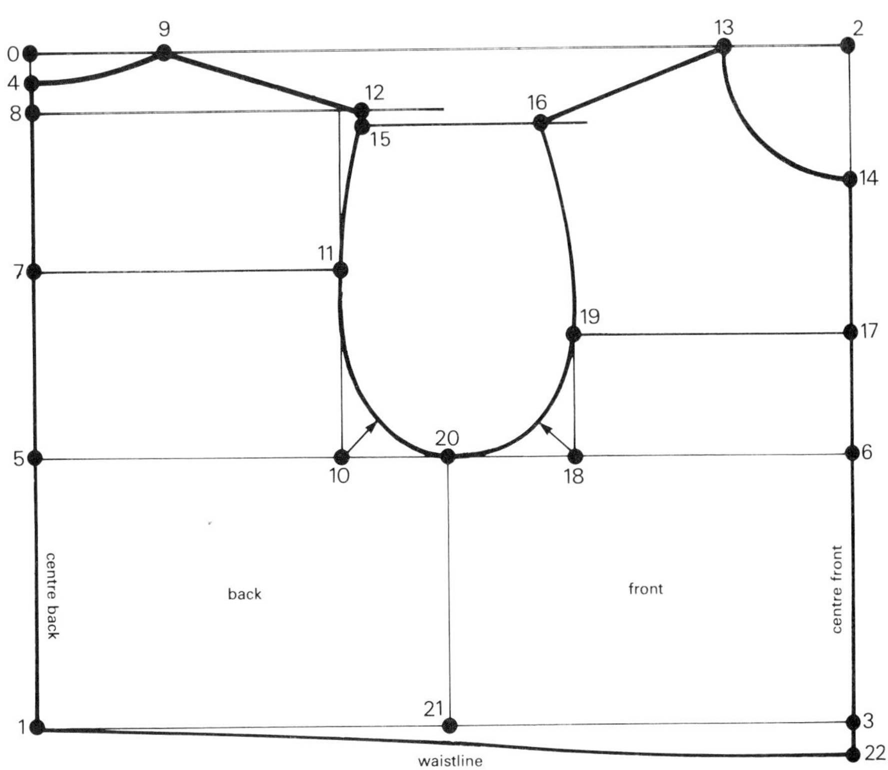

Shaping the bodice block

Bodice shaping without darts

Bodice shaping with darts

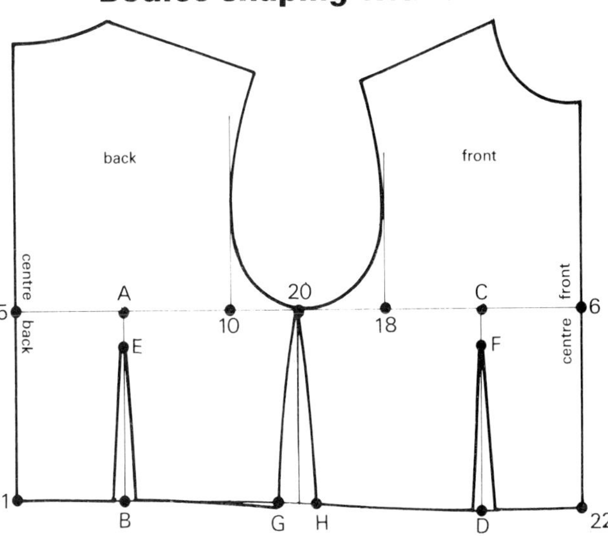

The Dress Block

For girls, sizes 92cm–152cm height

The dress block is constructed to knee length, this provides a consistent guide. Final length is marked at the pattern cutting stage.

A one-piece dress block for children is usually cut with an easy fit and avoids shaping directly in the waist area. Fitted dresses are not very suitable for small children as they tend to have rather large stomachs. The block is adapted to give high waist shaping as this flatters the figure.

Separate front and back bodice block.
Trace round bodice block, use the line 1–21 and 21–3 as the waistline to begin the draft.
Mark points 1, 3, 13, 20, 21.

Back

Square down from 1 and 21.

1–A Waist to knee measurement; square across to B.

B–C 5cm; join 21–C.

21–D The measurement 21–B, shape hem with a curve to D.

Curve in bodice side seam 20–21 0.75cm.

1–E Waist to hip measurement; square across.

Front

Square down from 3 and 21.

3–F Waist to knee measurement; square across to G.

G–H 3cm; join 21–H.

21–J The measurement 21–G.

F–K The measurement 3–22 on original body block; shape hem with a curve from K–J.

3–L The measurement F–K; join L to 21 with a curve.

3–M Waist to hip measurement; square across.

Sizes 92cm–122cm height

Young children have a forward stance, this means that extra fullness is required in the front block.

Square down from 13 to N: cut up the line and open block at hem line.

N–P Sizes 92cm–104cm height 2.5cm
110cm–122cm height 1.5cm.

Trace round new block shape; re-mark waistline, scye depth line and hip line.

The Sleeveless Dress Block

Back and front

Trace round dress block.
Mark point A at underarm point.
Raise scye depth line 1cm.

A–B 1cm; square up to C on new scye depth line.

Mark point D at shoulder point.

D–E 0.75cm; draw in new armscye shape from E–C as shown.

Mark point F at waistline. G at hemline.

F–H 0.75cm; draw in new side seam, join H–G; join C–H with a curve.

The dress block

The sleeveless dress block

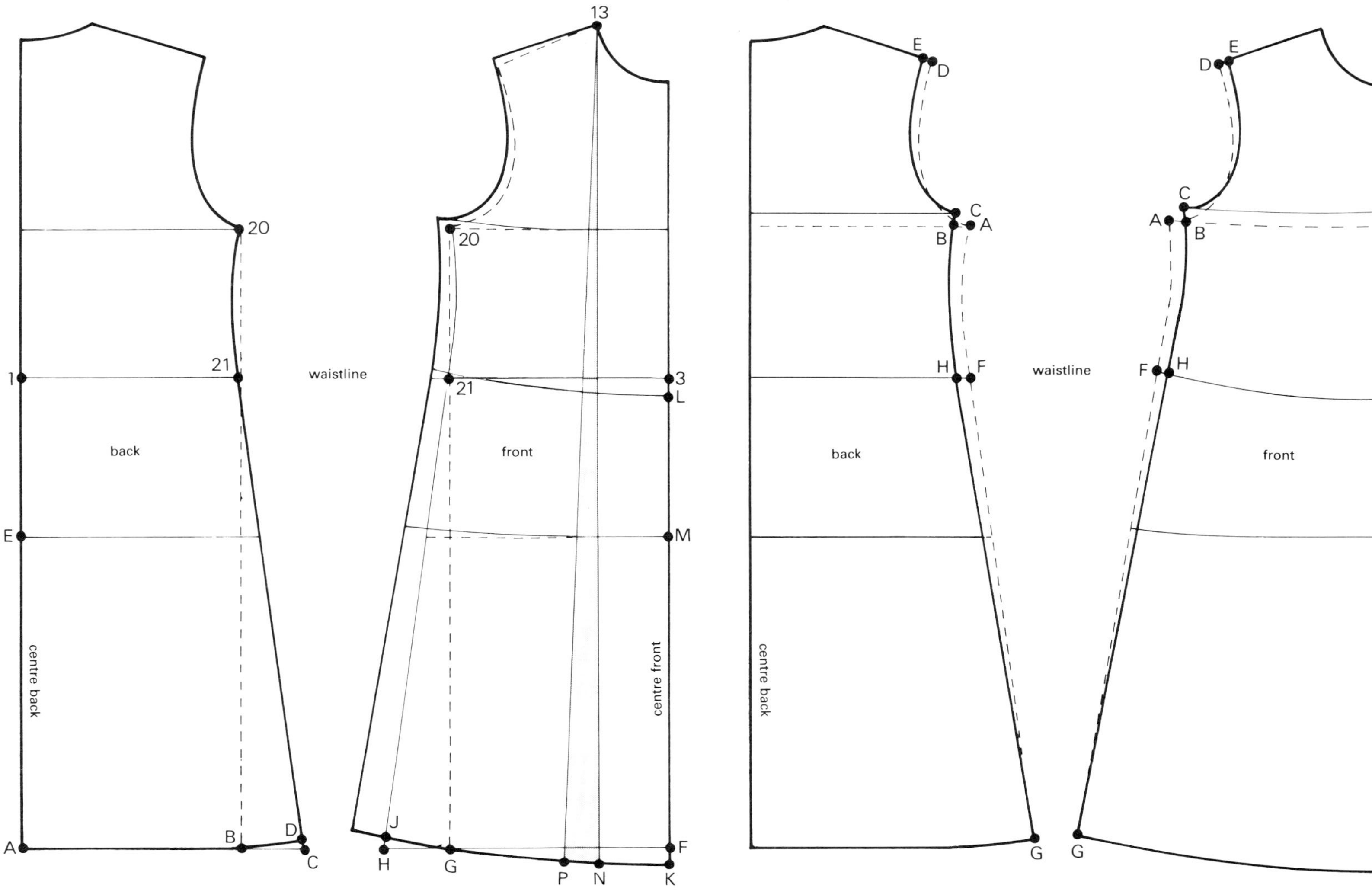

The Formal Coat Block

For boys and girls, sizes 92cm–122cm height
For girls (undeveloped figures), sizes 128cm–152cm height

A full-length block is required for formal coats. Trace round dress block. Mark points 11 and 19 on armscye.

Back and front
Mark points A and B at shoulder points C at underarm.
C–D 2cm, mark new scye depth line 2cm below previous scye depth line.
D–E 2.5cm.
Raise the shoulder line 0.5cm.
Square up from A to touch new shoulder line at F.
F–G 0.5cm. Correct neck curve.
Extend armscye line from B–11 and B–19 1cm.
Re-draw armscye line as shown.
Mark H at waistline, J at hipline, K at hem line.
Extend H, K, J 1.5cm; draw in new side seam.
Shape in line from underarm to waistline 0.5cm.

Sleeve
Draft one-piece sleeve (page 30) or two-piece sleeve (page 32) to fit new armscye measurement.

The Overgarment Block

For boys and girls, sizes 92cm–122cm height: approximate age 2–7 years

The overgarment block is a base for casual wear designs; i.e. anoraks, duffle coats. These garments require more ease in the body so that they can be worn over trousers, skirts and sweaters. For the smaller sizes (92cm–122cm) the basic block is adapted to provide a simple overgarment block.

Body sections
Cut out the basic bodice block, cut up side seam.
Draw round back block with a dotted line.
Mark points 1, 4, 9, 11, 12.
4–A Final length square across.
Extend scye depth line, waistline and hem line.
Mark B at underarm point.
B–C 5cm.
Square down from C to D, place front block correctly on extended lines to touch the line C–D; trace round.
Square down to E on hemline.
Mark points 3, 13,16, 19.
F midway B–C; square down to G to make new side seam.
F–H 2cm; draw in new scye depth line.
Raise shoulder line 0.5cm.
Square up from 9 and 13 to touch new shoulder lines at J and K.
J–L and K–M 0.5cm; correct neck curves.
Extend armscye line from 11–12 and 16–19 1.25 cm.
Re-draw armhole to touch new scye depth line.
Lower waistline 1–3 0.5cm.
E–N The measurement 3–22 on original bodice block.
Join G–N with a curve.

Sleeve
Draft one-piece sleeve (page 30) or a two-piece sleeve (page 32) to fit new armscye measurement.

The formal coat block

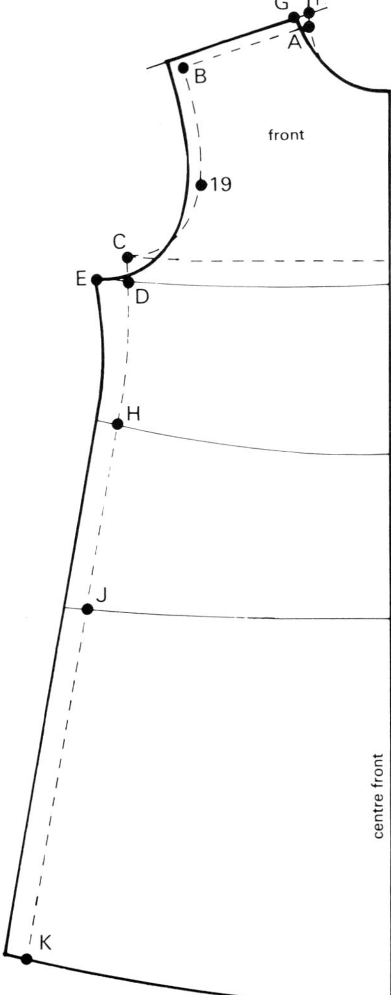

The overgarment block 2–7 years

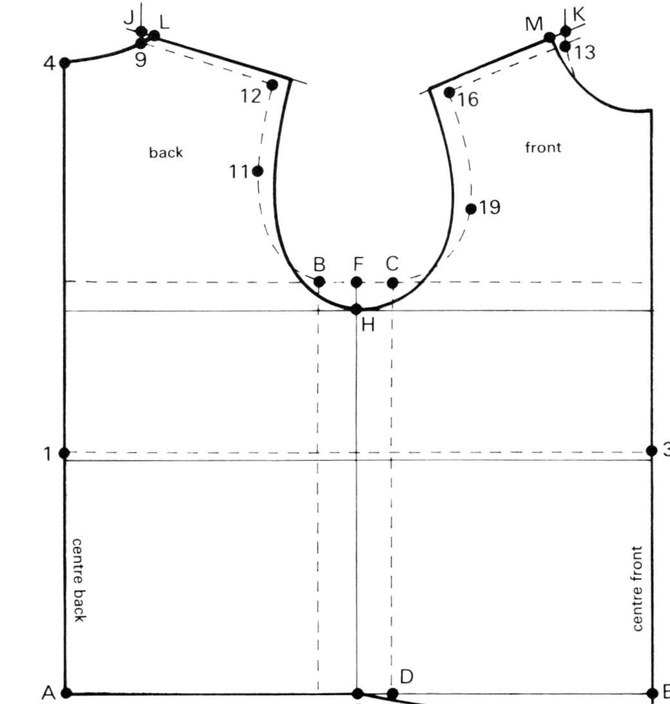

The Overgarment Block

For boys, sizes 128cm–170cm height
For girls (undeveloped figures), sizes 128cm–152cm height
Approximate age 8–14 years

The overgarment block is a base for casual wear designs; i.e. anoraks, duffle coats. These garments require more ease in the body so that they can be worn over trousers, skirts and sweaters.

MEASUREMENTS REQUIRED TO DRAFT THE BLOCK
(e.g. boy or girl size 134cm height)
Refer to the size charts (pages 18 and 19) for standard measurements.

	Girls	Boys
Chest	69cm	70cm
Across back	28.6cm	29.2
Neck size	31cm	31cm
Shoulder	10cm	10.5cm
Neck to waist	30.4cm	31.2cm
Scye depth	16.8cm	17.4cm
Waist to hip	15.6cm	15.6cm

Body sections
Square both ways from 0.

0 – 1 Neck to waist:
sizes 128cm–152cm height plus 2.25cm
158cm–170cm height plus 2.5cm.

0 – 2 ½ chest plus 10cm; square down, mark point 3 on waistline.

0 – 4 Sizes 128cm–152cm height 1.75cm
158cm–170cm height 2cm.

4 – 5 Scye depth:
sizes 128cm–152cm height plus 3cm
158cm–170cm height plus 3.5cm;
square across to 6.

4 – 7 ½ measurement 4–5; square out.

4 – 8 ¼ scye depth; square out.

5 – 9 ½ across back plus 2cm; square up to 10 and 11.

11–12 2cm; square out.

0 –13 ⅕ neck size plus 0.3cm; draw in neck curve.

12–14 Sizes 128cm–152cm height 1.5cm
158cm–170cm height 2cm; join 13–14.

Girls
Point 2 now becomes point 15.

15–16 ⅕ neck size plus 0.3cm.

16–17 ½ measurement 16–6 plus 2cm; square across.

6 –18 The measurement 5–9 minus 0.8cm; square up to 19.

Boys

2 –15 Sizes 128cm–134cm height 0.5cm
140cm–152cm height 1cm
158cm–170cm height 1.5cm; square across.

15–16 ⅕ neck size plus 0.3cm.

16–17 ½ measurement 16–6 plus 2cm; square across.

6 –18 The measurement 5–9:
sizes 128cm–152cm height minus 1cm
158cm–170cm height minus 1.25cm;
square up to 19.

15–20 ⅕ neck size; draw in neck curve.

Join 20 to point 11 with a straight line.

20–21 The measurement 13–14 minus 0.5cm.

21–22 Sizes 128cm–152cm height 1cm
158cm–170cm height 1.25cm.

18–23 ½ measurement 9–18 plus 0.5cm; square down; mark point 24 on waistline.

Draw in armscye shape as shown, measurement of curve:
Sizes 128cm–152cm height from 9 and 18 2.25cm
158cm–170cm height from 9 and 18 2.5cm.

4 –25 Finished length; square across to 26 and 27.

27–28 1cm; join 26–28 with a curved line.

1 –29 Waist to hip; square across.

Sleeve
Draft a one-piece sleeve (page 30) or a two-piece sleeve (page 32) to fit armscye measurement.

Note Separate instructions are required for the different sexes because a boy is developing a longer back length and wider back width than a girl at this period of his growth.

Boy's overgarment block

Girl's overgarment block

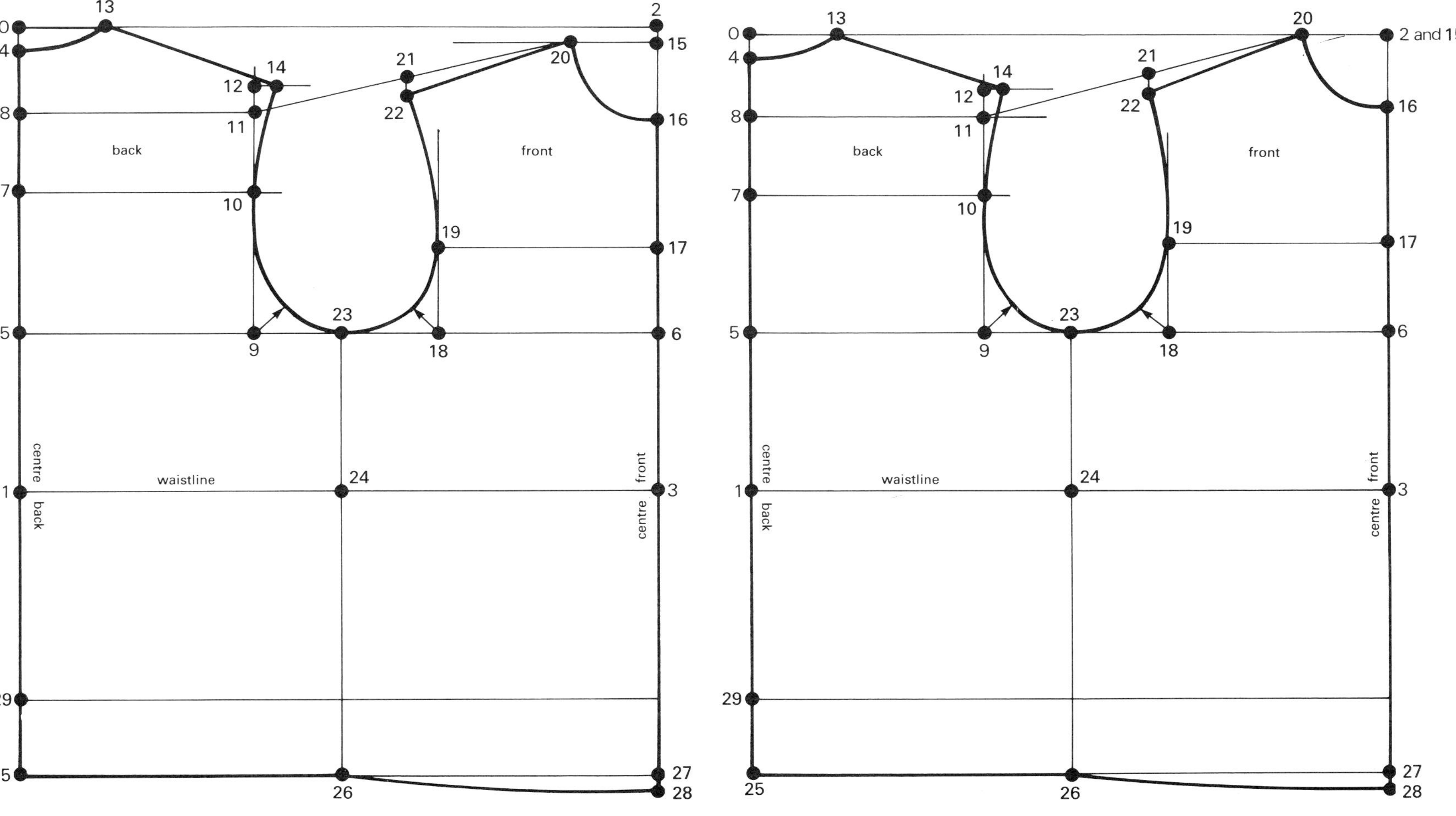

The Blazer Block

For boys, sizes 128cm–170cm height
For girls (undeveloped figures), sizes 128cm–152cm height
Approximate age 8–14 years

MEASUREMENTS REQUIRED TO DRAFT THE BLOCK
(e.g. boy or girl size 134cm height)
Refer to the size charts (pages 18 and 19) for standard measurements.

	Girls	Boys
Chest	69cm	70cm
Across back	28.6cm	29.2cm
Neck size	31cm	31cm
Shoulder	10cm	10.5cm
Neck to waist	30.4cm	31.2cm
Scye depth	16.8cm	17.4cm
Waist to hip	15.6cm	15.6cm

Body sections

Square both ways from 0.

0 – 1 Sizes 128cm–152cm height 1.75cm
158cm–170cm height 2cm.
1 – 2 Neck to waist; square across.
1 – 3 Finished length; square across.
2 – 4 Waist to hip; square across.
1 – 5 Scye depth:
sizes 128cm–152cm height plus 2.5cm
158cm–170cm height plus 3cm;
square across.
1 – 6 ½ measurement 1–5; square across.
1 – 7 ¼ scye depth; square across.
5 – 8 ½ across back plus 1.25cm; square up to 9 and 10.
10–11 2cm; square out.
0 –12 ⅕ neck size plus 0.25cm; draw in neck curve.
12–13 Shoulder length plus 1.5cm.
2 –14 1cm; square down to 15 and 16. Join 6–14.
0 –17 ½ chest plus 8cm; square down to 18,19 and 20.
18–21 The measurement 5–8 minus 0.5cm; square up.
21–22 ½ measurement 5–7 minus 2cm.
21–23 ½ measurement 21–18 minus 0.5cm; square up to 24 and down to hem line.

Girls

Point 24 and 25 are the same point.

Boys

24–25 Sizes 128cm–134cm height 0.5cm
140cm–152cm height 1cm
158cm–170cm height 1.5cm.

Join 25 to point 10; extend the line past point 25.
25–26 Sizes 128cm–134cm height 1.5cm
140cm–152cm height 1.75cm
158cm–170cm height 2cm.
25–27 The measurement 12–13 minus 0.5cm; square down 1cm to 28. Join 25–28 with slight curve.
21–29 ½ measurement 8–21. Mark 29 underarm point.
Draw in armscye shape as shown; measurement of curve:
Sizes 128cm–134cm height from 8 2.5cm; from 21 2cm
140cm–152cm height from 8 2.8cm; from 21 2.3cm
158cm–170cm height from 8 3cm; from 21 2.5cm.
29–30 ⅓ measurement 29–21; square down to 31 on waistline, 32 on hip/seat line.
31–33 ⅔ measurement 31–32; construct a 1cm dart on the line 30–33.
8 –34 ¼ scye depth minus 1cm; square across to 35 on armscye line. Square down to 36 on waistline.
8 –37 Sizes 128cm–152cm height 2cm
158cm–170cm height 2.5cm;
square down to 38, 39 and 40.
40–41 ⅙ measurement 5–8; draw in back seam line through points 35, 38, 41 and points 35, 36, 40.
18–42 ½ measurement 18–19 minus 2cm. 19–43 1.5cm.
43–44 The measurement 42–43. Mark points 42, 43 and 44 as buttonholes.
42–45 2cm; square up and down. Join 45 to point 26 and extend the line.
20–46 1.5cm; join 46 to 40 on back seam line.
46–47 ⅕ measurement 3–40 plus 1cm. Draw in front line of blazer from 45–47 as shown.
25–48 ⅛ neck size plus 0.5cm; square across to 49 on centre front line.
48–50 1.5cm; join 50–49 and extend the line.
49–51 1.5cm; draw in neckline with a curve to break line as shown. Draw in rever edge from 51–45 with a curve.

Pockets

23–52 ⅓ measurement 23–18.
52–53 Size 128cm height 7.5cm (add 0.5cm each size up).
53–54 1cm; size 128cm height square down 7.5cm from 52 and 54 (add 0.7cm each size up).
Draw in lower edge of pocket; curve the corners at bottom edge of pocket.
On the line from 24 mark point 55 on the waistline, 56 on hip/seat line.
55–57 ½ measurement 55–56 minus 2cm.
57–58 Size 128cm height 13.5cm (add 0.7cm each size up).
Draw two parallel lines from 57 and 58 parallel to the hem line.
57–59 Size 128cm height 12.5cm (add 0.5cm each size up).
Square down from 59 using the line 57–59 to complete pocket. Curve the corners at bottom edge of pocket.

Sleeve

Draft a two-piece sleeve (page 32) to fit armscye measurements.

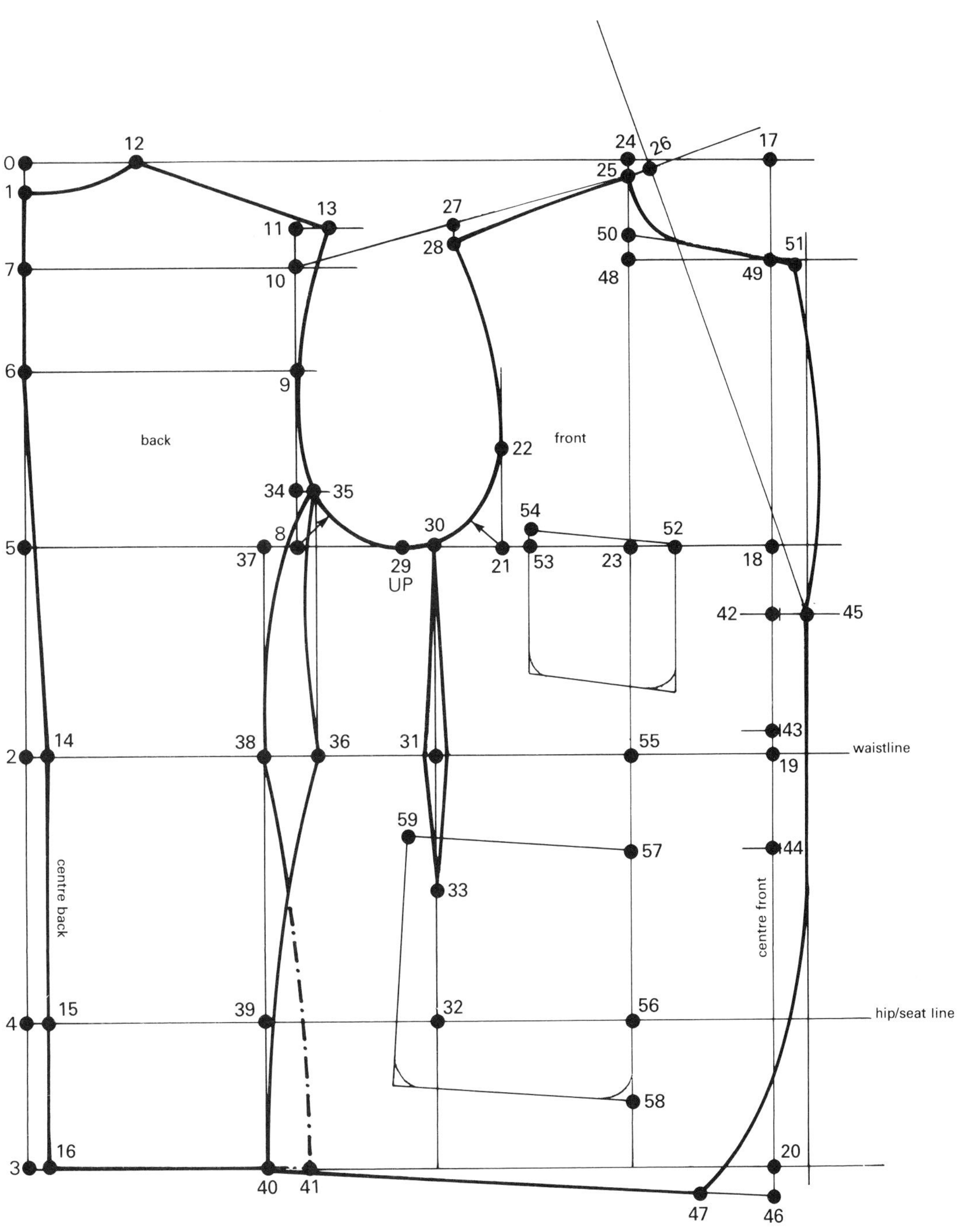

back
front
centre back
centre front
waistline
hip/seat line
UP

The One-piece Sleeve Block

To be used with all body blocks: boys and girls – all sizes

MEASUREMENTS REQUIRED TO DRAFT THE BLOCK
(e.g. size 110cm height)
Refer to the size charts (pages 18, 19 and 129) for standard measurements.

Armscye girth (measure the armscye)
Sleeve length 39.5cm
(For coats and overgarments add 1.25cm to sleeve length.)

Mark basic points on body block
(If the dress or formal coat block is used, draw a scye depth line and place armhole points together at A.)
Mark point A at underarm, B and C at shoulder points.
Square up from scye depth line to touch back and front armscye lines.
Mark points D and E on scye depth line.

Sleeve
Square up and across from 0.
0 – 1 ⅓ armscye girth plus 0.25cm; square across.
0 – 2 ½ measurement 0–1; square across.
0 – 3 ½ measurement 0–2.
On body block: E–F equals the measurement 0–3 on sleeve block.
Square out to FP (front pitch point) on armscye.
D–BP (back pitch point) equals the measurement 0–2 on sleeve block.
On sleeve:
3 – 4 The measurement C–FP measured in a curve:
sizes 92cm–122cm height plus 0.5cm
128cm–152cm height plus 0.75cm
158cm–170cm height plus 1cm; join 3–4.
4 – 5 The measurement B–BP measured in a curve:
sizes 92cm–122cm height plus 0.5cm
128cm–152cm height plus 0.75cm
158cm–170cm height plus 1cm; join 4–5.
3 – 6 The measurement FP–A measured in a curve minus 0.3cm; join 3–6.
5 – 7 The measurement BP–A measured in a curve minus 0.3cm; join 5–7.
Square down from points 4,6 and 7.
4 – 8 Sleeve length from shoulder; square across to 9 and 10.
Draw in outline of the sleeve head.
7 – 5 Hollow the curve:
sizes 92cm–122cm height 0.4cm
128cm–152cm height 0.5cm
158cm–170cm height 0.6cm.
5 – 4 Raise the curve:
sizes 92cm–122cm height 0.8cm
128cm–152cm height 1cm
158cm–170cm height 1.2cm.
4 – 3 Raise the curve at 11 ⅓ measurement 4–3:
sizes 92cm–122cm height 1.4cm
128cm–152cm height 1.6cm
158cm–170cm height 1.8cm.
3 – 6 Hollow the curve:
sizes 92cm–122cm height 0.6cm
128cm–152cm height 0.7cm
158cm–170cm height 0.8cm.
9 –12 ½ measurement 6–9; square across.
To shape side seams:
9 –13 ⅙ measurement 8–9.
10–14 ⅙ measurement 8–10.
Join 6–13 and 7–14.
Draw in line of wrist.
14– 8 Lower the curve:
sizes 92cm–122cm height 0.5cm
128cm–152cm height 0.7cm
158cm–170cm height 0.9cm.
8 –13 Hollow the curve:
sizes 92cm–122cm height 0.5cm
128cm–152cm height 0.7cm
158cm–170cm height 0.9cm.

Note It is important that all curved measurements are measured very accurately along the curved line, with the tape upright (see diagram).

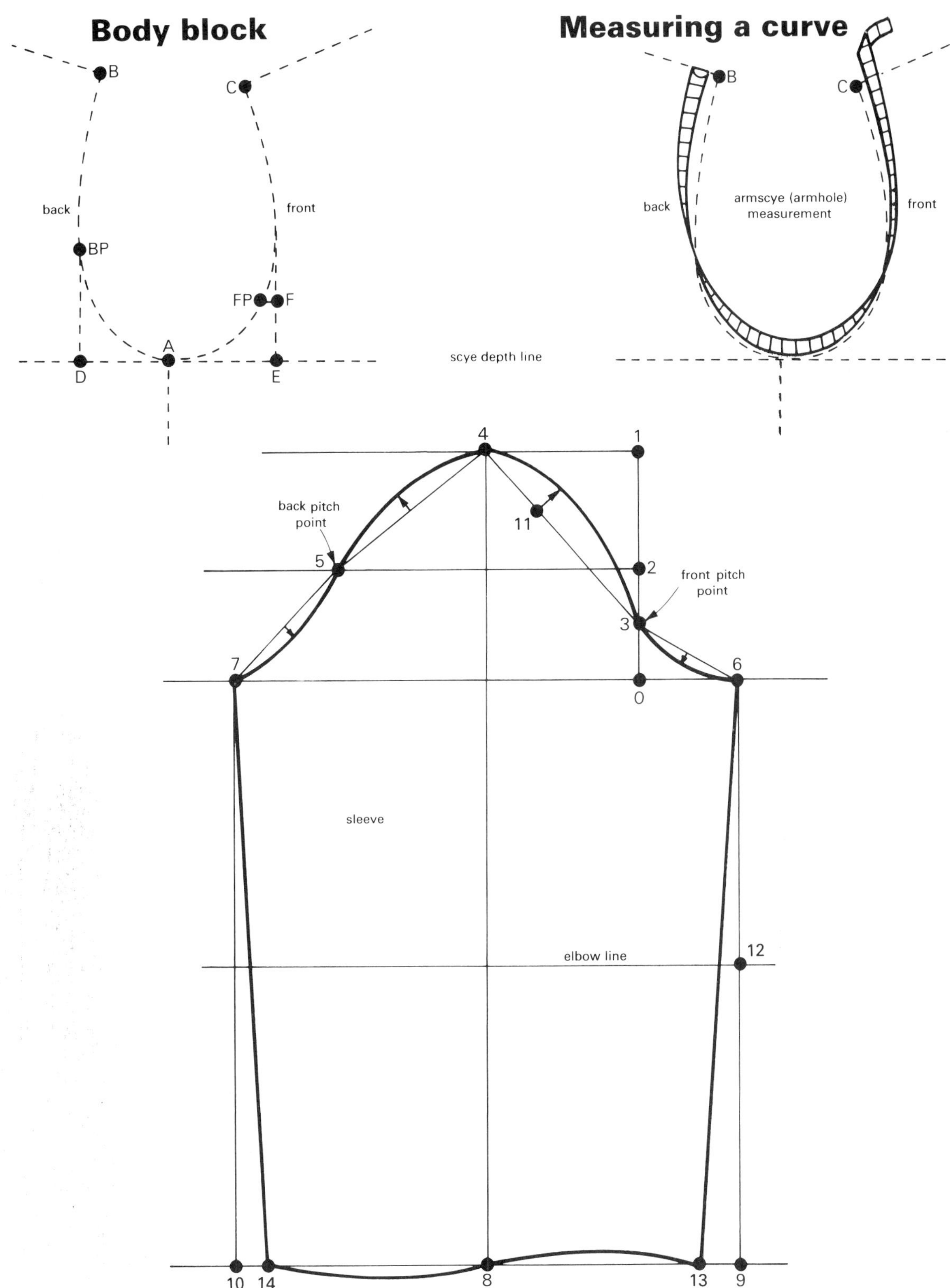
Body block
B
C
back
front
BP
FP
F
A
D
E
Measuring a curve
B
C
back
armscye (armhole)
measurement
front
scye depth line
4
1
back pitch
point
11
5
2
front pitch
point
3
7
6
0
sleeve
elbow line
12
10
14
8
13
9

The Two-piece Sleeve Block

To be used with all body blocks: boys and girls – all sizes

MEASUREMENTS REQUIRED TO DRAFT THE BLOCK
(e.g. size 110cm height)
Refer to the size charts (pages 18, 19 and 129) for standard measurements.

Armscye girth (measure the armscye)
Sleeve length 39.5cm
(For coats and overgarments add 1.25cm to sleeve length.)
Cuff size for two-piece sleeve.

Mark basic points on body block
(If the dress or formal coat block is used draw a scye depth line and place armhole points together at A.)
Mark points A at underarm, B and C at shoulder points.
Square up from scye depth line to touch back and front armscye lines.
Mark points D and E on scye depth line.

Sleeve
Square up and across from 0.

0 – 1 ⅓ armscye measurement plus 0.5cm; square across.
1 – 2 ⅓ measurement 0–1 plus 1cm; square across.
0 – 3 ¼ measurement 0–1.

On body block: E–F equals the measurement 0–3 on sleeve block.
Square out to FP (front pitch point) on armscye.
D–BP (back pitch point) equals the measurement 0–2 on sleeve block.

On sleeve:

3 – 4 The measurement C–FP measured in a curve:
sizes 92cm–122cm height plus 0.5cm
128cm–152cm height plus 0.8cm
158cm–170cm height plus 1cm; join 3–4.

4 – 5 The measurement B–BP measured in a curve:
sizes 92cm–122cm height plus 0.4cm
128cm–152cm height plus 0.6cm
158cm–170cm height plus 0.8cm; join 4–5.

0 – 6 The measurement A–E on body block:

0 – 7 sizes 92cm–122cm height 1.5cm
128cm–152cm height 1.75cm
158cm–170cm height 2cm; square across.

7–8 and 7–9
sizes 92cm–122cm height 1.25cm
128cm–152cm height 1.5cm
158cm–170cm height 1.75cm; square down.

1 –10 Sleeve length from shoulder; square across to 11 and 12.

10–13 Sizes 92cm–122cm height 2cm
128cm–152cm height 2.5cm
158cm–170cm height 3cm; square across.

10–14 Cuff size for two-piece sleeve; join 10–14 and 10–11.

7 –15 ½ measurement 7–10; square across (elbow line).

Curve inner sleeve seams inwards at elbow line, the measurement 7–8.
Draw in sleeve head.

5 – 4 Raise the curve:
sizes 92cm–122cm height 0.7cm
128cm–152cm height 0.8cm
158cm–170cm height 0.9cm.

Mark point 16, 4–16 is ⅓ measurement 4–3.

4 – 3 Raise the curve at 16:
sizes 92cm–122cm height 1.25cm
128cm–152cm height 1.5cm
158cm–170cm height 1.75cm; join 3–8.

6 –17 The measurement A–BP on body block, measured straight plus 0.5cm.

Join 6–17, draw a curve hollowed 1.5cm.
Join 6–9 with a slight curve.
Join 17–14 and 5–14.
Mark points 18 and 19 on elbow line.
Curve outer sleeve seams outwards the measurement 7–8 at points 18 and 19.

Note It is important that all curved measurements are measured very accurately along the curved line, with the tape upright (see diagram).

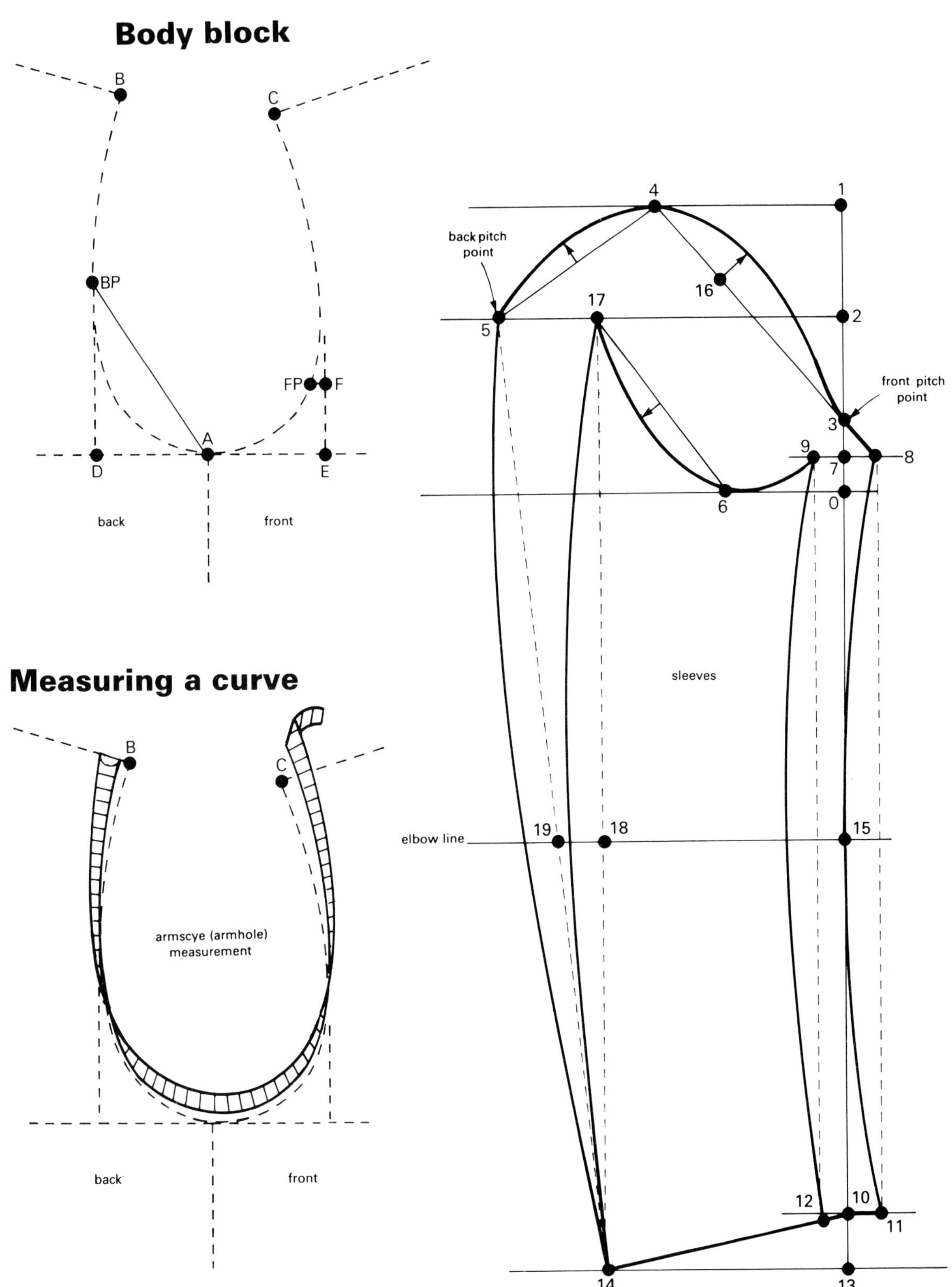
Body block
B
C
BP
FP
F
A
D
E
back
front
Measuring a curve
B
C
armscye (armhole)
measurement
back
front
back pitch
point
front pitch
point
1
2
3
4
5
6
7
8
9
0
16
17
sleeves
elbow line
19
18
15
12
10
11
14
13

From Block to Finished Pattern

The block pattern . . . is the basic pattern from which adaptations are made. The block chosen is traced or 'wheeled' on to pattern paper to produce a working pattern.
The working pattern . . . is used for cutting and adapting to achieve the final shapes required for the final pattern. Complicated designs may require a number of working shapes to be cut before the final shape is achieved. At this stage it is necessary to have as much information as possible written on the pattern.

The final pattern . . . is the pattern from which the garment will be cut. It must have all the information required to make up the garment written on the pattern. The final pattern has to be very accurate; all pattern pieces which have to be joined together should match exactly. If ease is included in a seam this should be marked by notches. The pattern should have smooth lines and curves. Curved rules and shapes are excellent aids in the making of 'professional' curves particularly at the neck and armhole.

Adapting the Blocks – Basic Points

The blocks include the correct amount of ease that is required for the function of the block (e.g. a coat block has more ease than a dress block). Before commencing any adaptation the following points should be considered.
1. Choose the correct blocks; e.g. if a baggy trouser style is required use the easy-fitting trouser block.
2. Decide the length; lengthen or shorten the block.
3. Decide if any easy-fitting armhole is required, (see lowered armhole page 36).

If this procedure is followed the correct basic shape will be achieved. This means that any styling will have the correct proportions.

Seam Allowances

Patterns used in industry have seam allowances added. Designers often adapt patterns from blocks which include seam allowances. This is a difficult task for a beginner. Students will find that it is easier to work with nett patterns (those without seam allowances) especially during the development of complicated styles. The seam allowance can be added when the adaptation of the pattern is completed. The amount of seam allowance required in specific places is usually:
basic seams (e.g. side seams, style seams) 1.5cm.
enclosed seams (e.g. collars, facings, cuffs) 0.5cm.
hem depth depends on shape and finish 1cm–5cm.
special seams (e.g. welt seam) often require different widths of seam allowance on matching seam lines.

Fabrics which fray easily may require a wider seam allowance.

The width of the seam allowance must be marked on each piece of pattern by lines or notches.

Nett patterns are often produced for individual garments and the seam allowances are chalked directly on to the fabric lay. These garments are often cut with a standard 1.5cm seam allowance around enclosed seams as well as basic seams. The enclosed seams of individual garments can be trimmed during making-up.

Pattern Instructions

To enable the garment to be made up correctly the following instructions must be marked on the pattern.
1. The name of each piece.
2. Centre back and centre front.
3. The number of pieces to be cut.
4. Folds.
5. Balance marks . . . these are used to ensure that pattern pieces are sewn together at the correct points.
6. Seam allowances . . . these can be marked by lines round the pattern or notches at each end of the seam. If the pattern is nett (has no seam allowance) this must be marked on the pattern.
7. Construction lines . . . these include darts, buttonholes, pocket placings, tucks, pleats, decorative stitch lines. Construction lines are marked directly on the pattern or indicated by punch holes.
8. Grain lines . . . these indicate how the pattern must be positioned on the fabric. Mark the grain lines on the separate pattern pieces before the working pattern is cut into sections. Once it is in pieces it can be difficult to establish the correct grain particularly if the pattern has been through a number of development stages.

3 THE SLEEVE

Special note The body block produces a basic fit for the body and at the armhole. If more ease is required in the body and armhole shape, the adaptation for a lowered armhole (page 36) must be completed before proceeding. For very easy-fitting styles a better shape can often be achieved by using the kimono block (ref. 17, page 46) as a base for the designs. Armhole shapes can be drawn and developed on this very adaptable block.

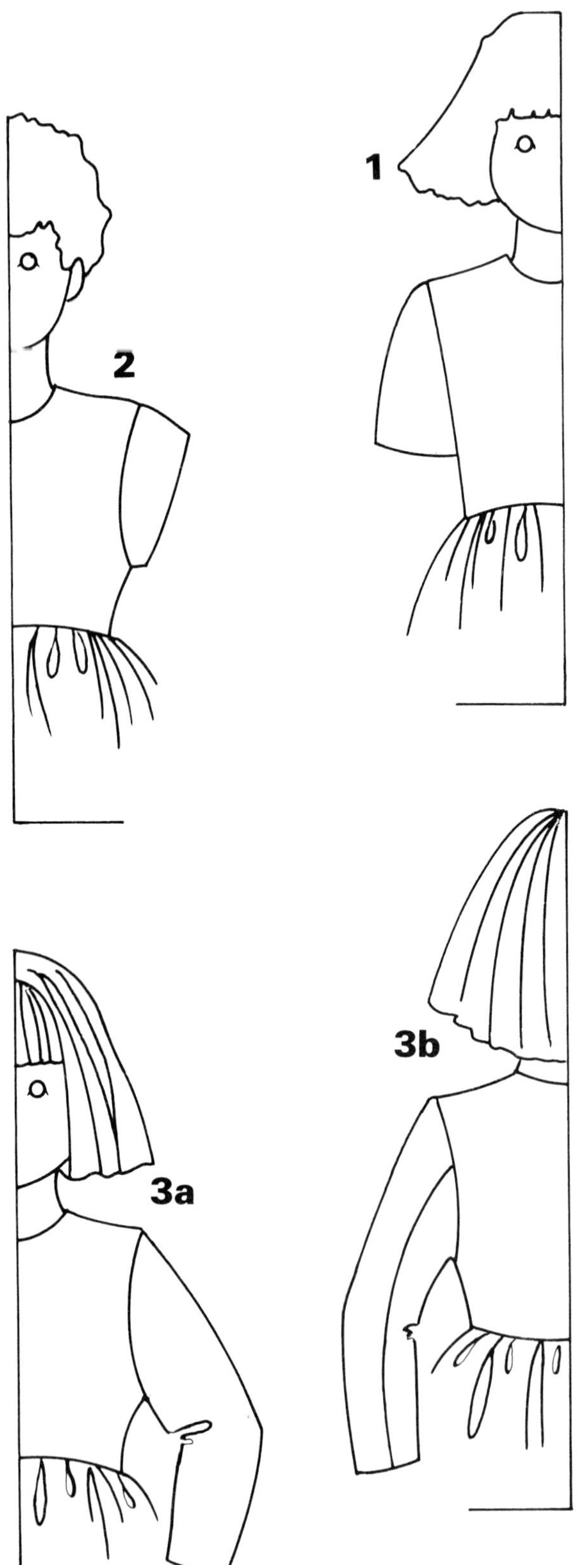

LOWERED ARMHOLE
For an easy-fitting body and armhole shape, complete this adaptation for the lowered armhole before continuing with further adaptations.

Body section Trace body section of block required; cut up side seam, open 3.5cm and draw a new side seam down the centre. Lower scye depth line 2.5cm.
Mark points A and B on each scye depth line.
Mark points C and D at front and back pitch points.
Draw in new armhole shape as shown.

Sleeve Trace one-piece sleeve block; draw a parallel line below armhole depth line, the distance is half the measurement A–B.
Mark points E and F at back and front pitch points.
Draw the curve E–G to new armhole depth line. The curve should equal the measurement of the curve C–B.
Draw the curve F–H to equal curve D–B.
Draw underarm seams, narrow at wrist if required.

Note The amount the block is widened and the armhole lowered can be varied but the proportions should remain constant.

1 SHORT SLEEVE
Trace round one-piece sleeve block to short sleeve length required. Shape in 1.5cm at the bottom of each side seam.

Sleeve facings Add 3cm to lower edge for facing. Fold along this line, wheel off the shape of the side seam line to complete the facing.

2 CAP SLEEVE
Square down from 0.
0–1 ¼ scye depth plus 0.5cm; square across.
1–2 3cm–4cm; square across.
0–3 and 0–5 ½ armscye measurement plus 0.5cm; square down to 4 and 6.
7 and 8 are midway between 0–3 and 0–5.
0–7 and 0–8 raise the curve 0.75cm.
3–7 and 8–5 hollow the curve 0.5cm.
4–9 and 6–10 1.5cm; join 3–9 and 5–10.
2–11 1.5cm; draw curve 9,11,10.

3a SEMI-SHAPED SLEEVE WITH DART
Cut from back elbow line to point A and from point A to wrist line. Pivot this section forward 2.5cm.
Halve the length of the dart made at back elbow.

3b SEMI-SHAPED SLEEVE WITH SEAM
Complete adaptation for 3a. Mark A and B on wristline. D at back pitch point E at dart point.
A–C ¼ measurement A–B. Join D–E and E–C, cut along line.
Close dart in back sleeve.
Curve both underarm seams as shown. Curve back and front sleeves outwards 0.5cm from D–E.

Lowered armhole

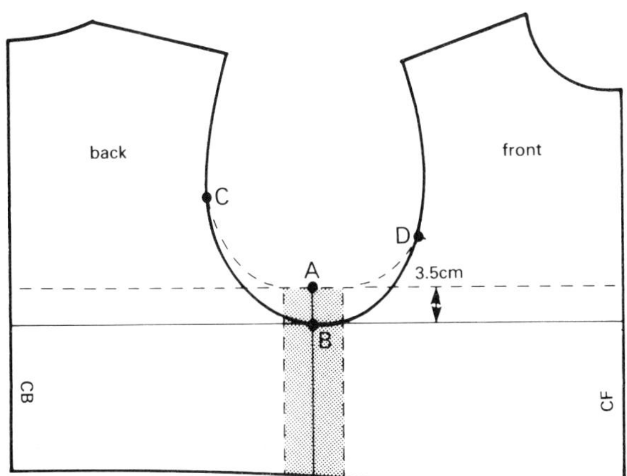

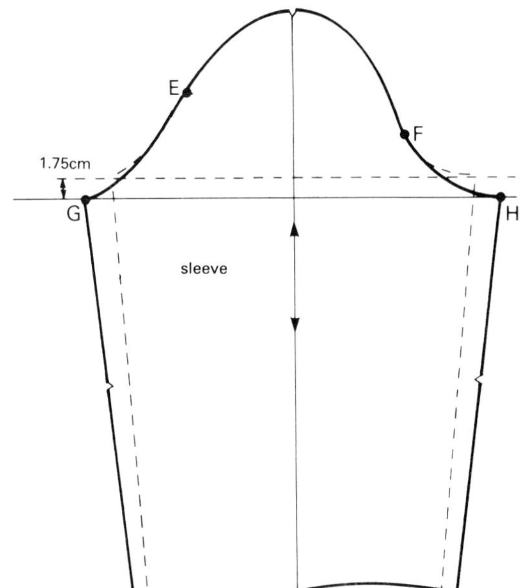

1 Short sleeve

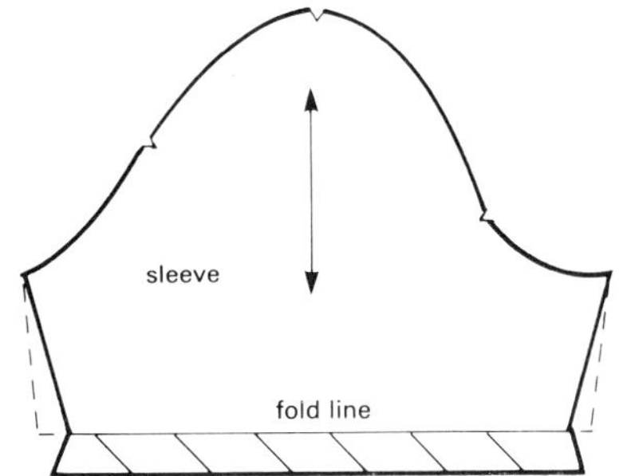

2 Cap sleeve

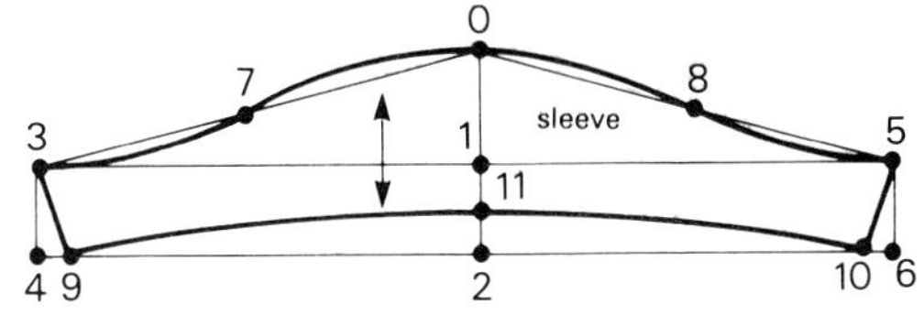

3 Semi-shaped sleeves

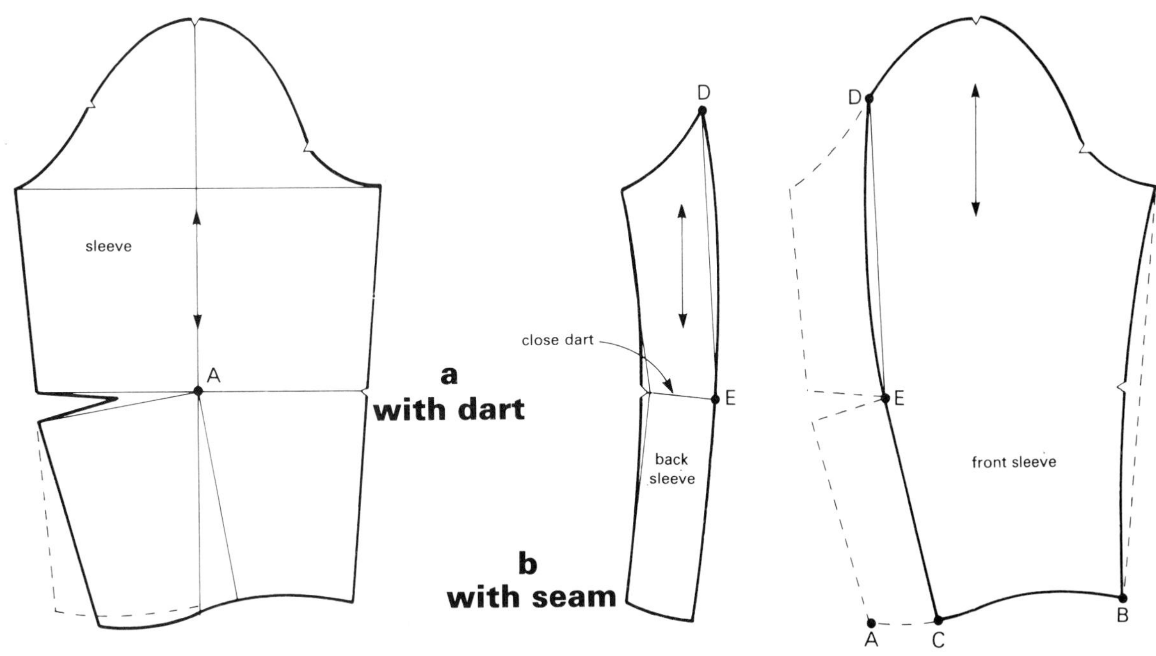

a with dart

b with seam

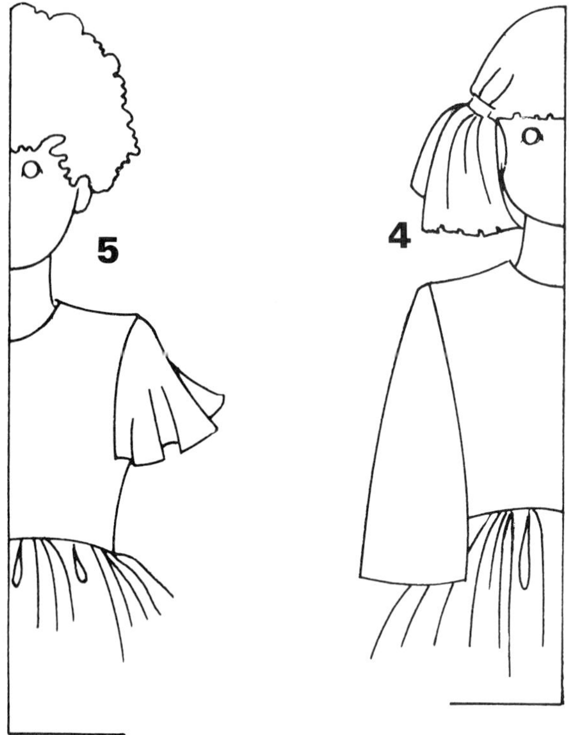

4 FLARED SLEEVES
Trace round one-piece sleeve block with straight hem to length required. Square down from front and back pitch points. Divide centre section into six.
Cut up lines, open approx. 1cm–2cm at the hem.
Grain line is in centre of the middle opening.
Trace round pattern.

4a FLARED SLEEVE WITH CUFFS
Flared sleeves of many different lengths can be gathered onto cuffs.
Trace off one-piece sleeve block with shaped hem.
Shorten sleeve the measurement of cuff depth.
Complete flare adaptation.
Draft relevant cuff (ref. 1a, page 50).

5 SLEEVE WITH EXTRA FLARE
Extra flare can be inserted between the sections.
Short sleeves Shape hem 1cm up at outer edges as shown.

6 SLEEVE WITH FLARED SECTIONS
Trace round flared sleeve to length required, mark points A and B.
Draw in section line; mark C and D. Draw in frill line; mark E and F.
Divide lower sleeve into eight sections.
Lower sleeve Cut away lower sleeve. Cut up lines, open for the required amount of flare (design shows 2cm).
Frill Measure the section line C–D.
Construct a circle the circumference is the measurement C–D (see 'constructing a circle', page 16).
G–H The measurement C–E.
Draw an outer circle from H.

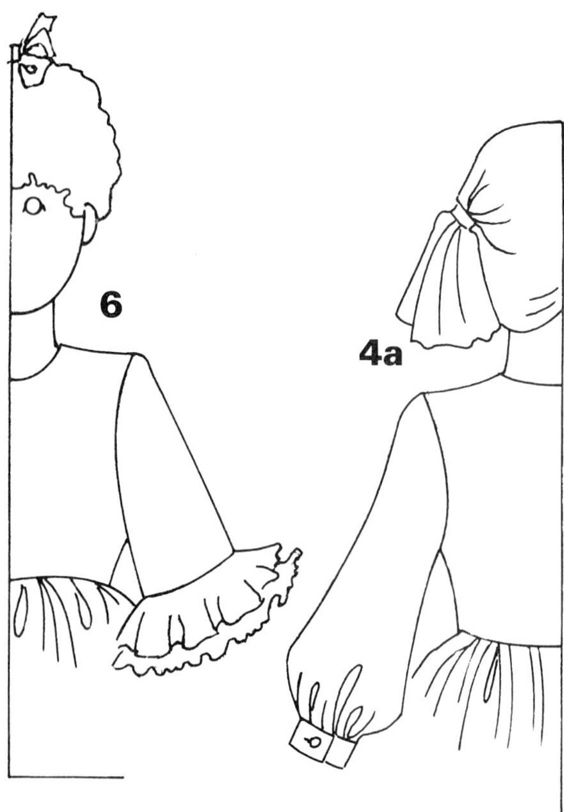

4 Flared sleeves

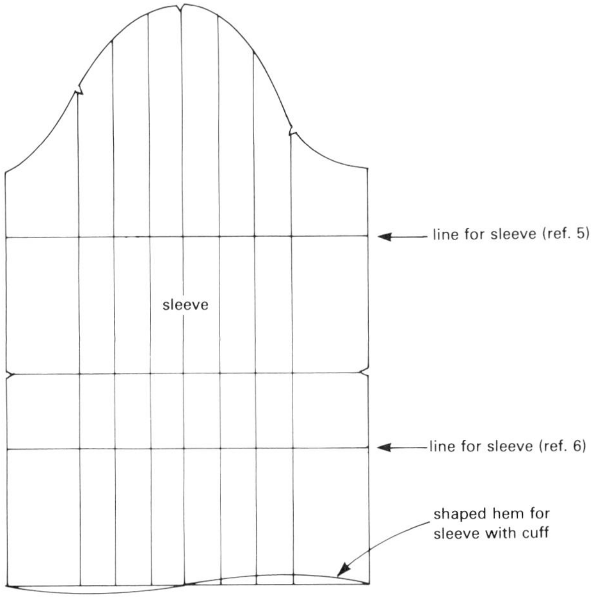

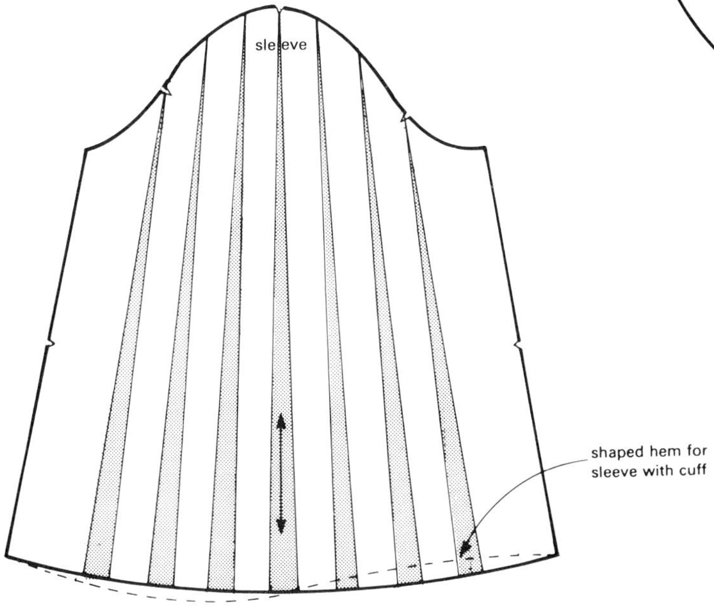

line for sleeve (ref. 5)

sleeve

line for sleeve (ref. 6)

shaped hem for sleeve with cuff

sleeve

shaped hem for sleeve with cuff

5 Sleeve with extra flare

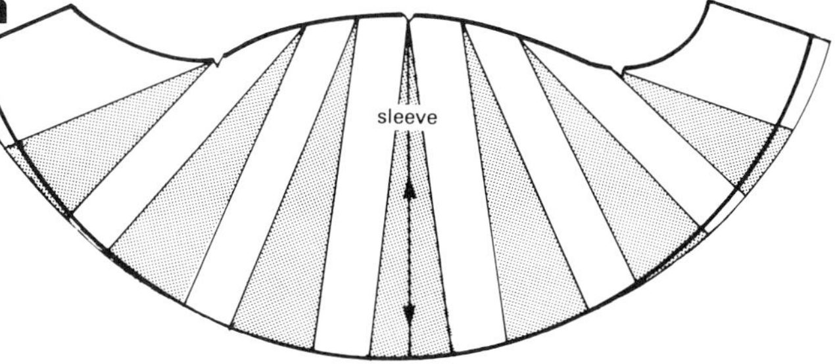

6 Sleeve with flared sections

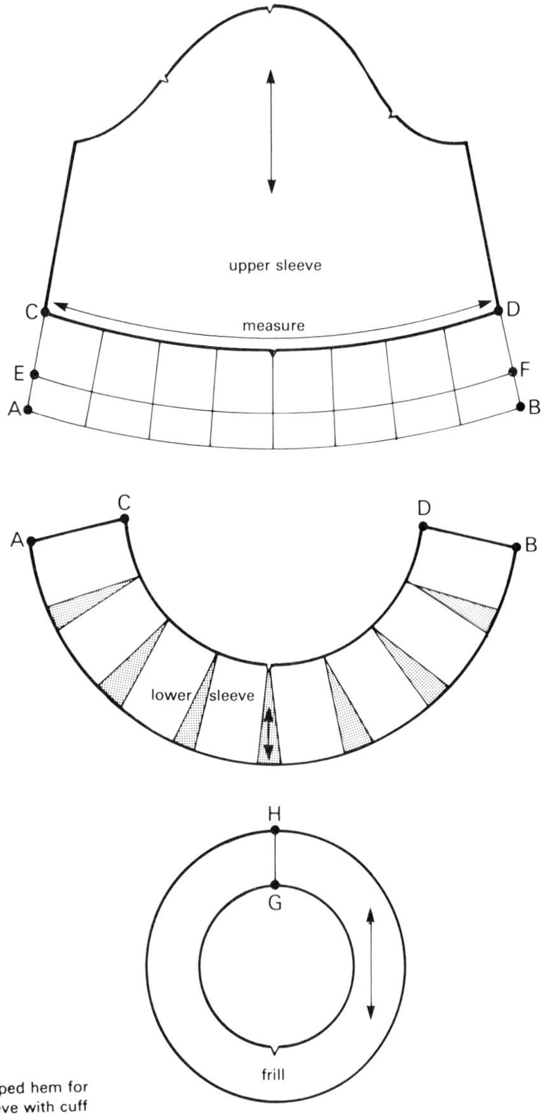

upper sleeve

C

D

measure

E

F

A

B

C

D

A

B

lower sleeve

H

G

frill

Note It is useful to number sections that are to be detached from the main pattern. This means that they can be placed in the correct order (e.g. ref. 7, gathered sleeve).

7 GATHERED (PUFF) SLEEVE
Trace round short sleeve. Square down from back and front pitch points. Divide centre section into six.
Open sections the amount required (example shows 2.5cm)
Add approx. 2cm extra depth to sleeve head and hem as shown.
Trace round pattern.

8 GATHERED SLEEVE HEAD
Trace round short sleeve. Square across from back pitch point. Divide sleeve head into six sections.
Mark balance points for gathers at points A and B.
Cut up the sections and open out the amount required (example shows 2cm).
Trace round pattern.

9 GATHERED AND FLARED SLEEVE
Trace round one-piece sleeve with straight side seams to the required length.
Square down from back and front pitch points.
Divide centre section into six. Open sections 1.5cm at sleeve head 3cm at hem (extra may be inserted).
Trace round pattern.
This sleeve can also be gathered onto a cuff.

Note It is necessary to make sure that when the pattern sections are opened at the sleeve head each section is laid on a line squared out from the line of previous section (e.g. line A–B).

10 GATHERED OR FLARED AND GATHERED SECTIONS (FRILLS)
Trace round one-piece sleeve block with shaping.
Draw in section line. Mark points A, B and C.
Square down from A, B and C.
A–D Depth of frill; square across to E and F.
Trace off top sleeve section.
10a Gathered section Measure the lengths A–C and C–B.
Construct the section, G–H and H–J are twice the measurements A–C and C–B; square down.
G–K The measurement A–D; square across to L.
10b Flared and gathered section Construct a half circle, the circumference of the whole circle is four times the measurement A–B (see 'constructing a circle', page 16). Mark points G and H.
G–J Twice measurement A–C.
G–K and H–L are the measurement A–D.
Complete outer sleeve line.

7 Gathered (puff) sleeve

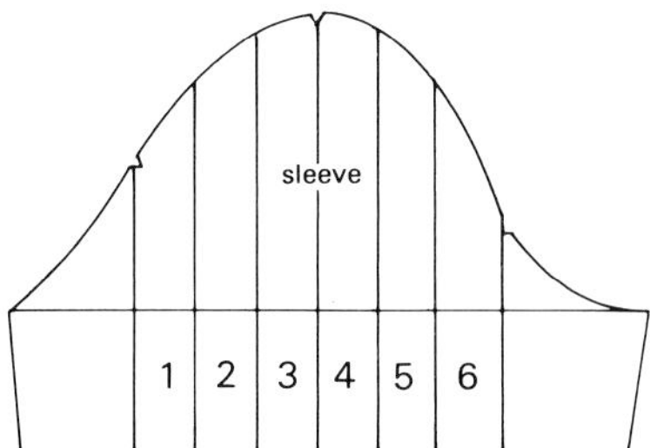

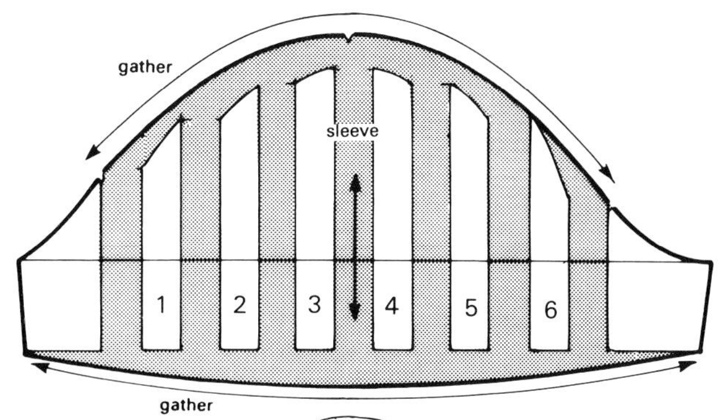

8 Gathered sleeve head

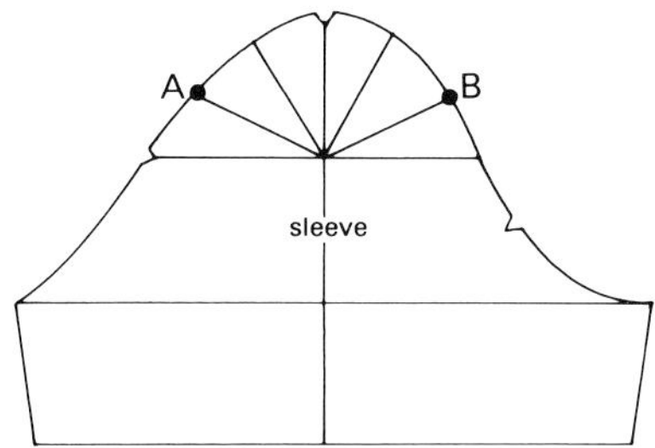

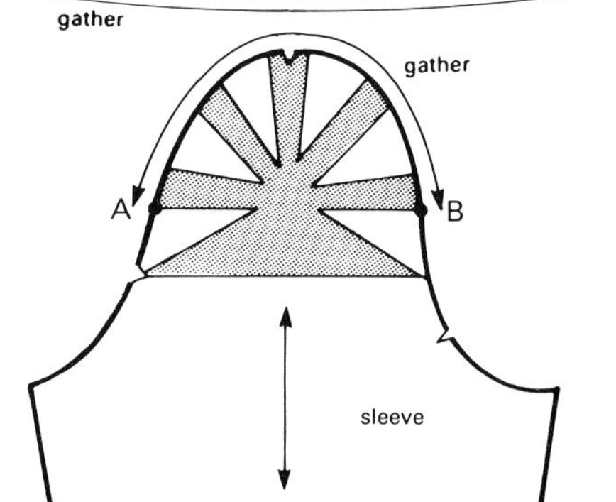

9 Gathered and flared sleeve

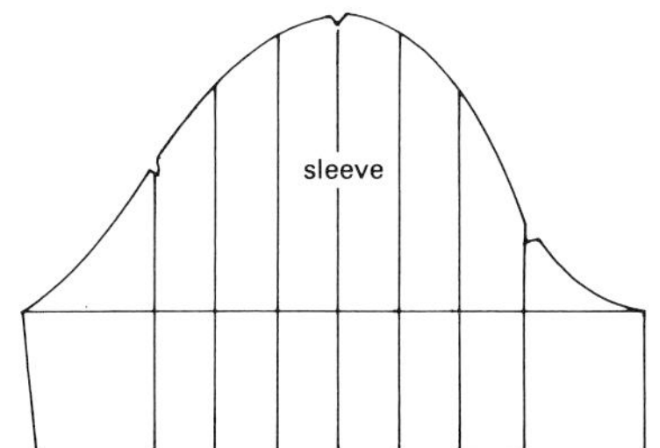

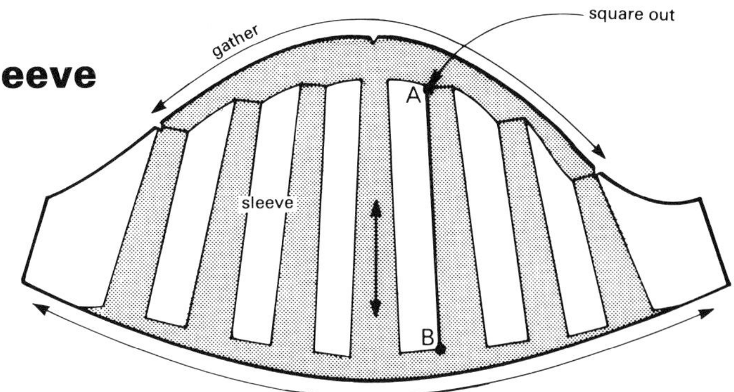

10 Gathered or flared and gathered sections

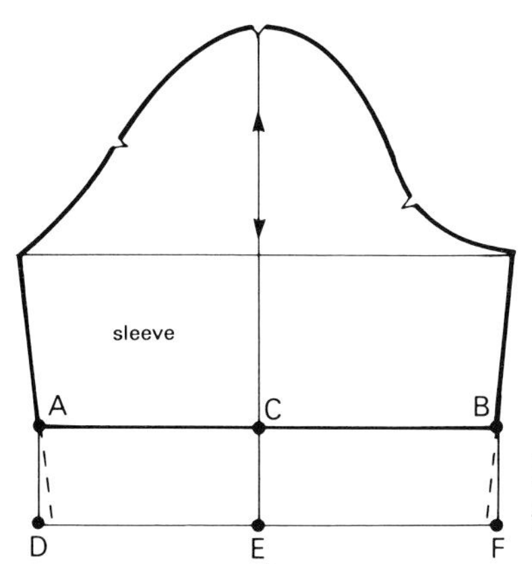

a gathered section

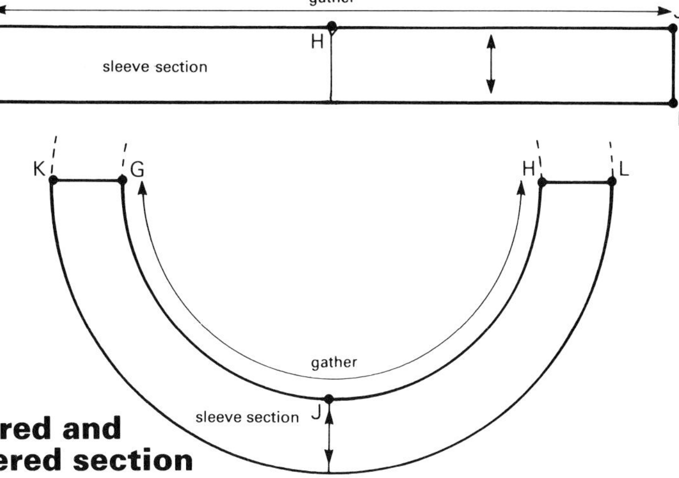

b flared and gathered section

11 EXTENDED SLEEVE WITH YOKE

Body section Trace body section of block required. Mark points A and B at pitch points on body block. Draw in yoke lines; mark points C and D at armhole edge. Trace off yoke sections.

Sleeve Trace one-piece sleeve, cut up centre line. Mark points E and F at pitch points on sleeve block.

E–G The measurement A–C on back body section.

F–H The measurement B–D on front body section.

Back yoke Place sleeve to yoke matching point C to G.

Front yoke Place sleeve to yoke with point H opposite D and sleeve head touching shoulder point. The top of the sleeve head will rise above the shoulder on both yokes, raise shoulder line at armhole edge to make a smooth continuous line at sleeve head.

Front bodice D–J the measurement D–H on yoke, draw new armhole shape.

Note For deep yokes use kimono block (ref. 17, page 46) as placing deep yokes to a sleeve head creates problems.

12 DROPPED SHOULDER

Body section Trace body section of block required. Mark points A and B at pitch points on body block. Extend shoulder to shape required.

Mark points C and D at base of extended shoulder.

Sleeve Trace one-piece sleeve block. Mark points E and F at pitch points on sleeve block, G at sleeve head.

E–H The measurement A–C on back body section.

F–J The measurement B–D on front body section.

G–K The measurement the shoulder has been extended.

Draw new sleeve head H, K, J.

12a WITH FLARED SLEEVE

The new sleeve shape can be flared (ref. 4, page 38) or gathered (ref. 7, page 40) or gathered and flared (ref. 9, page 40) to create different styles.

13 DROPPED SHOULDER WITH LOWERED ARMHOLE

Body section Mark points A and B at pitch points. Cut up side seam widen required amount draw new scye depth line (ref. lowered armhole, page 36). Extend shoulder line and raise 0.5cm at shoulder edge. Draw new armhole shape. Mark points C and D where old and new armhole shapes touch.

Sleeve Trace one-piece sleeve block.

Mark points E and F at pitch points on sleeve block.

E–H The measurement A–C on back body section.

F–J The measurement B–D on front body section.

Draw new armhole depth line (ref. lowered armhole, page 36). Mark point L at underarm point on side seam.

The curve H–M is the measurement of the curve C–L.

The curve J–N is the measurement of the curve D–L.

Complete the head of the sleeve H, K, J as for the dropped shoulder. Check sleeve head measurement; it is often necessary to widen the sleeve at K as shown.

11 Extended sleeve with yoke

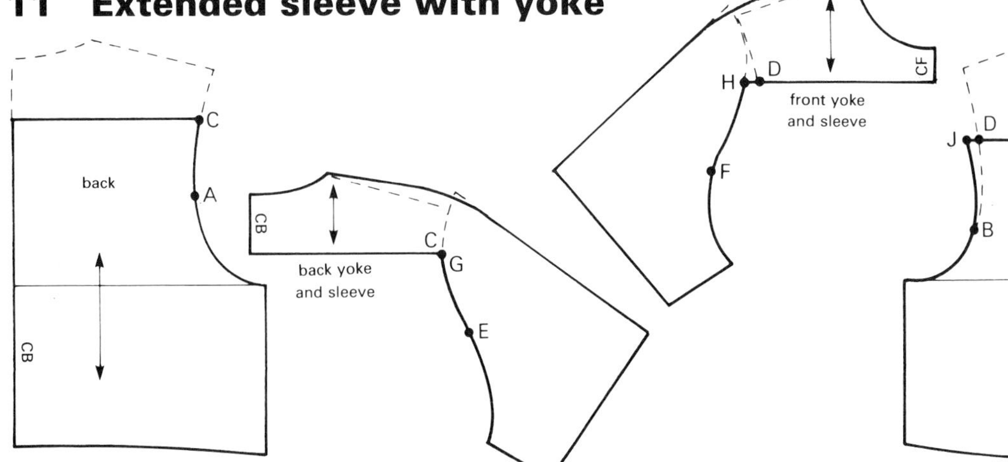

12 Dropped shoulder

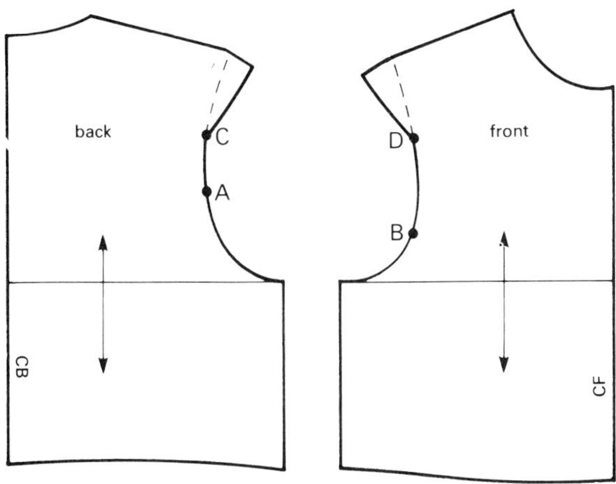

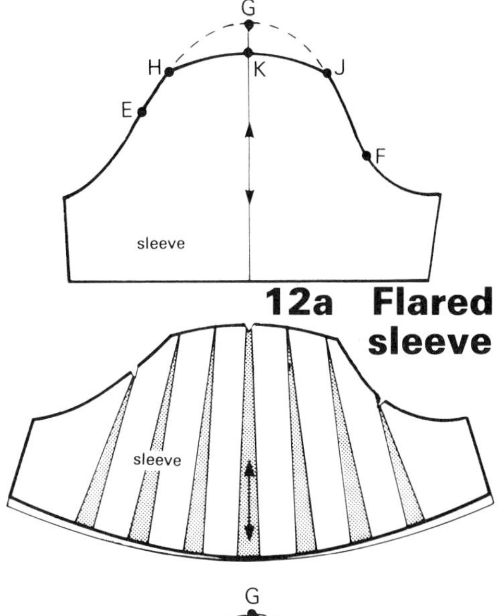

12a Flared sleeve

13 Dropped shoulder with lowered armhole

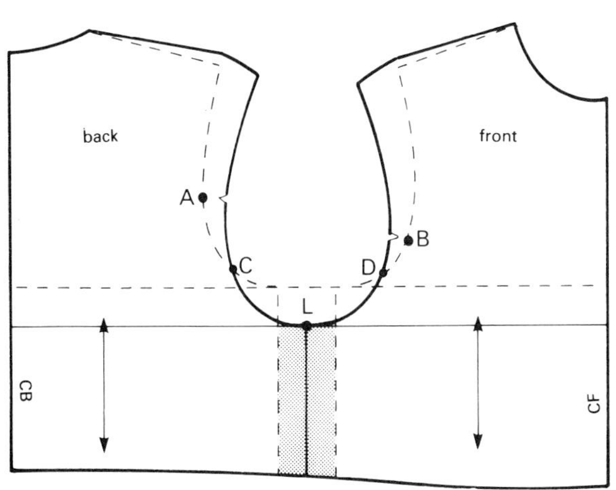

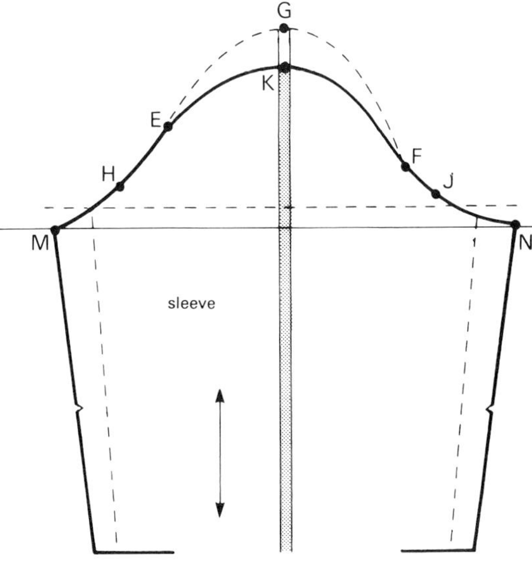

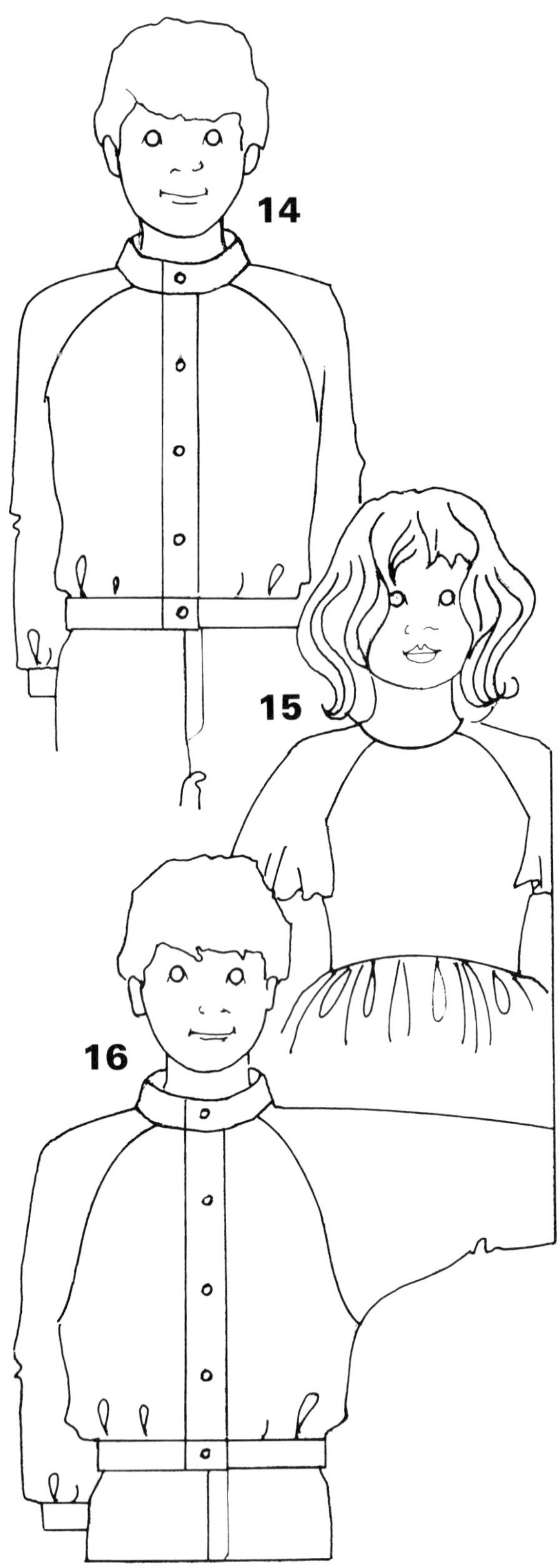

14 RAGLAN SLEEVE

Body section Trace body section of block required.
Add to back shoulder line: 92cm–122cm height 0.3cm
128cm–152cm height 0.6cm
158cm–170cm height 0.9cm.
Remove the above amount from front shoulder line.
Mark A and B at new shoulder points.
A–C and B–D: 92cm–122cm height 2.25cm
128cm–152cm height 2.5cm
158cm–170cm height 2.75cm
Mark E and F at pitch points on body block. E–G 1cm.
Mark H on front armhole directly opposite point G.
Draw curved lines from C–G and D–H; draw dart on back shoulder, size is amount of shoulder ease.
Cut off shaded sections. Close back shoulder dart.

Sleeve Trace one-piece sleeve block; draw centre line of sleeve. Mark J at sleeve head; J–K is the amount added to the back shoulder; square down from K.
Mark L and M at pitch points.
L–N The measurement E–G on back body block.
M–P The measurement F–H of front body block.
Cut up line from K.
Place back body section to back sleeve; place G to touch N, place shoulder point to touch sleeve head.
Place front body section to front sleeve; place H to touch P, place shoulder point to touch sleeve head.
Add 0.5cm to the centre line of each sleeve. Mark point Q 5cm down from the top of the sleeve head.
Draw shoulder lines to Q with curved lines as shown.

15 FLARED RAGLAN SLEEVE

Mark points A and B at the centre of the neckline on the back and front sleeve. Draw curved lines to the hem line. Cut up the lines. Place back and front sleeve together; open approx. 4cm at the hem line.
Open the curved lines approx. 4cm at the hem line.
Shorten neck dart 3cm. Shape up hem 1cm at outer edge.

Note The sleeve can be gathered onto a cuff.

16 EASY-FITTING RAGLAN SLEEVE

Complete adaptation for lowered armhole (page 36).

Body section Adapt shoulders as for raglan sleeve.
Mark points A, B, C, D.
Mark E at back pitch point. F at front pitch point.
Mark G on back armhole directly opposite point F.
Draw curved lines from C–G and D–F; draw in dart on back shoulder, size is amount of shoulder ease.
Cut off shaded sections. Close back shoulder dart.

Sleeve Adapt centre line of sleeve as raglan sleeve.
Mark H at sleeve head, J and K at sleeve pitch points.
J–L The measurement E–G on body block.
Complete the adaptation for the classic raglan placing G to L on back sleeve and F to K on front sleeve.

14 Raglan sleeve

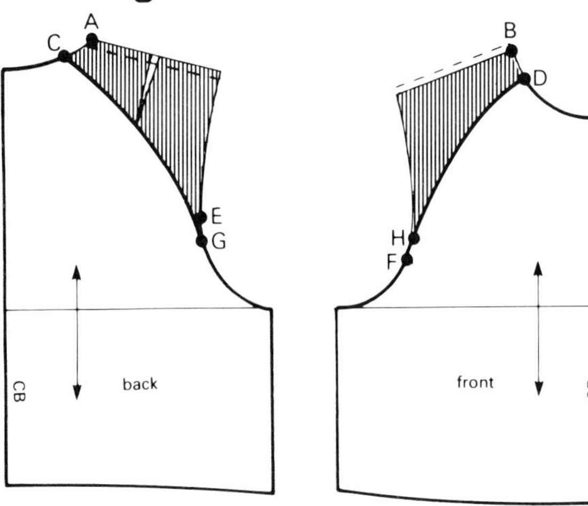

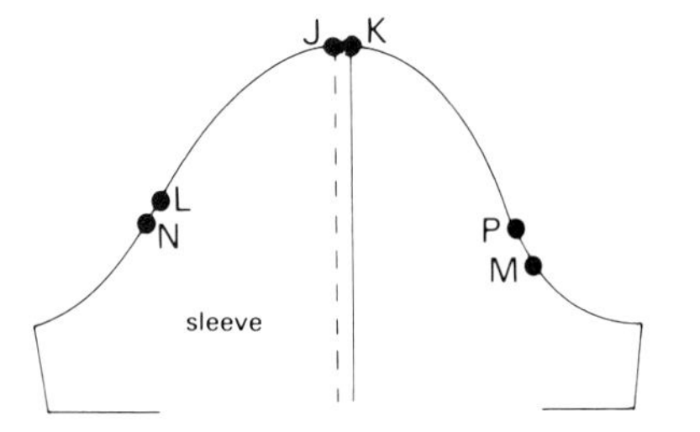

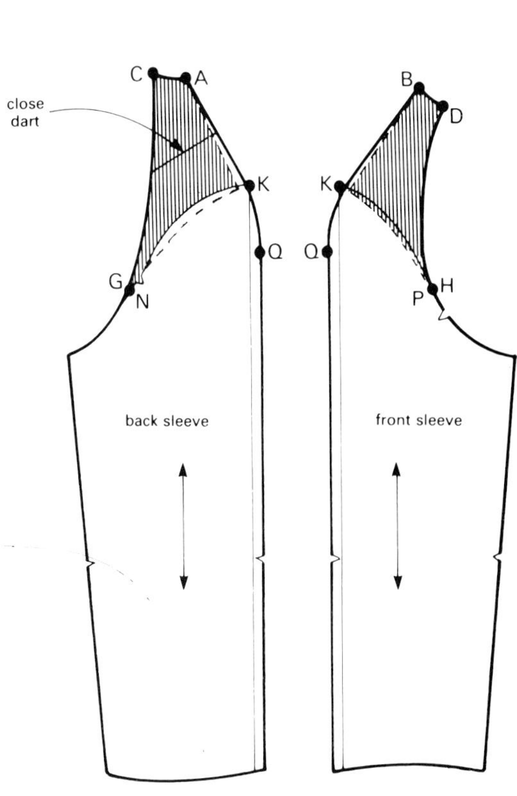

15 Flared raglan sleeve

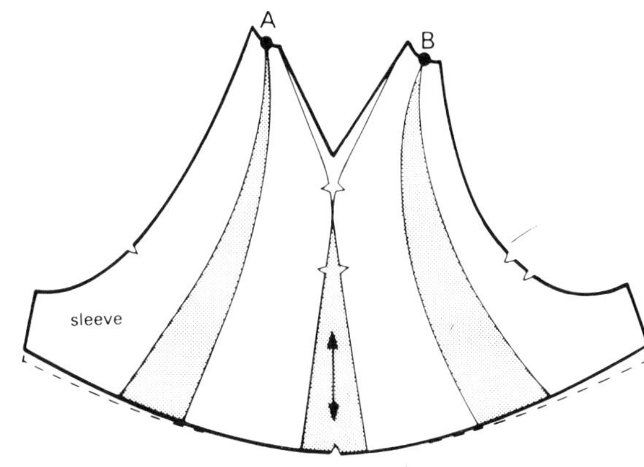

16 Easy-fitting raglan sleeve

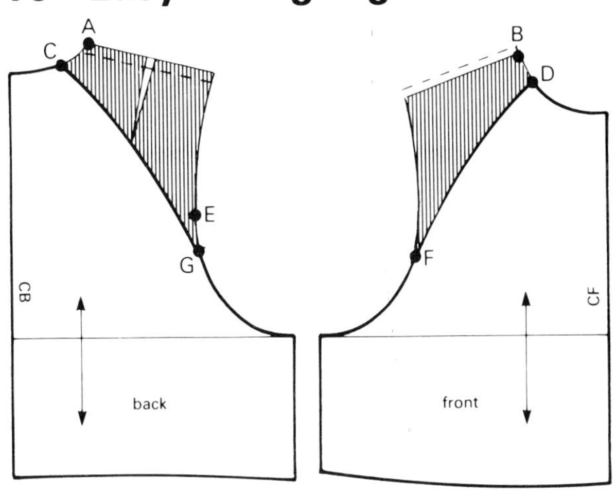

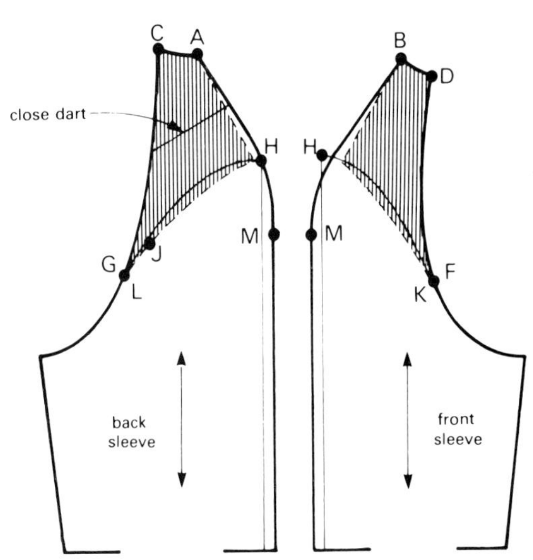

KIMONO SLEEVES

The basic kimono block is a base for easy-fitting designs. Gussets are not suitable for children's wear; they are a weak construction point but ease under the arm can be inserted in the pattern shapes during adaptation (ref. 19, page 46; ref. 20, page 48).

17 BASIC KIMONO BLOCK

Back Trace round body section of block required. Mark points 0 and 1 on side seam; square out.
1–2 92cm–122cm height 1.5cm
128cm–152cm height 2.5cm
158cm–170cm height 3.5cm; square up to 3
Mark 4 at shoulder point, 5 at neck point.
Split sleeve from balance point at sleeve head.
Place back sleeve head to touch shoulder point 4 and underarm of sleeve to touch line 2–3. Mark point 6.
0–7 ⅓ measurement 0–1 minus 0.5cm.
Join 7 to wrist at base of underarm sleeve.
7–8 and 7–9 92cm–122cm height 4cm
128cm–152cm height 4.5cm
158cm–170cm height 5cm.
Join 8–9 with a curve.
4–10 0.5cm; join 5–10 and 10 to wrist point 11.

Front Trace round body section of block required. Mark points 12 and 13 on side seam; square out.
12–14 92cm–122cm height 1.5cm
128cm–152cm height 2cm
158cm–170cm height 2.5cm; square up to 15.
15–16 The measurement 3–6 on back section.
Place underarm of front sleeve to point 16 and the sleeve head to shoulder (it will rise approx. 0.5cm above shoulder point).
Mark sleeve head point 17; neck point 18. Join 17–18.
Complete front as for back section.

18 KIMONO CAP SLEEVE

Trace back and front sections of the kimono block without underarm curve. Mark point 7. Square out.

Body sections Mark A at shoulder. A–B 1.5cm, B–C 3.5cm, 7–D 1.5cm. Join B–7 and C–D with a curve.

Sleeve Draw a perpendicular line E–F. Place back and front sleeve sections to E–F, open sections 1.5cm at F.

19 DEEP DOLMAN SLEEVE

Back Trace round basic kimono block. Mark points 8, 9 and 10. Draw in armhole curve A-B from required position on shoulder to centre of underarm curve.
B–C ½ measurement A–B; draw in 1cm dart from B–C.
C-D ⅓ measurement C–B. Join D–9.
Construct front using the same instructions.

Sleeve Draw a perpendicular line. Trace off sleeves from body sections; place to line.
Cut along line 9–D, open 3cm. Raise sleeve head 1cm at A with curve. Curve line from C–B.

17 Basic kimono block

18 Kimono cap sleeve

19 Deep dolman sleeve

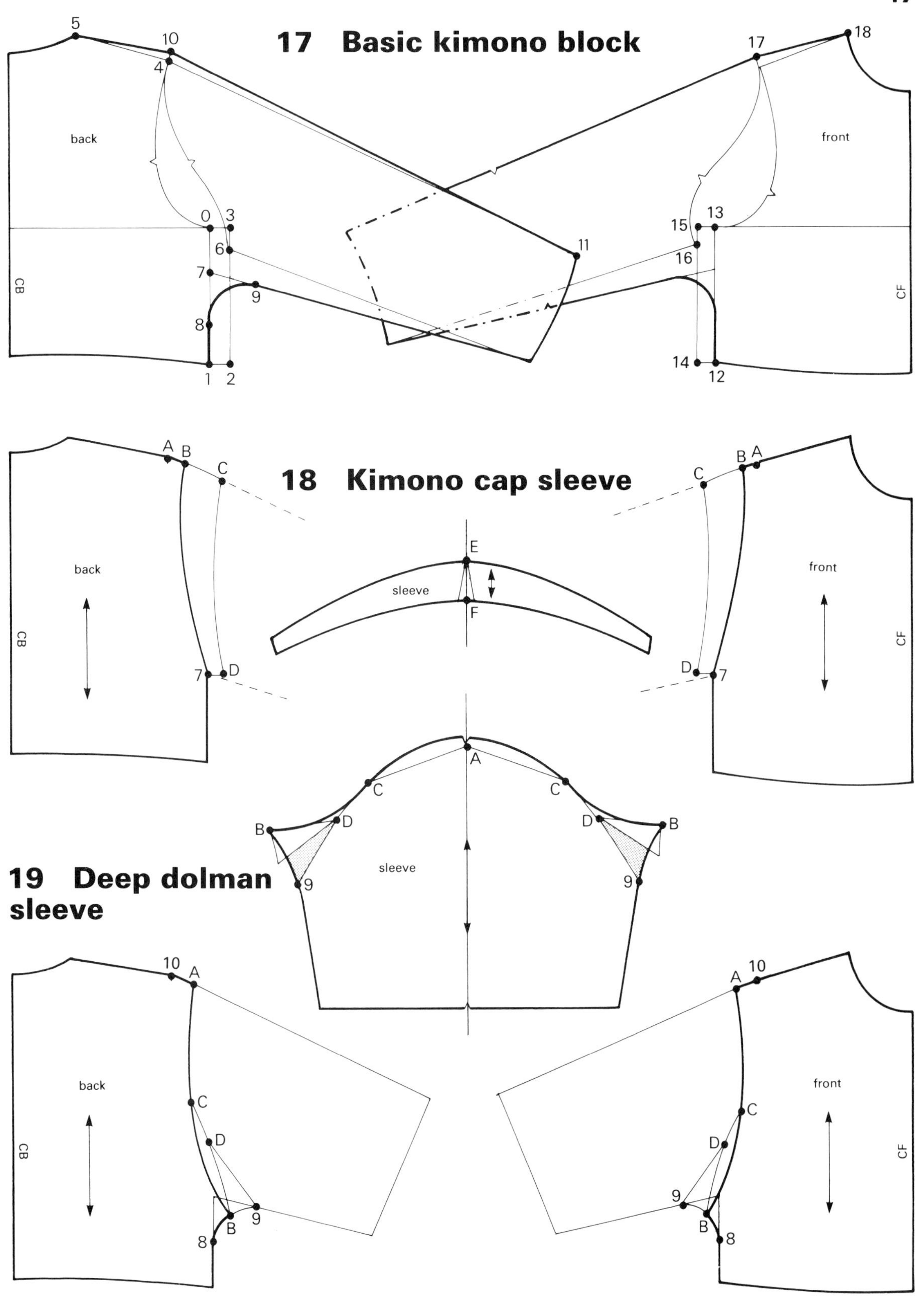

20 STYLED KIMONO SLEEVE

Body sections Trace round basic kimono block to sleeve length required. Mark points 8 and 9.
Draw curved panel seams on back and front.
Draw line from neck point to centre of underarm curve.
Mark points A and B, mark point C on panel line.
C–D ⅓ measurement C–B; join D–8 and D–9.
Trace off back and front sections.
Trace off back and front panels. Cut up lines 8–D and open 3cm. Join 8–B with curves. Curve lines D–B.
Sleeve Draw a perpendicular line. Trace off sleeve sections, place to centre line at E as shown.
Cut up lines 9–D and open 3cm. Join 9–B with curves.
Curve lines D–B.
Raise sleeve head 1cm with a curve.

21 STYLED KIMONO SLEEVE

Body sections Trace basic kimono block to body length and sleeve length required. Mark points 8 and 9.
Draw yoke seams.
Draw line from neck point to centre of underarm curve.
Mark points A and B. Mark C on yoke line.
Draw a 1.5cm dart on the line B–C.
Mark D and E on both yoke lines.
Divide C–D into three sections; square down.
Divide C–E into three sections; draw parallel lines down the sleeve.
Trace off back and front sections; cut up lines and open required amount (example shows 1.5cm at yoke, 2.5cm at hem).
Trace round outlines making good yoke curves.
Add 1cm flare at side seams.

Note It is necessary to make sure that when the pattern sections are opened each section is laid on a line squared out from the line of the previous section (e.g. line F–G).

Yokes Trace off yoke sections.
Sleeve Draw perpendicular line.
Trace off sleeve sections, place to line.
Cut up section lines and open top of sleeve required amount (the example shows 1.25cm).
Trace round new outline making a good yoke curve.

Note Designs which are cut with extra fullness in the body rarely need to have 'gusset ease' inserted at the armscye.

20 Styled kimono sleeve

21 Styled kimono sleeve

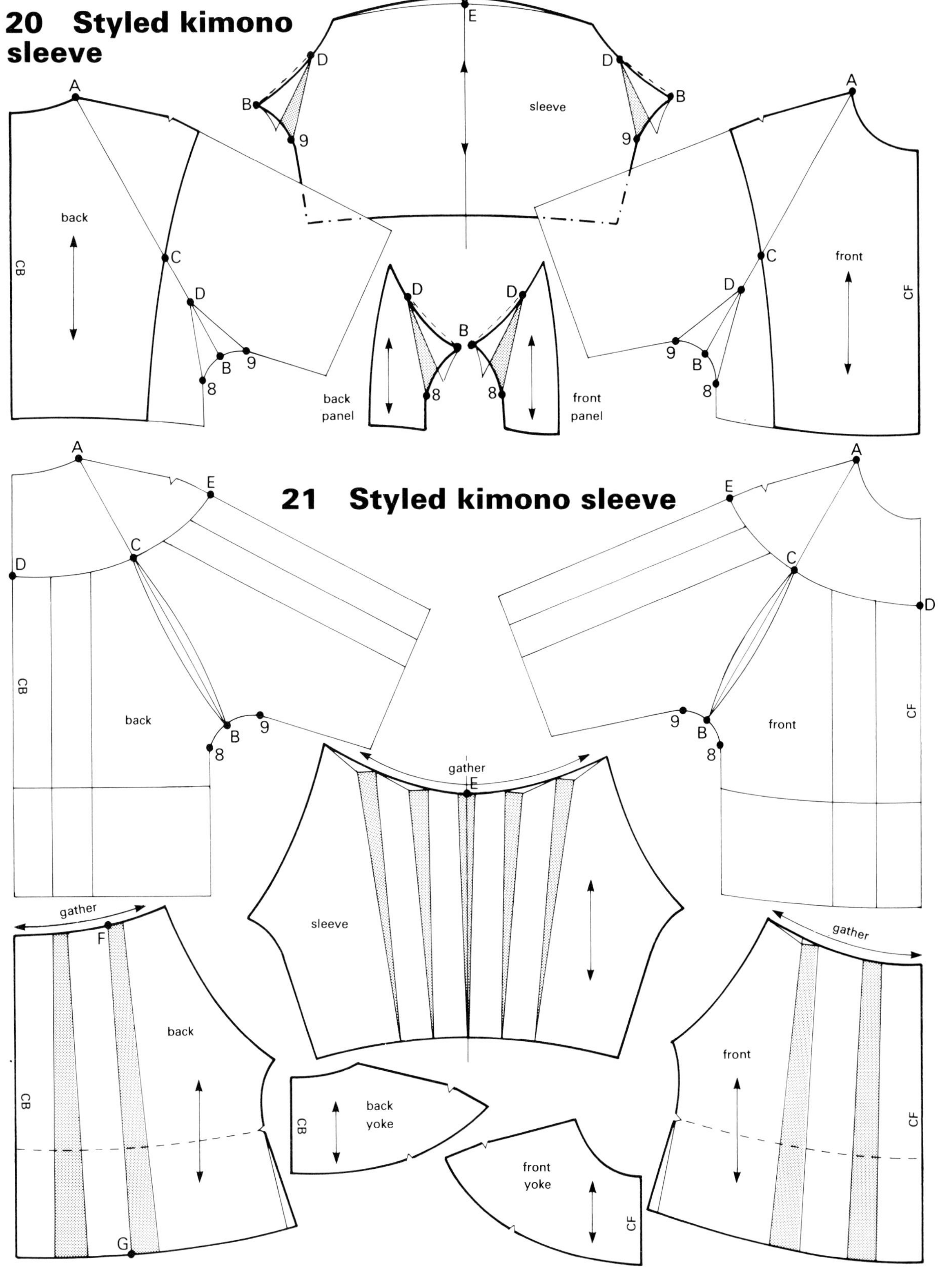

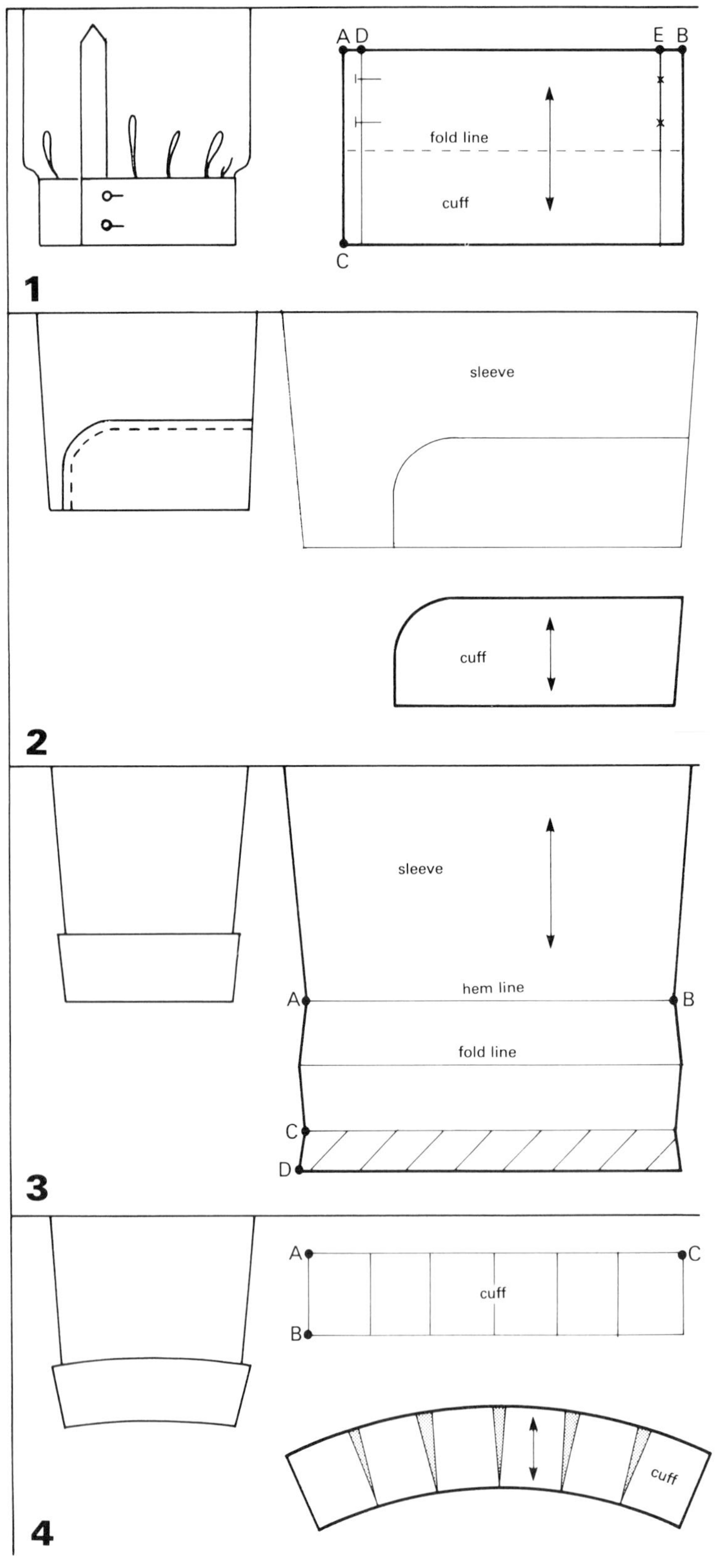

1 STRAIGHT CUFFS

If a sleeve pattern is the finished length required, shorten sleeve pattern by the measurement of the cuff depth.

1a Shirt cuff A–B cuff size plus 2cm; square down.

A–C Twice cuff depth; square across.

A–D and B–E 1cm; square down.

Draw the fold line through centre.

Mark buttonholes and button placings on the lines as shown.

1b Simple straight cuff This cuff is similar to the shirt cuff but it has no opening. Construct pattern as for the shirt cuff but make the following alterations.

Long sleeve A–B is cuff size, omit button stand lines and button placings.

Short sleeve A–B top arm measurement plus 3cm, omit button stand lines and button placings.

2 SLEEVE FACING (MOCK CUFF)

Trace round lower edge of sleeve with straight hem line.

Draw in line of facing on sleeve.

Trace off facing.

3 ATTACHED CUFF

Trace round lower edge of sleeve with straight hem line.

Mark A and B at side seam.

A–C Twice cuff depth; square across.

Mark fold line through centre.

C–D Facing depth (approx. 3cm); square across.

Fold back cuff and facing to finished position; trace through side seam to obtain cuff shaping.

4 SHAPED CUFF

This cuff is attached to a straight hem line.

A–B Depth of finished cuff; square across.

A–C The measurement of base of the sleeve; square down.

Divide rectangle into six sections; square down. Cut up lines from outer edge; open out top edge to width required at top of cuff.

Trace round new shape.

4 OPENINGS – COLLARS – HOODS

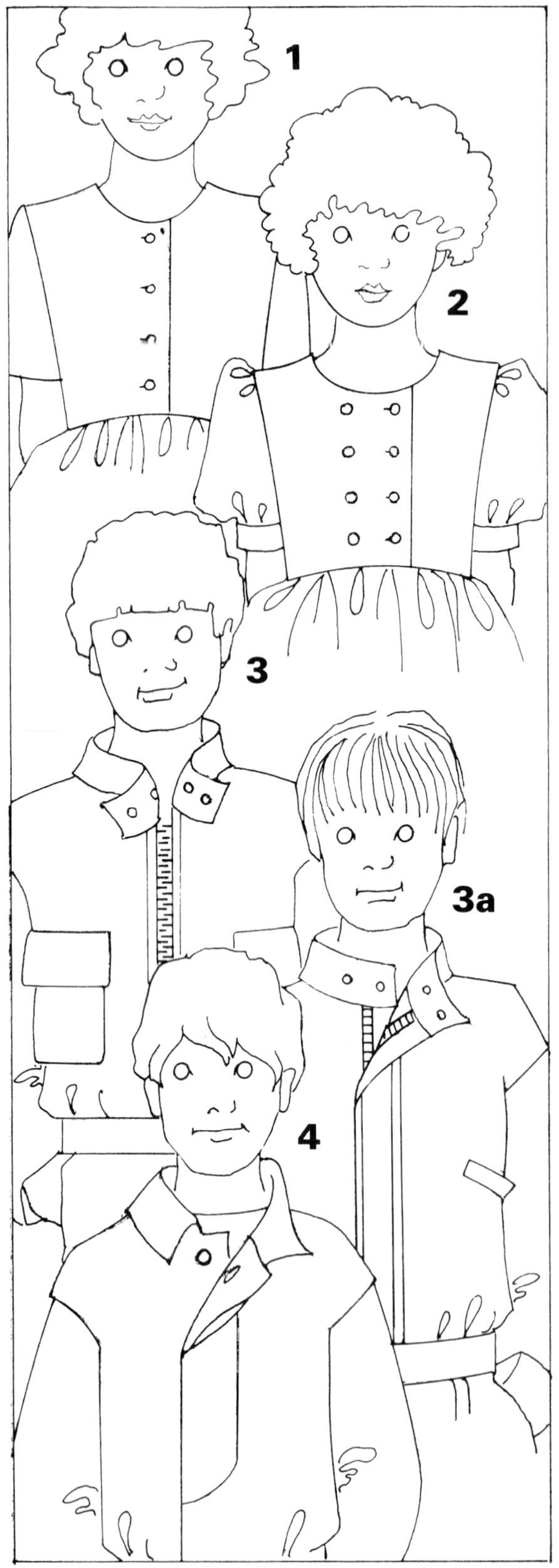

FRONT OPENINGS

When drafting designs with front openings it is necessary to be aware that the centre front is a stable position and cannot be moved. Any movement will alter the fit of the garment, therefore care must be taken when button stands or straps are added. If the neckline requires lowering, this must be done before working the instructions for front openings. It is the convention that the front of girls' garments overlaps towards the left while boys' garments overlap towards the right. Garments designed for both sexes usually have centre openings.

1a STANDARD FRONT

Mark buttonholes on centre front line (buttonholes overlap the line by 0.2cm). Add button stand approx. 2cm (varies with size of button).
Draw in back and front facings, trace round neck edges, front edge of pattern and facing lines to construct facings.

1b EXTENDED FACING

Mark buttonholes; add button stand.
Fold front edge line, trace through facing line and neckline to construct an extended facing.

2 DOUBLE BREASTED FRONT

Draw two button lines at equal distances each side of centre front. Mark buttonholes, button placings; add button stand. Construct facing as for standard front.

3 STANDARD ZIP FRONT (ZIP EXPOSED)

Measure width of zip to be exposed. Mark in from centre front half this distance and mark this zip line, front edge line. Rub out centre front line.
Construct facing as for standard front.

3a STRAP FOR ZIP FRONT

Mark strap line on front section. Mark A at top of strap line, B at centre front.
Construct strap twice the measurement A–B. Mark fold line at outer edge. Mark centre front.

CONCEALED ZIP

Construct front and facing as for standard zip front but work to centre front line. Add 2cm seam allowance to centre front line of front and facing.
Place zip between front and facing and top-stitch.

4 SIMPLE FLY FRONT

Fly front Add button stand to centre front, mark stitch line. Add extension to front edge 2cm below top edge to 5cm below stitch line. The extension must be 1.5cm wider than width of stitch line.
Trace off facing with the same extension. Mark vertical buttonholes on centre front line of facing.
Buttoned front Construct as a standard front.

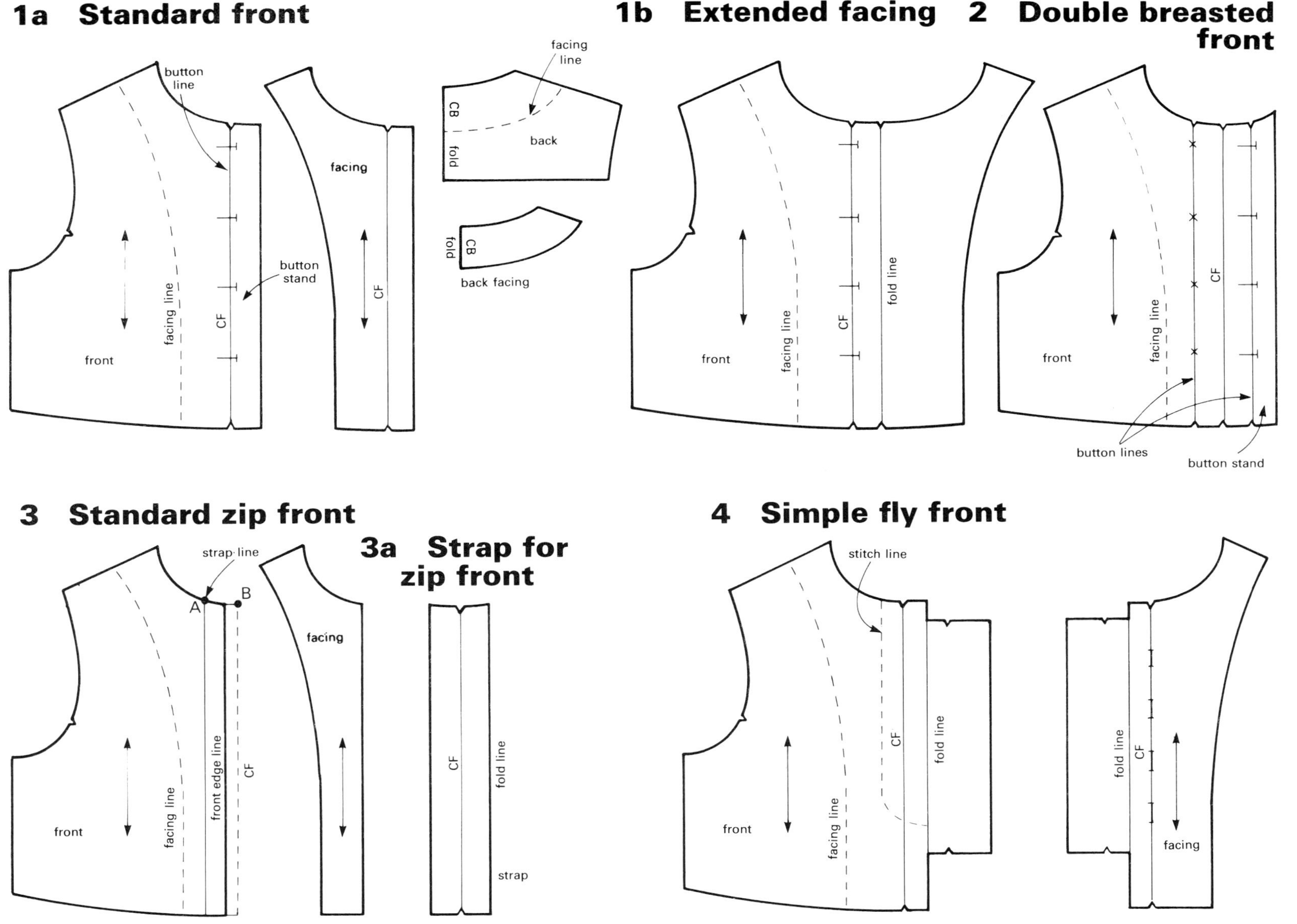
1a Standard front
button line
button stand
facing line
CF
front
facing
CF
facing line
CB
fold
back
CB
fold
back facing
1b Extended facing
front
facing line
CF
fold line
2 Double breasted front
front
facing line
CF
button lines
button stand
3 Standard zip front
strap line
A
B
front
facing line
front edge line
CF
facing
3a Strap for zip front
CF
fold line
strap
4 Simple fly front
stitch line
front
facing line
CF
fold line
fold line
CF
facing

TERMS USED FOR COLLAR CONSTRUCTION

Neckline Line where the collar is joined to the neck.
Style line Outer edge of collar and rever.
Roll line The line where the collar rolls over.
Stand Rise of the collar from neckline to roll line.
Fall Depth of the collar from roll line to style line.
Break point Where the rever turns back.
Break line Line along which the rever rolls back.

Note The break line and the roll line are sometimes referred to as crease lines.

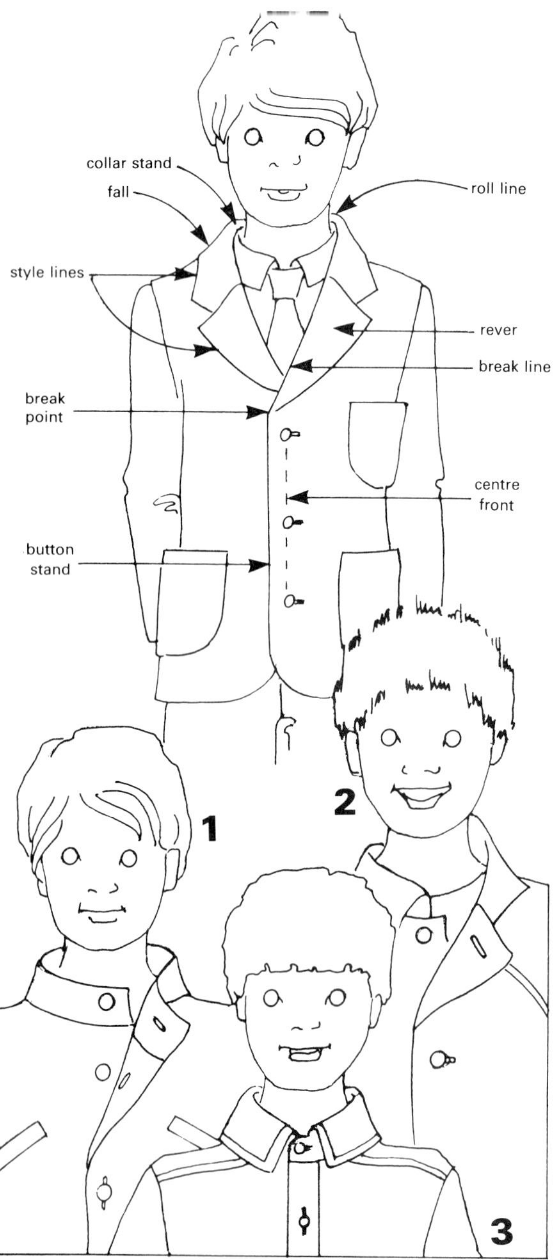

Before drafting a collar
Alter neckline if required, mark any button lines, buttonholes and button stands.

Collar shapes
Although the style line determines the shape of the outer edge of the collar, the length of the outer edge determines where it sits on the body. If the outer edge of a collar is tightened it sits higher in the neck, increasing the stand. If it is widened it reduces the stand (see diagram).

Top collars
Add approx. 0.25cm (depending on thickness of fabric) to outer edge of top collars from A–B. Some collar designs require 0.25cm on back neckline from C–D.

STANDING COLLARS

Measuring the neckline
If the neckline is to be lowered, complete this first. Place back shoulder to front shoulder, measure the neckline accurately from centre back to centre front with the tape measure upright (see diagram); this gives ½ *neckline measurement*. This measurement is not ½ the neck size body measurement as the neckline measurement is drafted to include the ease required for the garment.

1 STANDING STRAIGHT COLLAR

0 – 1 ½ neckline measurement; 1–2 button stand; square up from 0 and 2.
0 – 3 Collar depth; square across to 4.
4 – 5 1.25cm; 5–6 equals 1–2; 0–7 ½ measurement 0–1.
2 – 8 1cm; join 5–8 and 6–1.
Joint 7–8 with a curve. Mark any buttonholes.

2 CONVERTIBLE COLLAR

0 – 1 ½ neckline measurement; square up from 0 and 1.
0 – 2 ¾ measurement 0–1 minus 1cm; square up.
0 – 3 Collar depth; square across to 4 and 5.
0 – 6 0.5cm; 1–7 0.8cm; shape neckline of collar from 6–7. Draw style line of collar from 4–7.

Note If depth of collar exceeds 7cm, the outer edge from 3–4 is cut and spread to sit lower on shoulder.

3 SHIRT COLLAR

0 – 1 ½ neckline measurement; square up from 0 and 1.
0 – 2 Collar and stand depth (approx. 6cm–8cm); square across.
0 – 3 ¾ measurement 0–1; square up to 4.
0 – 5 ½ measurement 0–2 minus 1cm; square across to 6.
1 – 7 Button stand measurement; square up.
0 – 8 0.25cm; 7–9 0.75cm; join 8–3 and 3–9 with a curve.
6 –10 0.5cm. Draw outline of collar as shown.

3a SHIRT COLLAR WITH BAND

Trace round collar. Mark points 5, 9, 10.
5 –11 0.5cm; 10–12 0.25cm. Join 11–12–9.
Trace round collar and stand as shown.

Collar shapes

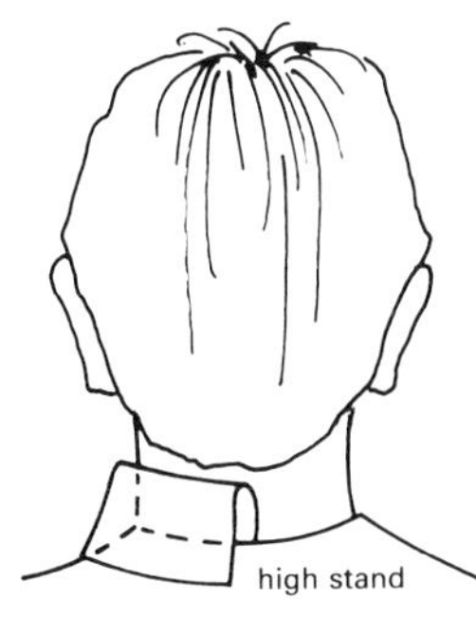

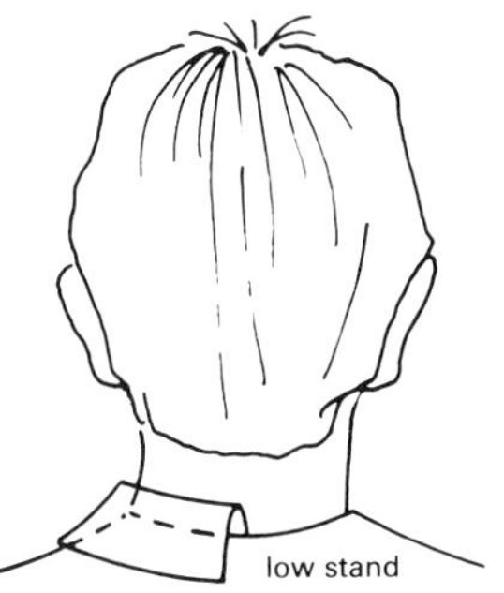

Measuring the neckline

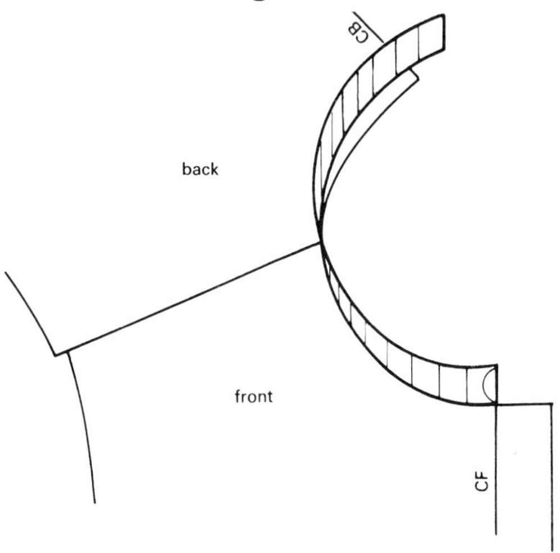

Top collars

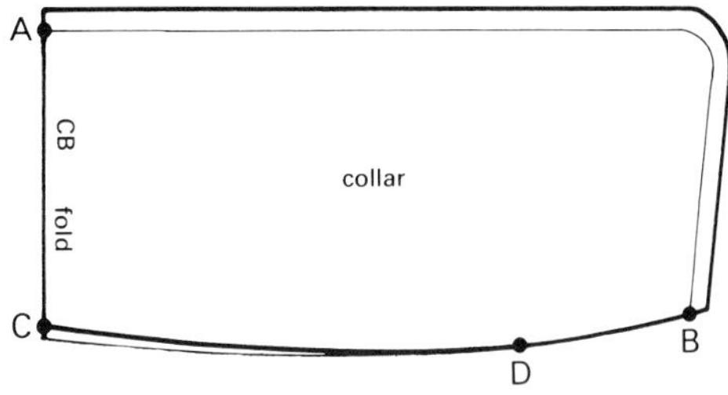

1 Standing straight collar

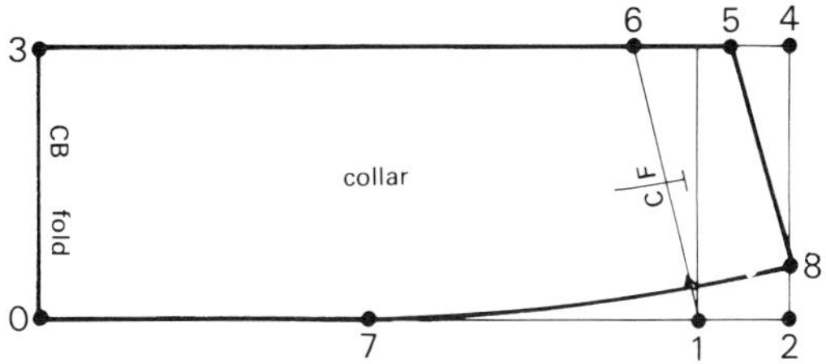

2 Convertible collar

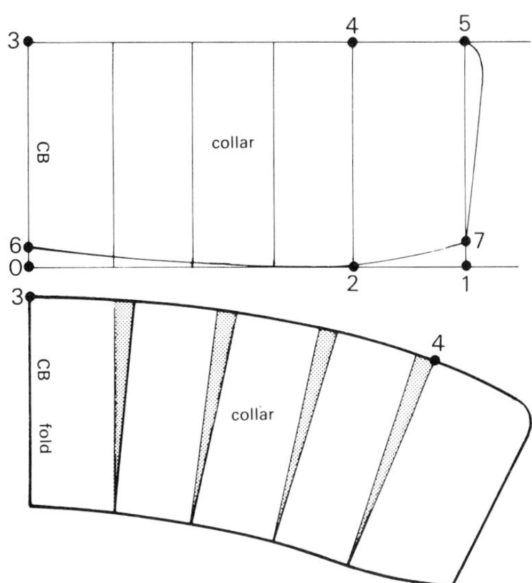

3 Shirt collar

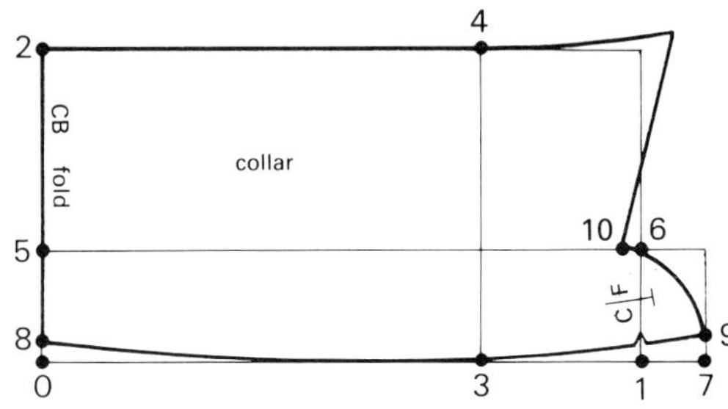

3a Shirt collar with band

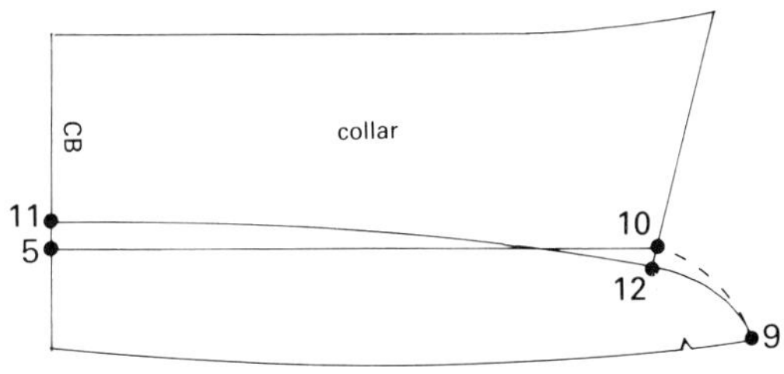

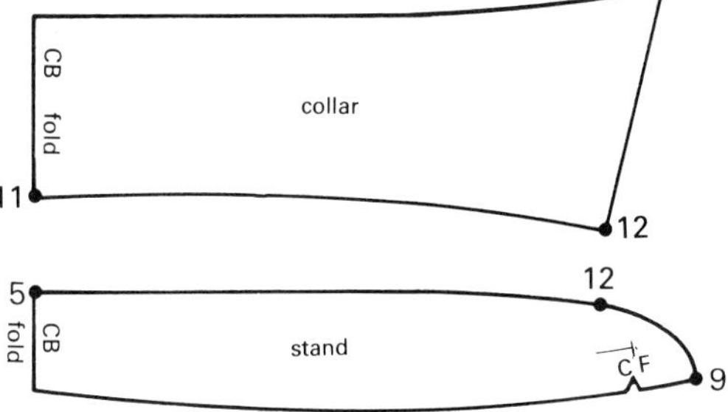

4 BASIC FLAT COLLAR (PETER PAN)
Many shapes of flat collar can be drafted from this adaptation by changing the style line (example shows classic peter pan shape).
Dotted line shows two-piece collar for back opening.
Place shoulder of back bodice to shoulder of front bodice, neck points touching.

Overlap outer shoulders: 92cm–122cm height 1cm
128cm–152cm height 1.5cm
158cm–170cm height 2cm.
Draw in collar shape. Trace off collar.

5 ETON COLLAR
Construct a peter pan collar.
Divide the collar into six sections as shown.
Cut up the lines, overlap the outer edge 0.5cm.
Trace round new collar shape with a smooth line.

6 LOWERING THE NECKLINE
Draw in new neckline on front and back bodice.
Place shoulder of back bodice to shoulder of front bodice, neck points touching.
Overlap shoulders amount given for peter pan collar.
Draw in collar shape.
Trace collar; trace bodice sections with new neckline.

7 SAILOR COLLAR
Place shoulder of back bodice to shoulder of front bodice, neck points touching.
Overlap shoulders amount given for peter pan collar.
Draw in 'V' neckline. Draw in collar as shown.
The collar is 1cm wider than the shoulder line.
Trace off collar pattern. The collar can be cut in one-piece or have a join at the shoulder.

8 FRILLED COLLAR
Measure the total neckline. Construct a circle, the circumference is twice the measurement of the neckline (see 'constructing a circle', page 16).
Mark point A at top of circle. A–B is depth of frill.
Draw outer circle.
Mark points C and D 1.5cm each side of A; square up.
Mark balance points E and F. C–E and D–F are twice the measurement of back neckline.

Note For extra frilling construct a circle with a greater circumference.

9 SIMPLE ROLL COLLAR
Trace round front bodice. Mark buttonholes, add button stand. Mark point 1 at break point. Mark point 2 at neckline; square up from 2.
2–3 back neck measurement.
3–4 92cm–122cm height 2.5cm
128cm–152cm height 3cm
158cm–170cm height 3.5cm.
2–4 The measurement 2–3. Join 2–4 with a slight curve.
Square out from the line 2–4.
4–5 6cm–9cm approx.
5–6 1cm. Draw in style line of collar as shown.
Draw in facing line. Trace off facing.
Add 0.5cm (depending on the thickness of fabric) to rever edge from 6–1.

4 Basic flat collar (peter pan)

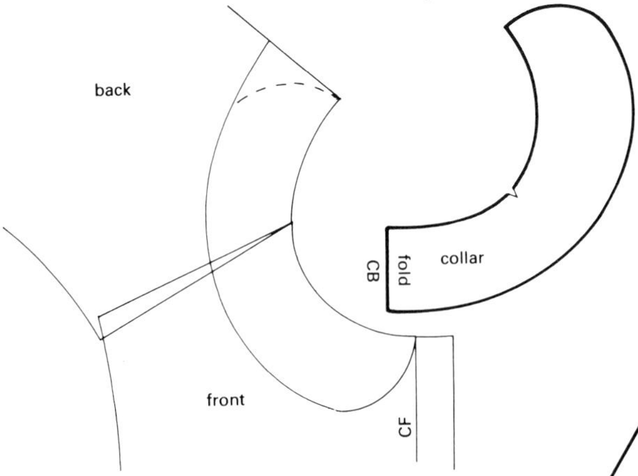

back
collar
CB
fold
front
CF

5 Eton collar

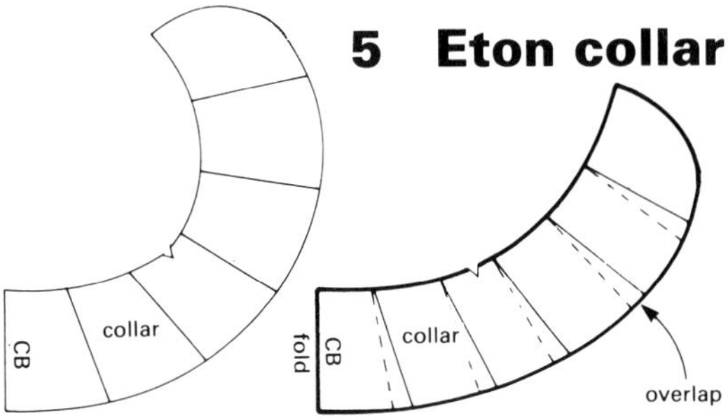

collar
CB
collar
CB
fold
overlap

6 Lowering the neckline

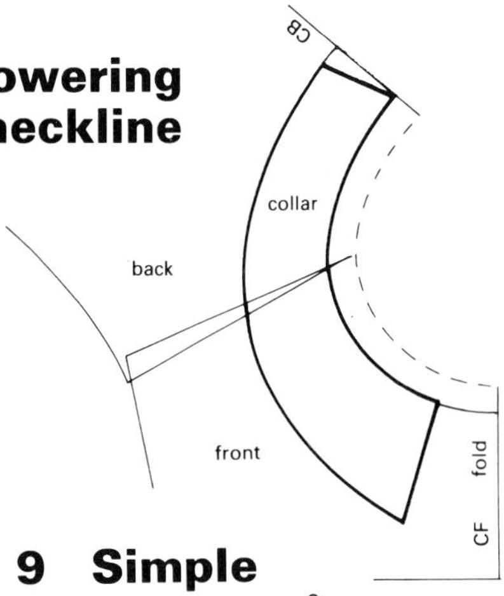

CB
collar
back
front
fold
CF

7 Sailor collar

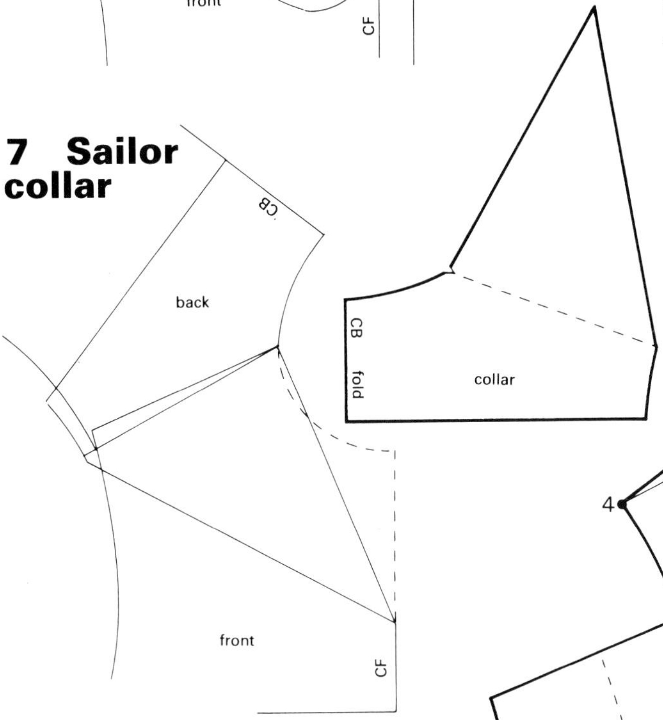

CB
back
CB
fold
collar
front
CF

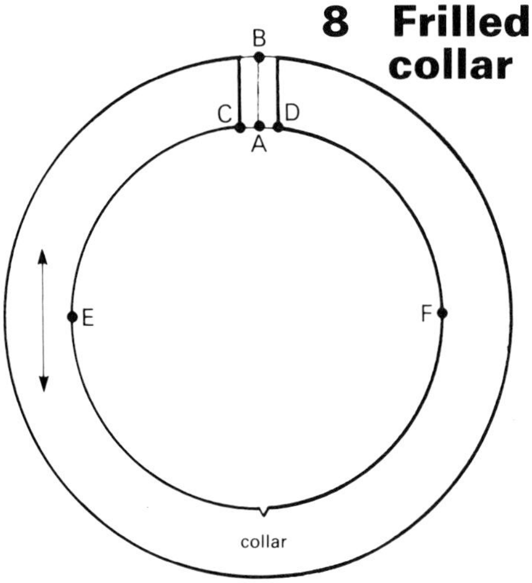

9 Simple roll collar

6
5
4
3
2
front
facing line
CF
1
6
CB
collar and facing
1

8 Frilled collar

B
C
D
A
E
F
collar

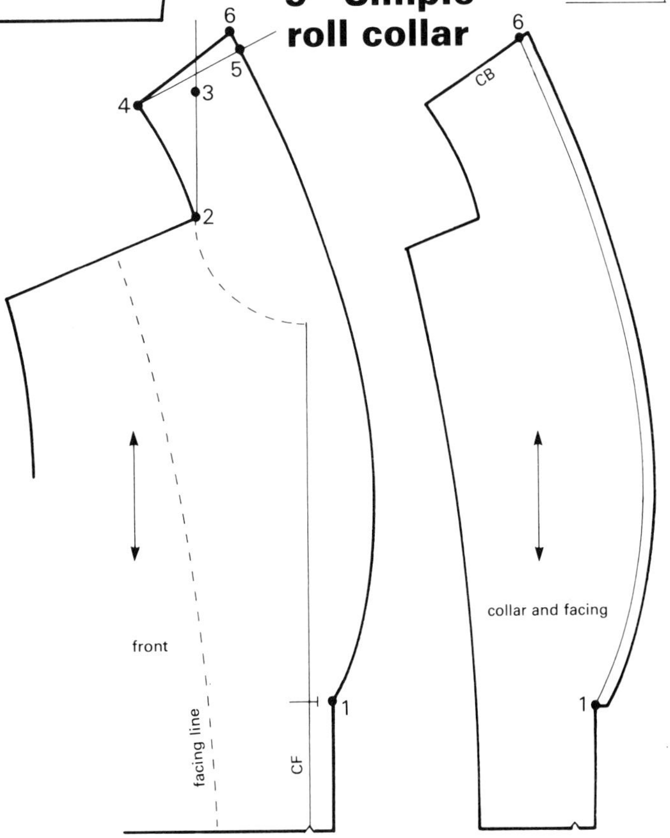

10 STANDARD BLAZER COLLAR
Trace round front section of the blazer block; extend the shoulder line. Draw in facing line, break line, centre front. Extend the break line.
Mark point 1 at break point, 2 at neckline, square down from 2. Re-mark point 26 point 3.

3–4 Back neck measurement plus 0.5cm.
4–5 1.5cm; make 3–5 the same measurement as 3–4.

92cm–122cm height	5–6 2cm;	5–7 3cm
128cm–152cm height	5–6 2.25cm;	5–7 3.25cm
158cm–170cm height	5–6 2.5cm;	5–7 3.5cm.

Draw a line from 6 parallel to the line 5–3 to touch the line squared down from 2. Mark point 8.
Mark point 9 where break line crosses neckline, draw a curve from 8–9.
Mark collar point 10 1cm from centre front line.

10–11 92cm–122cm height 2cm
128cm–152cm height 2.5cm
158cm–170cm height 3cm.

Draw style line of collar; curve outer edge inwards. Trace off facing and collar.

Note 1 Add 0.5cm (depending on thickness of the fabric) to rever from point 1–10. Draw in roll line on collar as shown.

Note 2 Under-collars of tailored garments are cut on the cross. The grain line of the rever is placed parallel to the rever edge.

11 STANDARD REVER COLLAR FOR BODICE, COAT AND OVERGARMENT BLOCKS
Trace round block required. Extend shoulder line.
Raise front neckline 1cm. Re-draw neck curve.
Mark buttonholes, button stand. Draw in facing line.
Square down from 2.

2–3 92cm–122cm height 1.5cm
128cm–152cm height 1.75cm
158cm–170cm height 2cm.

Draw in break line from 1–3; extend line.

3–4 Back neck measurement plus 0.5cm.
4–5 1.5cm; make 3–5 the same measurement as 3–4.

92cm–122cm height	5–6 2.5cm	5–7 3.5cm
128cm–152cm height	5–6 2.75cm	5–7 3.75cm
158cm–170cm height	5–6 3cm	5–7 4cm.

Draw a line from 6 parallel to the line 5–3 to touch the line squared down from 2. Mark point 8.
Mark point 9 where break line crosses neckline, draw a curve from 8–9. Mark point 10 on centre front line.
Draw in style line of collar from 7–10. Draw in style line of rever from 10–1. Trace off facing and collar.
See Notes 1 and 2 of classic blazer collar to complete pattern.

Wider collar shape The fall of the collar can be increased but the style line of the collar will have to be cut and opened at A, B and C (the amount varies with the depth of the collar).

12 CHANGING THE STYLE LINE
(e.g. double breasted reefer collar)
Using the standard collar and rever draft, the style line of the collar and rever can be changed.
Trace round front section of the block required.
Mark buttonholes and button stand for double breasted front (ref. 2, page 52); mark break point.
Construct standard collar and rever drawing in style lines for reefer collar and rever as shown.

Note For other designs, the neckline can be lowered or raised and the rever angle changed.

10 Standard blazer collar

11 Standard rever collar

12 Changing the style line

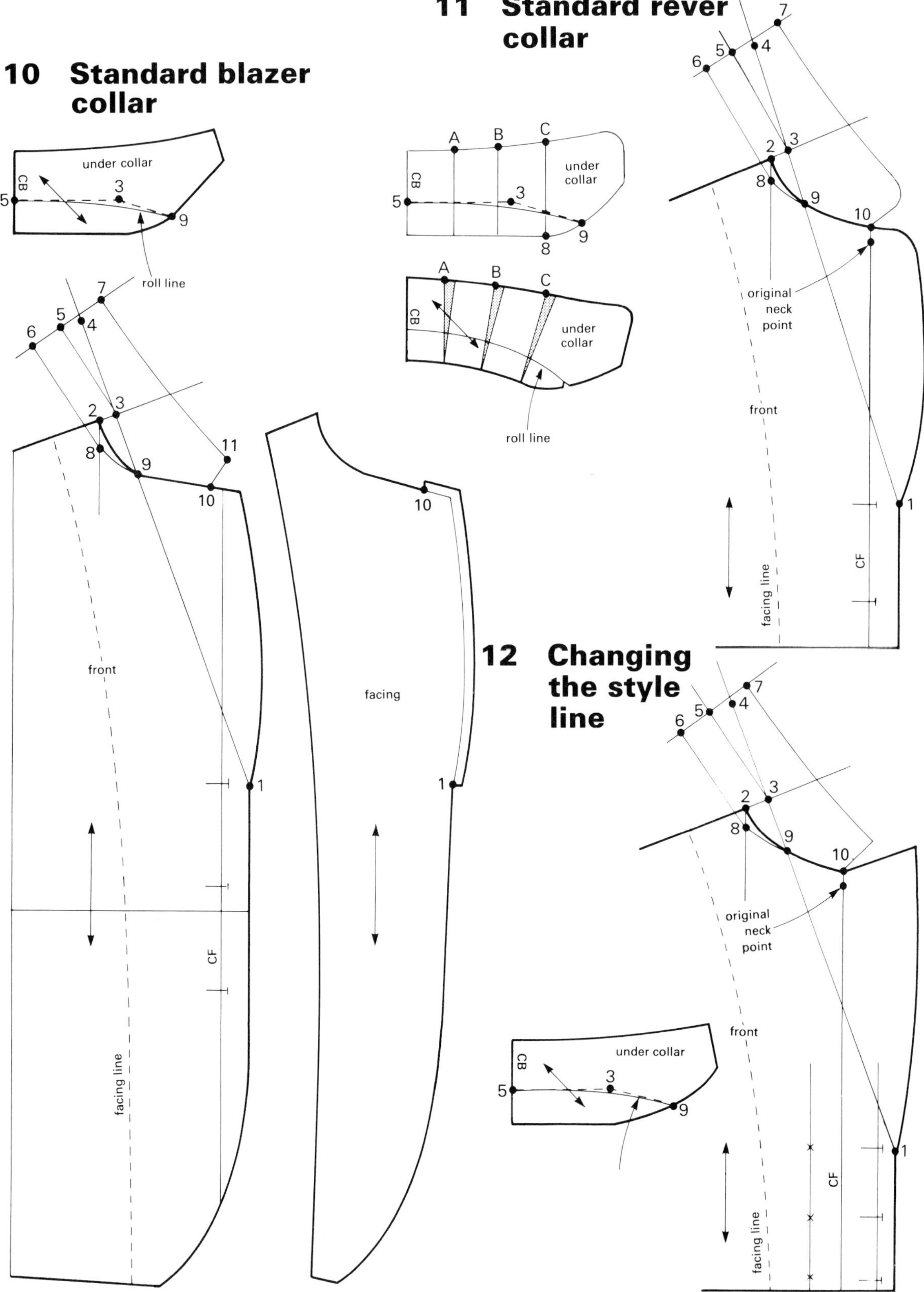

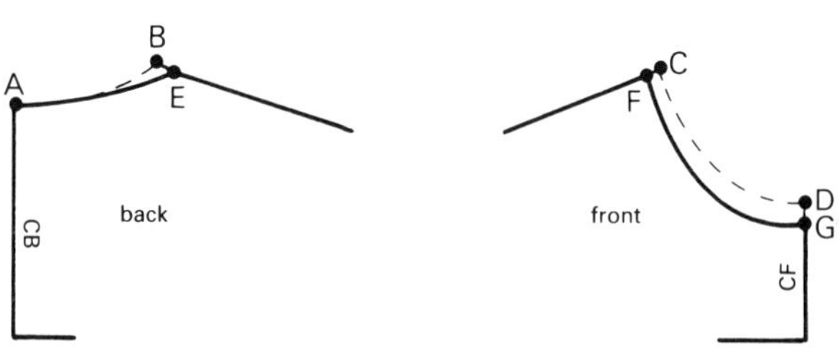

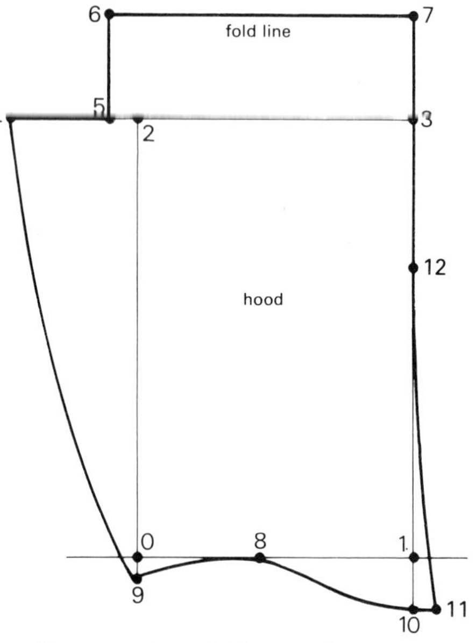

13 Attached hood

Both hoods are illustrated on page 76

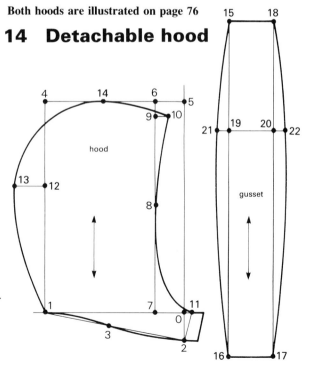

14 Detachable hood

MEASUREMENT REQUIRED FOR BOTH BLOCKS
Cervical to head crown This measurement is calculated height minus cervical height.

13 ATTACHED HOOD
Body sections Mark points A, B, C, D at neckline. B–E and C–F 0.5cm, D–G 1cm–1.5cm. Draw new neckline.
Measure new neckline, A–E plus F–G is ½ neckline measurement.
Hood Square both ways from 0.
0 – 1 ½ neckline measurement minus 1cm; square up.
0 – 2 Cervical to head crown plus 4cm; square across.
Mark point 3.
2 – 4 ⅓ measurement 2–3 plus 2cm.
4 – 5 ⅓ measurement 2–3 plus 0.5cm; square up.
5 – 6 The measurement 4–5; square across to 7.
0 – 8 ½ measurement 0–1 minus 1cm.
0 – 9 0.75cm; join 9–8 and 9–4 with curves.
1 –10 ⅕ measurement 0–1; square out.
Join 8–10 with a curve. 10–11 1cm.
3 –12 ⅓ measurement 1–3; join 11–12 with a curve.

14 DETACHABLE HOOD
Measure the neckline (see page 54).
Square up and down and across from 0.
Hood
0 – 1 ½ neckline measurement plus 1.5cm; square up.
0 – 2 ⅕ measurement 0–1; join 1–2.
2 – 3 ½ measurement 1–2 plus 1cm.
Curve the line 1–3 0.5cm, and 2–3 0.5cm.
1 – 4 Cervical to head crown:
92cm–122cm height plus 4cm
128cm–152cm height plus 4.5cm
158cm–170cm height plus 5cm;
square across to 5.
5 – 6 ⅕ measurement 4–5; square down to 7.
6 – 8 ½ measurement 6–7.
6 – 9 1.5cm; square out. 9–10 1.5cm.
Square up from the line 1–2 to touch the line 0–1 at 11. Draw in face curve 10, 8, 11.
Add the same button stand as garment from line 2–11.
4 –12 ⅓ measurement 1–4 plus 2cm.
12–13 ⅕ measurement 0–1 plus 0.5cm.
4 –14 ½ measurement 4–6: Draw in head curve 1, 13, 14, 10.
Hood gusset Square down and across from 15.
15–16 Length of outer line of hood from 1–10; square across.
16–17 92cm–122cm height 5cm
128cm–152cm height 6cm
158cm–170cm height 7cm; square up to 18.
15–19 ¼ measurement 15–16; square across to 20.
19–21 1.5cm; 20–22 1.5cm. Draw curved outer lines.

Note The hood is attached to garment from points 1–3, usually a zip or studs.

5 ADAPTATIONS OF THE BODY BLOCKS

DRESSES

OVERGARMENTS

1 PINAFORE DRESS
Trace off bodice block and skirt block.
On bodice block shape waist without darts (page 20).
Back bodice Mark points A and B at waistline, C and D at neckline, E and F at armhole.
A–G ½ measurement A–B.
C–H 1cm, D–J 2.5cm, draw in new neckline curve.
E–K 1.25cm, F–L 4cm, G–M ½ measurement G–K plus 1cm.
Join K–G and M–L with curves.
Draw in armhole facing on side section, depth 3cm.
Trace off back, side back and facing.
Front bodice Mark points N and P at neckline.
N–Q 2cm. P–R 2.5cm; draw in new neckline curve.
R–S The measurement J–K on back.
Construct remainder of bodice as for back.
Facing Join facing pieces at side seam, trace round pattern.
Back skirt T–U the measurement A–B on bodice block; join U to hem line.
T–V The measurement A–G on bodice block; square down.
V–W and W–X are pleat width approx. 2cm; square down from W and X. Cut up lines and open each section twice pleat width. Draw a fold line down centre of each pleat.
Fold pleats to finished position, cut out pattern.
Front skirt Construct front skirt as for back skirt.

Note 1 Front and back sections of bodice are self-faced.

Note 2 The skirt could be gathered instead of pleated to make an alternative design.

2 PINAFORE DRESS
Trace off dress block.
Back section Mark points A and B at neckline, C and D at armhole.
A–E 1.5cm, B–F 2.5cm; draw in new neckline curve.
C–G and D–H 1cm; draw in new armhole line.
Join H to hem line. E–J approx. 5cm.
H–K 3cm; draw in yoke curves. Mark point L.
Divide J–L into three sections; mark points M and N.
Square down from M and N. Cut off yoke and trace round.
Cut up lines on main section at M and N and open required amount (example shows 2.5cm at yoke line, 4.5cm at hem line). Trace round new pattern.

Note It is necessary to ensure that when curved pattern pieces are opened at the top each section is laid on a line squared out from the line of the previous secton (e.g. P–Q).

Front section Mark R and S at neckline. R–T and S–U 2.5cm. Draw in new neck curve.
T–V The measurement F–G on back.
Complete front section as for back section.

Note The yoke is self-faced.

1 Pinafore dress

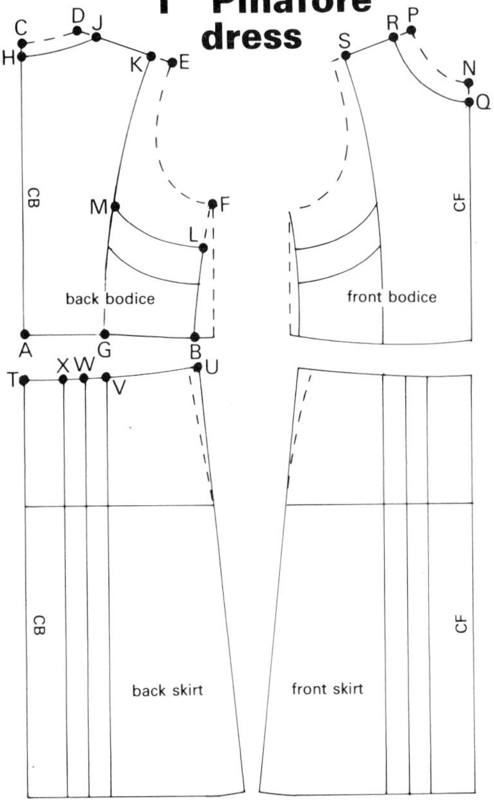

C D J H K E S R P N Q
CB
M F L
CF
back bodice
front bodice
A G B
T X W V U
CB
CF
back skirt
front skirt

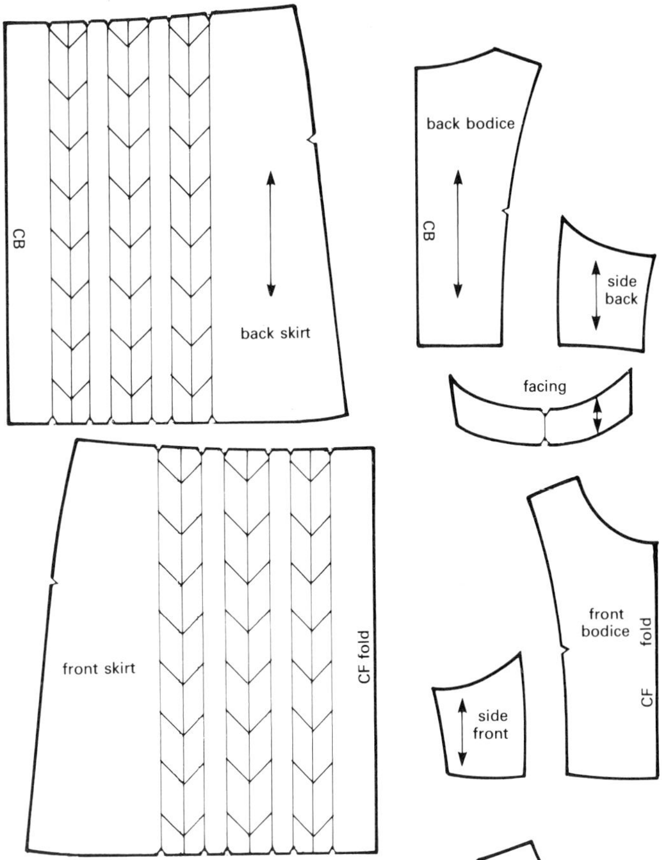

CB
back skirt
front skirt
CF fold

back bodice
CB
side back
facing
front bodice
fold
CF
side front

2 Pinafore dress

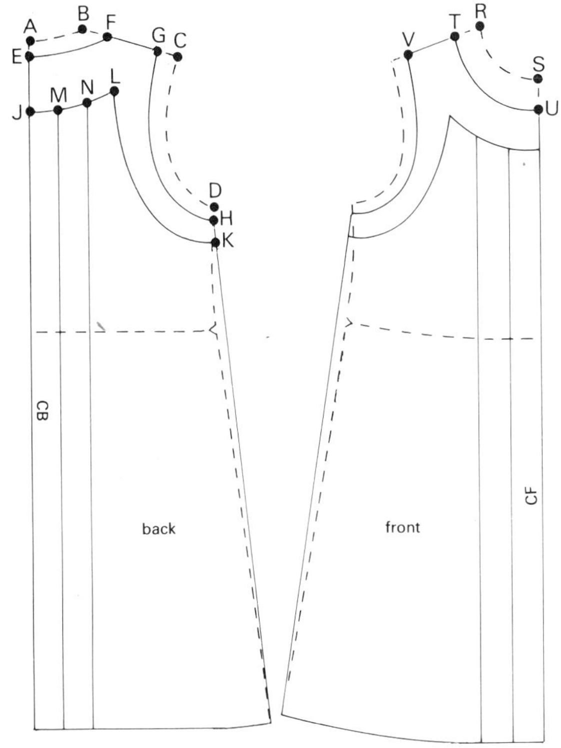

A B F G C E J M N L D H K
V T R S U
CB
CF
back
front

gather
P
back yoke
CB
front yoke
CF fold
gather
CB
back
front
fold
CF
Q

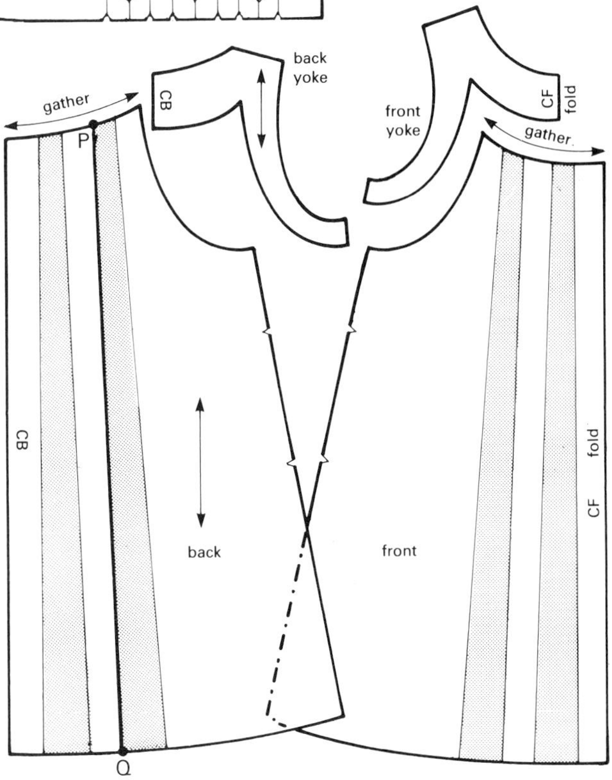

3 CLASSIC BLOUSE WITH YOKE
Trace off bodice block and one-piece sleeve block.
Body section Mark point A at centre back neckline, B at centre back waistline.
B–C Waist to hip measurement plus 4cm; square across.
A–D ⅕ measurement A–B; square across to E.
Mark in front yoke line approx. 3cm–5cm in depth.
Divide front yoke line into three sections, mark points F, G; square down from F and G.
Mark buttonholes, button stand. Add 3.5cm to front edge line for facing, curve neckline.
Back Trace off back. D–H ⅓ measurement D–E; square down.
Front Trace off front. Cut up lines from F and G, open approx. 2cm–3cm. Trace round pattern.
Yokes Trace off back and front yokes.
Collar Construct convertible collar (ref. 2, page 54).
Sleeve Design shows short sleeve (ref. 1, page 36).

Note A long sleeve with shirt cuff is often used with this design (ref. 1, page 50).

4 CLASSIC DRESS WITH YOKE
Trace off dress block and one-piece sleeve block.
Back Mark point A at centre back neckline, B at centre back waistline.
A–C ¼ measurement A–B; square across to D.
Divide C–D into four sections, mark points E, F, G; square down from E, F, G.
Trace off back, cut up lines from E, F, G and open required amount (example shows 2.5cm at top, 4cm at hem line). Trace round pattern.

Note It is necessary to ensure that when pattern pieces are opened at the top each section is laid on a line squared out from the previous section (example shows line H–J).

Front Mark point K at neckline, L at front waistline.
K–M ¼ measurement K–L: square across to N.
Divide M–N into four sections, Mark points P, Q, R; square down from P, Q, R.
Trace off front, cut up lines from P, Q, R and open required amount (example shows 2.5cm at top, 4cm at hem line). Trace round pattern.
Yokes Trace off front and back yokes.
Sleeve Design shows gathered sleeve (ref. 7, page 40), many styles of inset sleeve are used with this design.

3 Classic blouse with yoke

4 Classic dress with yoke

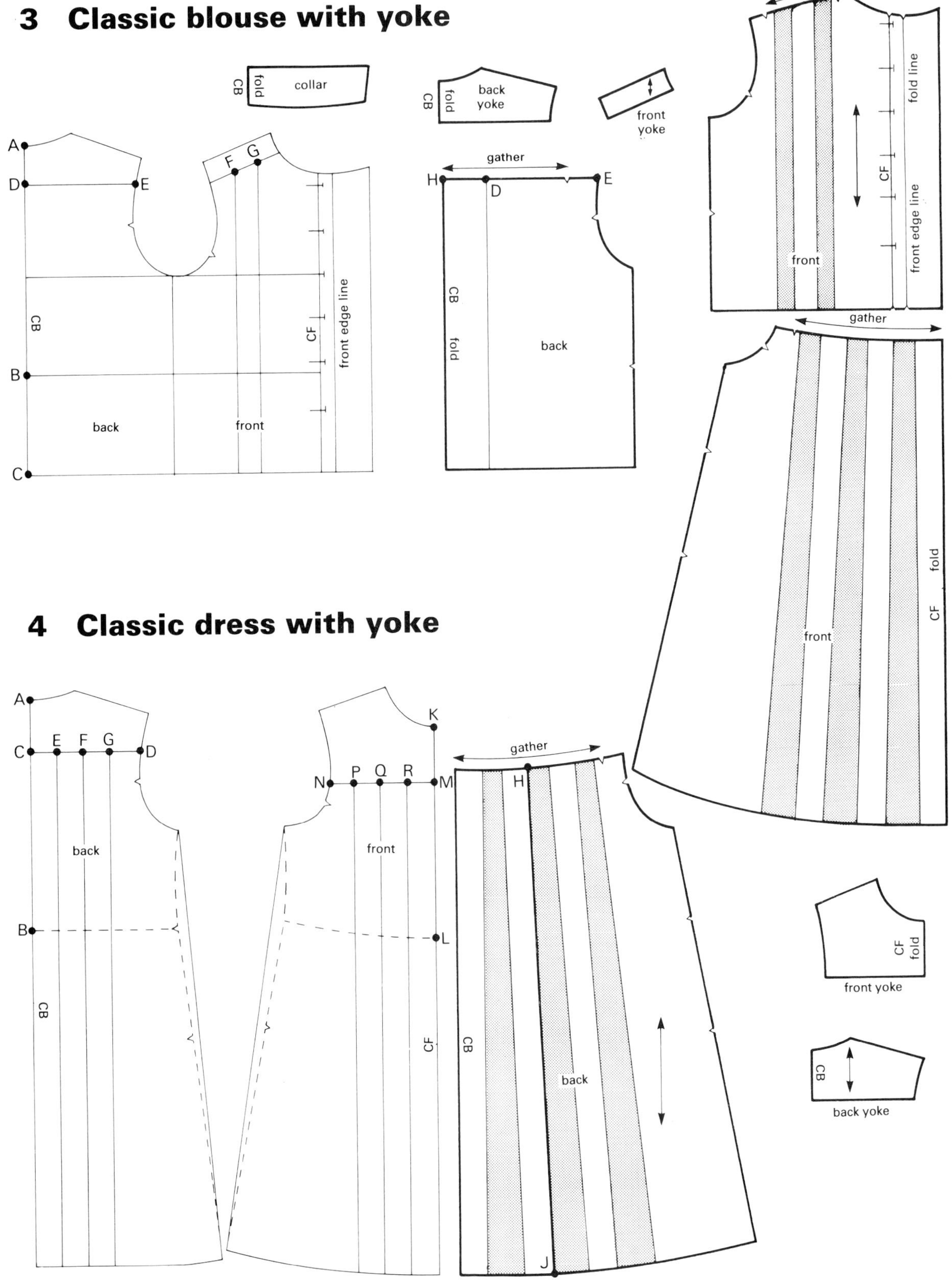

Note It is necessary to ensure that when pattern pieces are opened at the top, each section is laid on a line squared out from the line of the previous section (e.g. ref. 5 shows line N–P).

5 SLEEVELESS DRESS
Trace off sleeveless dress block.
Back and front sections Lower neckline the required amount (example shows 1cm at A, 1.5cm at B, C and D).
Mark E, F, G, H at hem line. E–J, F–K, G–L, H–M are depth of frill. Draw in frill lines J–K and L–M parallel to hem line.
Draw in buttonholes, button stand; add extended facing.
Draw in back facing.
Divide J–K and L–M into four sections; square down from lines J–K and L–M. Cut off frill, cut up lines and open required amount (example shows 4cm at top of frill, 6cm at hem line). Trace round patterns.
Trace off back facing.

6 LOW WAISTED DRESS
Trace off dress block and one-piece sleeve block, draw in waistline.
Back Mark A and B at waist. A–C and B–D are depth of new waistline; draw in new low waistline.
Mark E and F at hem line. C–G and D–H are depth of frill.
Draw in frill line G–H parallel to hem line of garment.
Draw in back facing.
Divide lower section and frill into four sections.
Square down from line C–D.
Trace off frill. Cut off lower section.
Cut up lines and open required amount (example shows lower section 2.5cm at top, 4cm at bottom; frill 5cm at top, 7.5cm at bottom). Trace round patterns.
Trace off back facing.
Front Construct front as back.
Sleeve Design shows gathered and flared sleeve (ref. 9, page 40).

5 Sleeveless dress

6 Low waisted dress

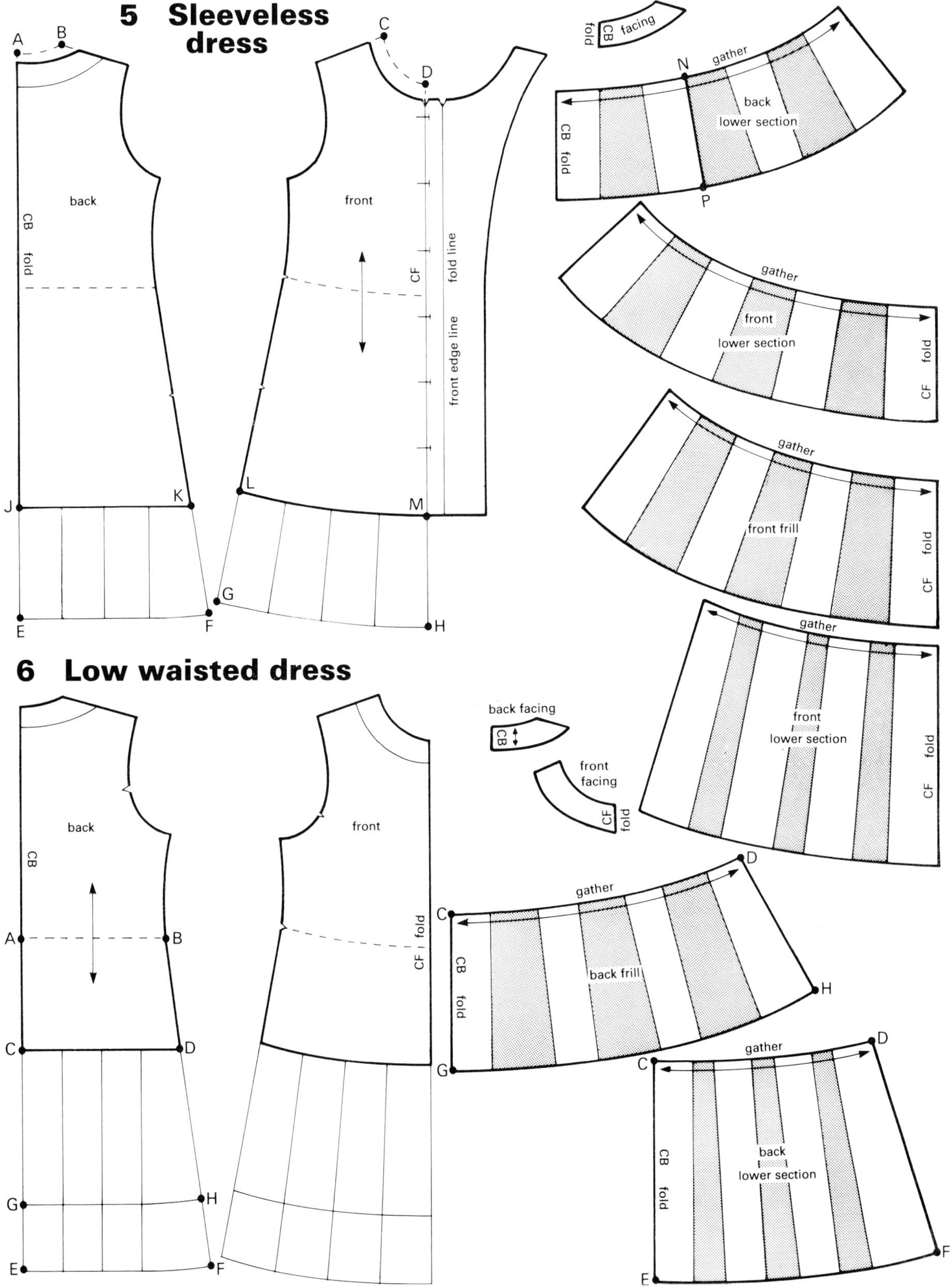

7 DRESS WITH YOKE

Trace off dress block and one-piece sleeve block.
Add to back shoulder line: 92cm–122cm height 0.3cm
128cm–152cm height 0.6cm
158cm–164cm height 0.9cm.
Remove the same amount from front shoulder.
Move centre line of sleeve forward the amount added to back shoulder.

Body section Mark A and B at sleeve pitch points. Mark C at front armhole opposite back pitch points. Draw in yoke lines, mark points D and E. E–F approx. ⅓ measurement E–D. Draw in raglan lines A–F and C–F.
Divide D–F on both yoke lines into three sections. Mark points G and H; square down from G and H. Draw in back dart, width is amount of shoulder ease. Mark point J at base of armhole. Join J to hem line. Cut off yoke and raglan sections; cut up lines on body sections and open at hem required amount (example shows 3cm at yoke line, 5 cm at hem line). Trace round pattern.

Note It is necessary to ensure that when curved pattern pieces are opened at the top each section is laid on a line squared out from the line of a previous section (e.g. line K–L).

Yoke Join yoke sections along shoulder line.
Sleeve Mark points M, N and P at sleeve pitch points.
N–Q The measurement B–C on front. P–R 4cm.
Close back shoulder dart. Place raglan sections to sleeve at points M and Q and to sleeve head. Extend shoulders to R. Divide sleeve into four sections. Mark points S and T. Open 4cm at hem, 1cm at S and T. Shape up hem 1cm at outer edge. Trace round pattern.

8 SIMPLE WAISTED DRESSES

Trace off bodice block, skirt block and one-piece sleeve block.
Back bodice Mark A and B on waistline.
Front bodice Mark C and D on shoulder line, mark E and F on waistline. C–G ⅓ measurement C–D.
E–H ½ measurement E–F plus 1cm. Draw in panel line.
Mark buttonholes, button stand, add extended facing. Trace off front and side front.
Back skirt Mark J at waistline, J–K the measurement A–B on bodice block. Join K to hem line.
J–L ½ measurement J–K; square down.
Front skirt Mark M on waistline, M–N the measurement E–F on bodice block. Join N to hem line.
M–P ½ measurement M–N; square down.
Collar Construct flat collar (ref. 4, page 56).
Sleeve Design shows short sleeve (ref. 1, page 36).
Waist tie Construct tie length approx. 50cm, width 5cm. Mark fold line down centre.

8a HIGH WAISTED DRESSES

A high waisted dress flatters young children.
Approx. 4cm can be taken off the depth of the bodice and added to the skirt length.

7 Dress with yoke

8 Simple waisted dress

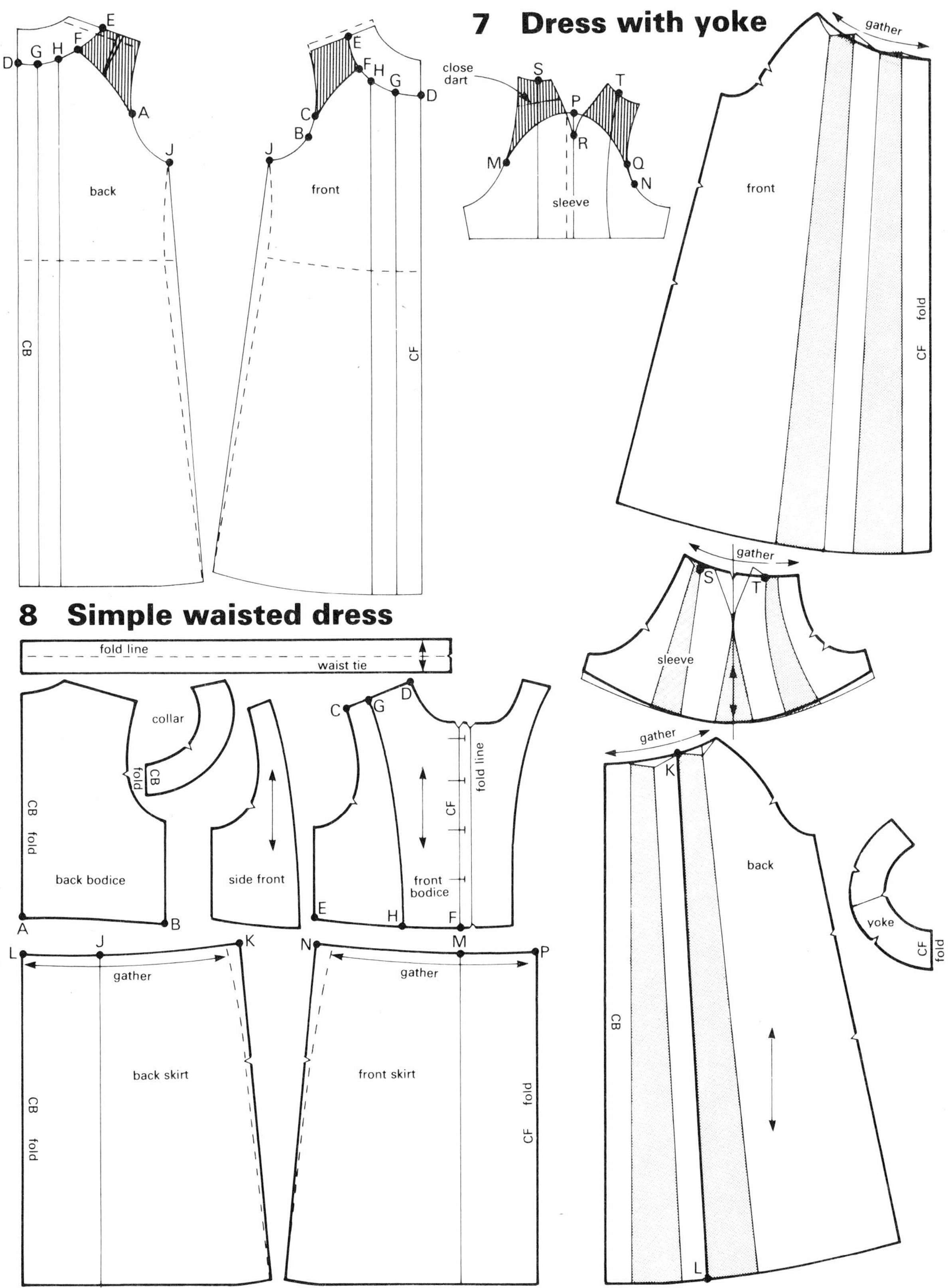

9 PLEATED DRESS

Trace off bodice block and one-piece sleeve block.

Back and front bodice Mark points A and B on side seam.

B–C ½ waist to hip measurement. Draw new low waistline from C parallel to original waistline.

For waist shaping – draw a curved line from A–C, curve inward 0.5cm at a point mid-way between A and B.

Mark D at centre front and centre back of new waistline.

Draw in facing line. Trace off facing.

Back and front skirts Square both ways from E.

E–F is three times the measurement D–C on back bodice block; square down.

E–G Skirt length minus the measurement B–C on bodice block; square across.

Construct front skirt as back skirt.

Collar Construct a flat collar (ref. 4, page 56).

Sleeve Construct semi-shaped sleeve (ref. 3b, page 36).

Neck tie Construct rectangle, length approx. 50cm, width approx. 8cm. Draw fold line down centre.

Note On pleated skirt the two rectangles are seamed and divided by number of pleats required (e.g. 20). The pleat fold is the same width as pleat.

10 PANELLED DRESS

Trace off dress block and one-piece sleeve block.

Back and front Mark points A and B at shoulder line, C and D at waistline.

A–E ½ measurement A–B; C–F ⅓ measurement C–D; square down to G.

Draw in panel lines E, F, G.

Extend shoulder lines for dropped shoulder (ref. 12, page 42).

Cut up panel lines, add 2.5cm flare at G at hem of side panels; add 1.5cm flare at G at hem of back and front.

On back section mark buttonholes, button stand; add extended facing.

Add 1cm flare to hem line at H on side seam of side back and side front. Join H to underarm point.

Collar Construct a two-piece flat collar (ref. 4, page 56).

Sleeve Complete instructions for a dropped shoulder.

Remove cuff depth from bottom of sleeve.

Mark points J and K at hem line.

J–L ¼ measurement J–K; square up approx. 6cm.

Cuff Construct shirt cuff (ref. 1, page 50).

Waist tie Construct rectangle, length approx. 50cm, width approx. 5cm. Draw fold line down centre.

9 Pleated dress

10 Panelled dress

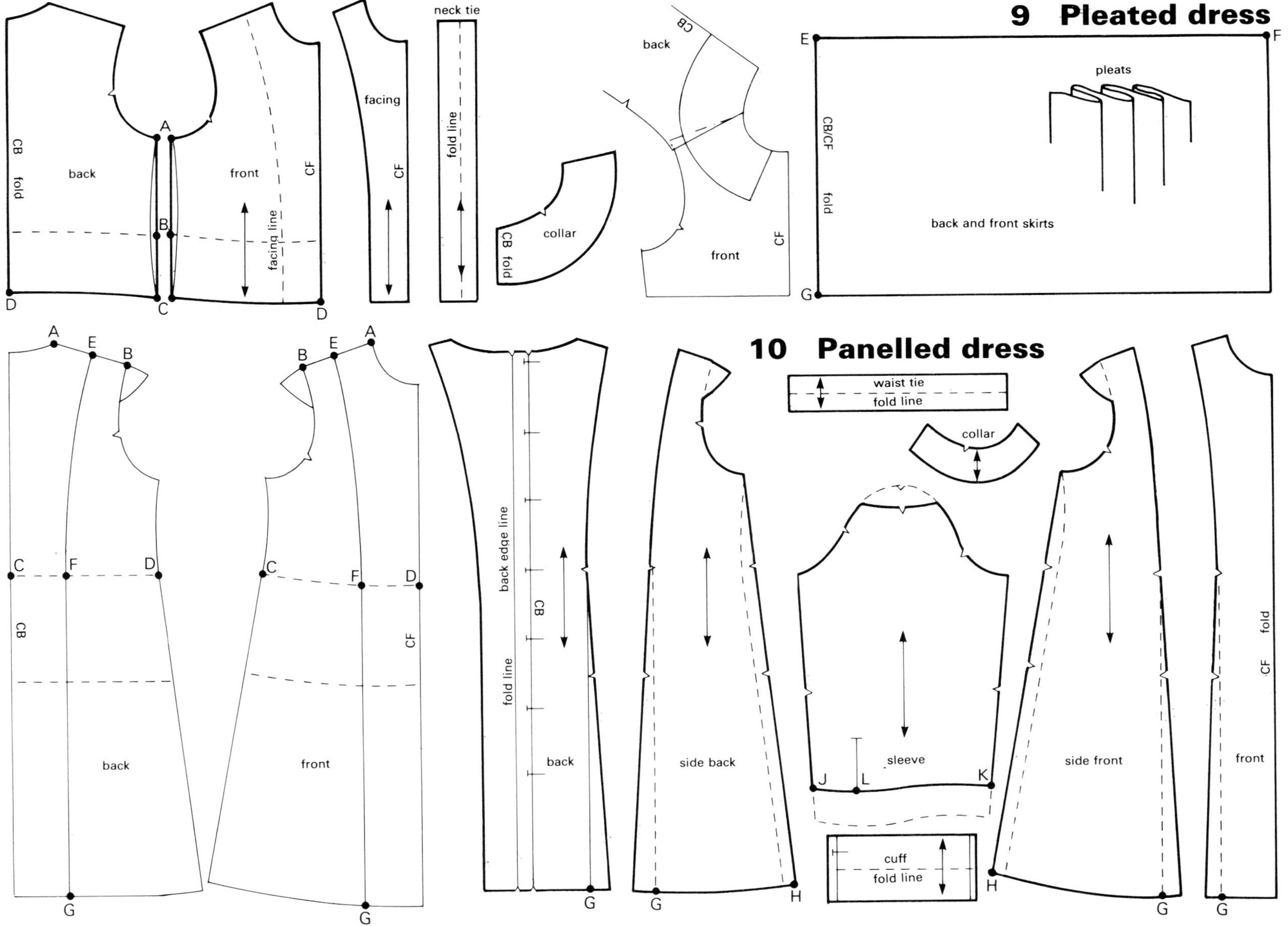

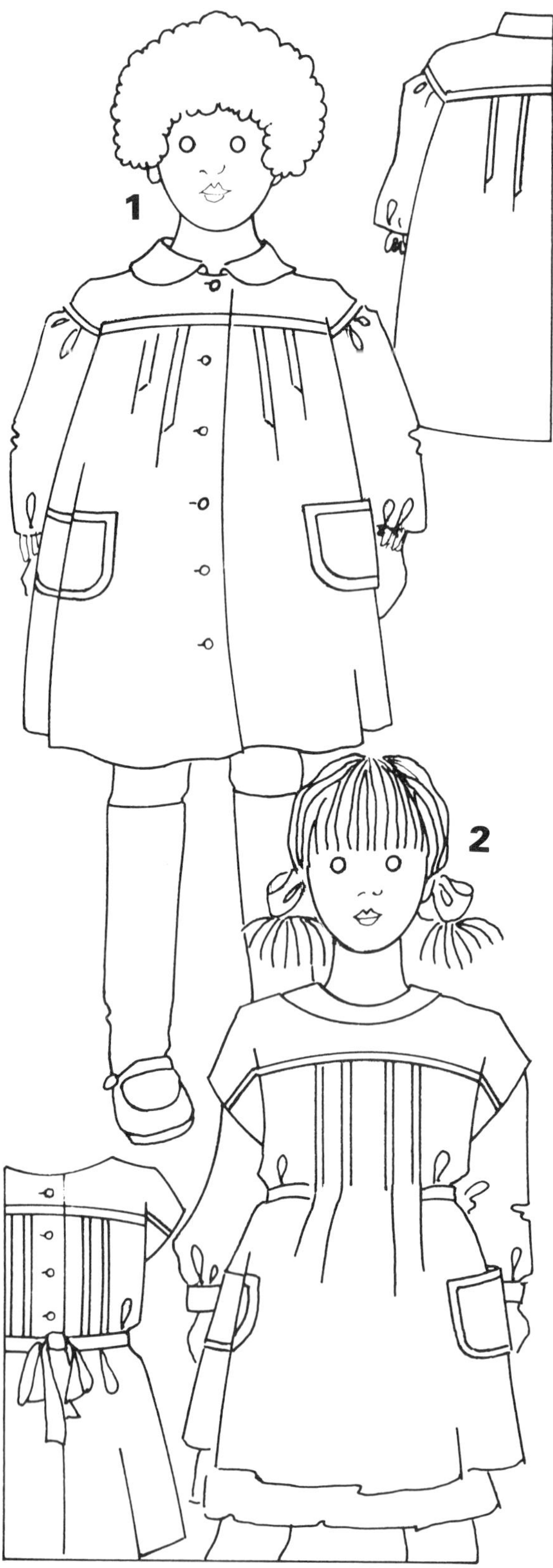

1 SMOCK COAT (KIMONO BASE)
Trace off overgarment block to finished length (curved front hem line) and one-piece sleeve block.
Body sections Complete kimono adaptation, mark points 8 and 9.
Mark points A, B, C and D at neckline, E and F at shoulder.
E–G ½ measurement B–E minus 1cm.
F–H ½ measuurement C–F minus 1cm.
J and K are mid-way between 8 and 9, draw in armhole curves G–J and H–K.
Mark point L at centre back waistline. M at centre front waistline.
A–N ⅕ measurement A–L.
D–P ⅕ measurement D–M.
G–Q ¼ measurement G–J plus 1cm.
H–R ⅓ measurement H–K plus 1cm.
Draw in yoke curves N–Q and P–R.
Draw in 1cm darts from Q–J and R–K.
Q–S ½ measurement Q–J.
R–T ½ measurement R–K. Joint S–9 and T–9.
Draw in vertical pleat lines.
Mark points U and V at waistline, W and X at hem line.
W–Y 4cm. X–Z 6cm.
Easy-fitting shape Join J–Y and K–Z.
Semi-fitting shape Join U–Y and V–Z.
Mark buttonholes, button stand. Add 6cm extended facing.
Draw in pocket shape.
Back and front Trace off back and front sections, cut up pleat lines and open approx. 5cm for pleats.
Trace round patterns.
Yokes Trace off back and front yokes.
Collar Construct Eton collar (ref. 5, page 56).
Sleeve Draw a perpendicular line; trace off sleeve sections, place to this line opening the sleeve 7.5cm at sleeve head, 2.5cm at hem line.
Cut up lines S–9 and T–9, open a 3cm wedge.
Curve underarm seams and lines S–J and T–K.
Draw in new sleeve head raising 1cm.
Add 4cm casing for elastic at wristline.
Pocket Trace off pocket.

2 SMOCK PINAFORE (KIMONO BASE)
Adapt body sections and back and front yokes as for a smock coat but change buttoned opening from centre front to centre back as shown.
Draw in armhole facings. Trace off facings.
Yokes are self-faced.
Waist ties Draw a rectangle length approx. 30cm, width 5cm. Draw fold line down centre.

1 Smock coat (kimono base)

2 Smock pinafore

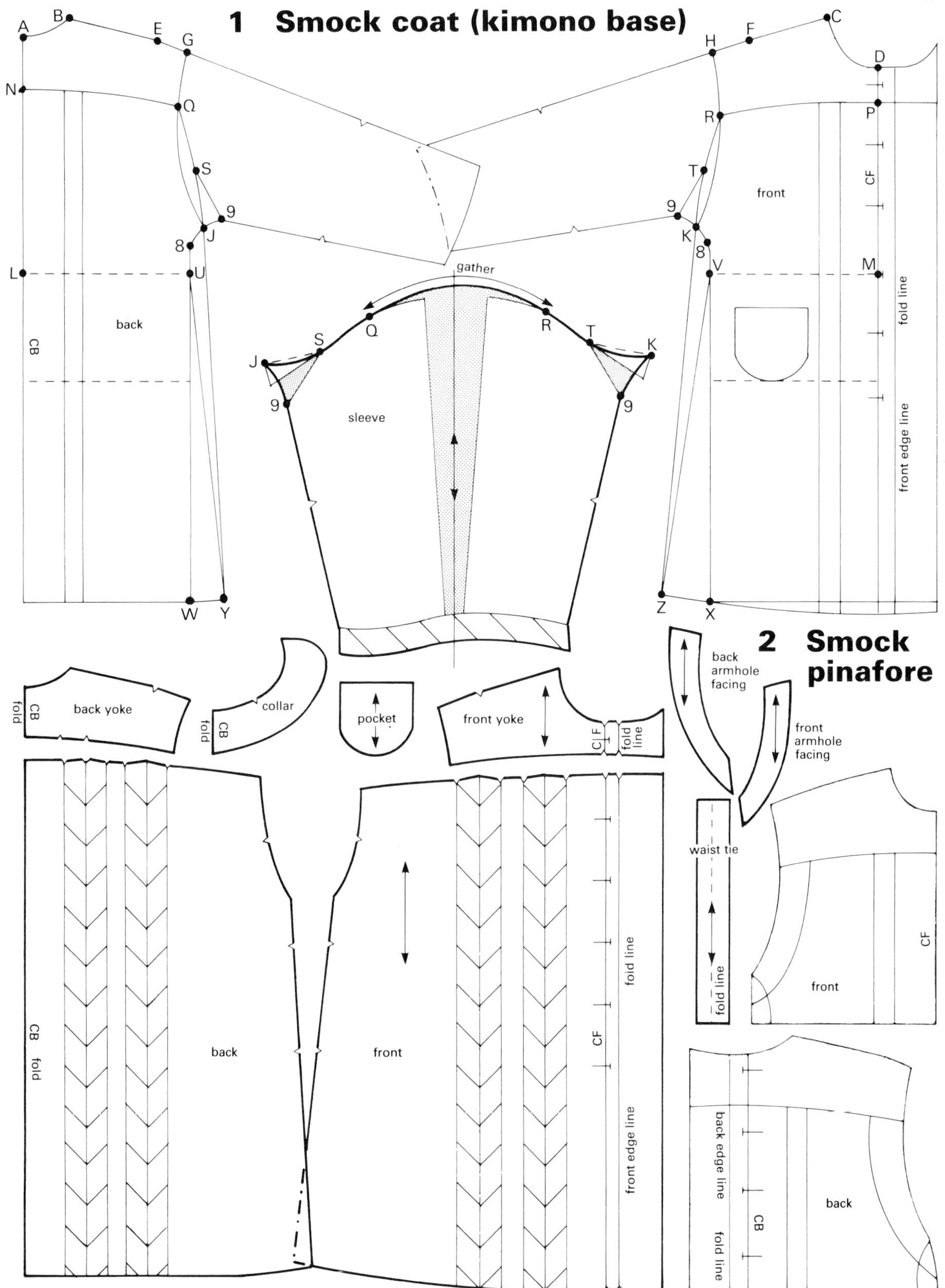

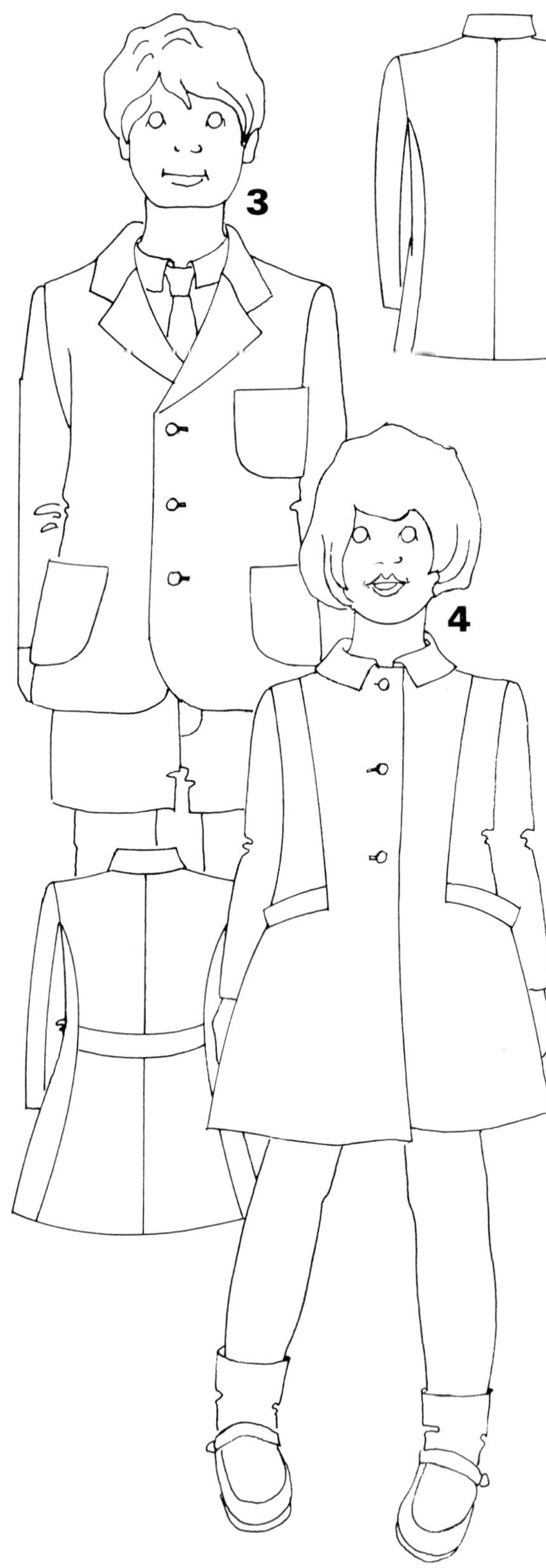

3 CLASSIC BLAZER
Trace off blazer block.
Back Trace off back section.
Front, collar and facing Trace off front section. Construct collar and facing (ref. 10, page 58).
Sleeves Construct a two-piece sleeve for blazer block (page 32).
Pockets Trace off pockets. Add 3cm facing to top of each pocket.

4 CLASSIC FORMAL COAT
Trace off formal coat block.
Back Mark point A at neckline, B at waistline, C at sleeve pitch point. D at underarm point.
B–E 1cm; square down. A–F ⅓ measurement A–B: Join E–F.
Square down from C to G on waistline, H on hem line.
Join D to hem line with straight line. Mark point J.
G–K 2cm. H–L 2cm. Draw in back seam line C, K, L.
Curve line from C–K.
Trace off back section.
Front Mark M and N at shoulder points, P at front waistline. Q at front pitch point. R at underarm point.
Join R to hem line with a straight line. Mark point S.
Q–T ½ measurement Q–R. S–U the measurement H–J minus 2cm. U–V 2cm.
Join T–V. Mark W on waistline. Curve line from T–W 0.5cm.
W–X ½ measurement W–P plus 1cm. Square down 2cm to Y.
W–Z 5cm. Draw in panel line from shoulder through Y to Z.
Draw in welt pocket, depth 2cm.
Mark buttonholes, button stand, facing line.
Trace off front section.
Trace off side front; add 3cm pocket facing from Y–Z.
Side section Draw a vertical line. Trace off back and front panels, place to line, square down from C and T to waistline. Join new waist points to hem line.
Facing Trace off facing.
Collar Construct Eton collar (ref. 5, page 56).
Sleeve Construct two-piece sleeve for the formal coat block (page 32).
Pocket Trace off welt pocket and pocket bag.
Belt Construct rectangle, length measurement E–K on back, width 7cm. Draw fold line down centre.

3 Classic blazer

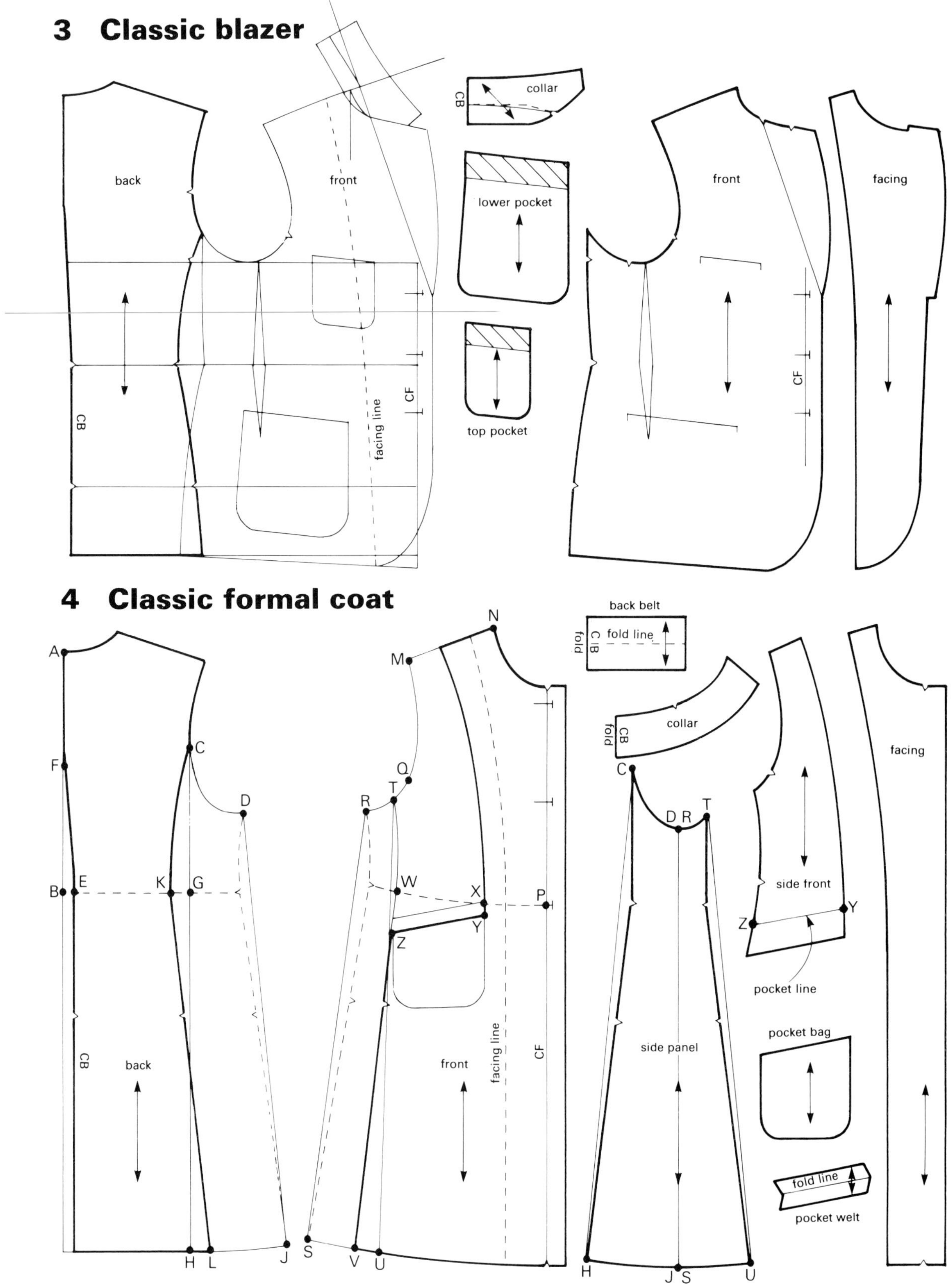

4 Classic formal coat

5 ANORAK
Trace off overgarment block and one-piece sleeve block.
Draw in finished length with straight hem line.
Complete adaptation for dropped shoulder with lowered armhole (ref. 13, page 42) on body and sleeve sections.
Body section Draw in yoke line and lowered waistline 3cm–5cm below natural waistline. Mark points A, B, C.
C–D ¼ measurement B–C. Draw in waist flap from A–D depth 3cm–4cm.
Draw in patch pocket shape and breast pocket opening:

92cm–122cm height	length 11cm
128cm–152cm height	length 13cm
158cm–170cm height	length 15cm.

Draw in pocket bag.
Draw in zip line and front strap line see strap for zip front (ref. 3a, page 52).
Back Trace off back yoke, main back section and lower back.
Front Trace off main front section and lower front.
Complete instructions for constructing front strap.
Waist flap Trace off waist flap, make it twice the depth and mark fold line, mark stitch line for cord.
Pockets Trace off patch pocket shape add 3cm facing at top.
Construct welt pocket, E–F length of pocket opening, E–G twice finished width. Draw fold line through centre. Trace off pocket bag.
Collar Construct standing straight collar (ref. 1, page 54).
Hood Construct detachable hood (ref. 14, page 60).
Sleeve Add 5cm facing to hem line of adapted sleeve.

6 DUFFLE COAT
Trace off overgarment block and one-piece sleeve block.
Draw in finished length with curved front hem line.
Mark points A and B at underarm points, C and D at hem line.
Extend shoulder 1cm.
Back C–E 2cm; join A–E.
Front D–F 3.5cm; join B–F. Draw in yoke line.
Add 2.5cm button stand, draw in toggle line 3.5cm in from centre front line, mark toggle positions.
Mark hood position 1cm in from centre front.
Draw in facing line. Draw in pocket shape.
Yoke Trace off yoke.
Facing Trace off facing.
Pocket Trace off pocket add 3cm facing.
Hood Measure neckline to hood position; construct attached hood (ref. 13, page 60).
Sleeve Lower point at sleeve head 1cm; draw new sleeve head to front and back pitch points.

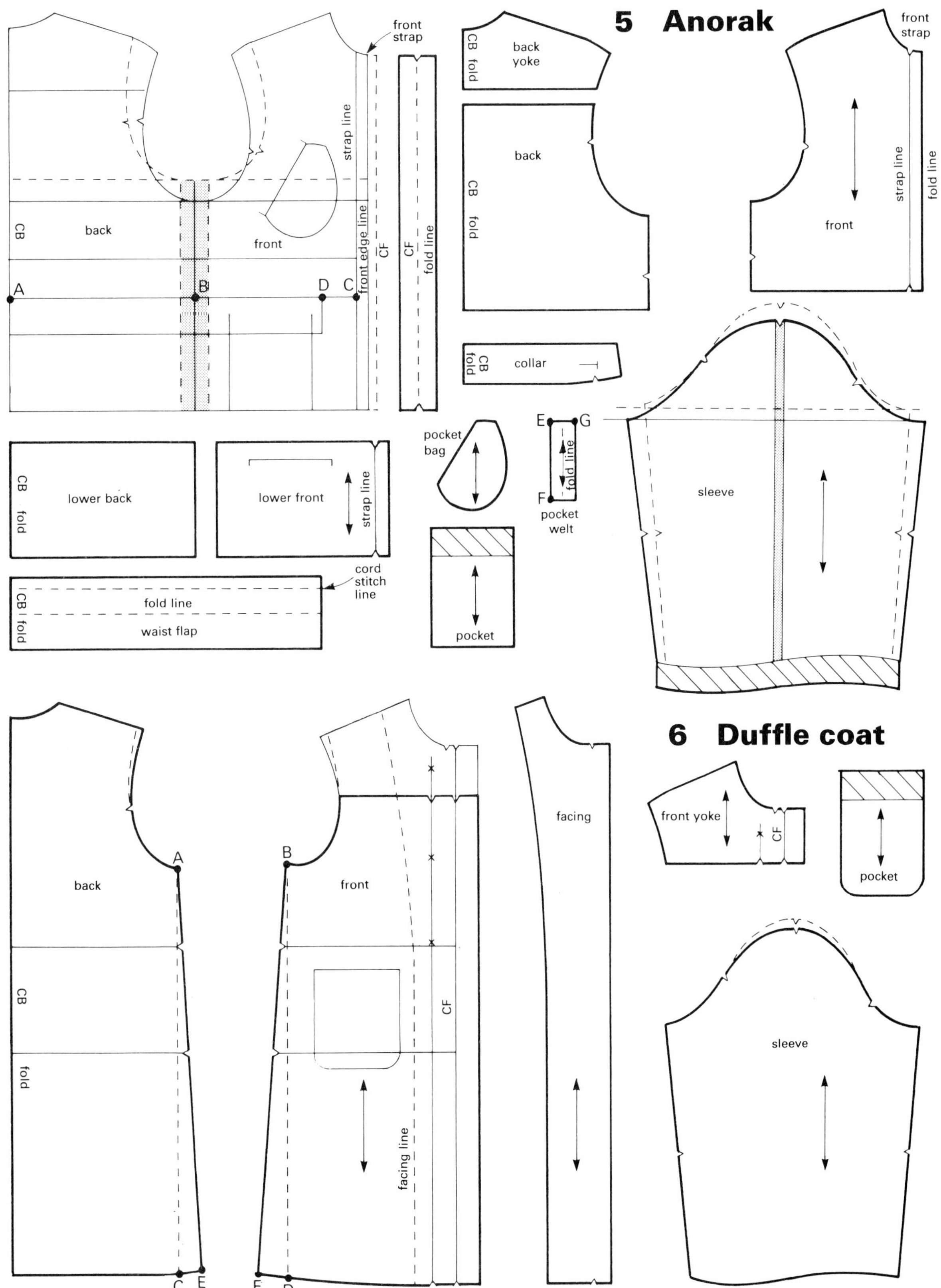
5 Anorak
back
front
CB
front strap
strap line
front edge line
CF
fold line
A
B
D
C
back yoke
CB fold
collar
pocket bag
pocket welt
E
G
F
sleeve
lower back
lower front
cord stitch line
waist flap
pocket
6 Duffle coat
front yoke
facing
facing line

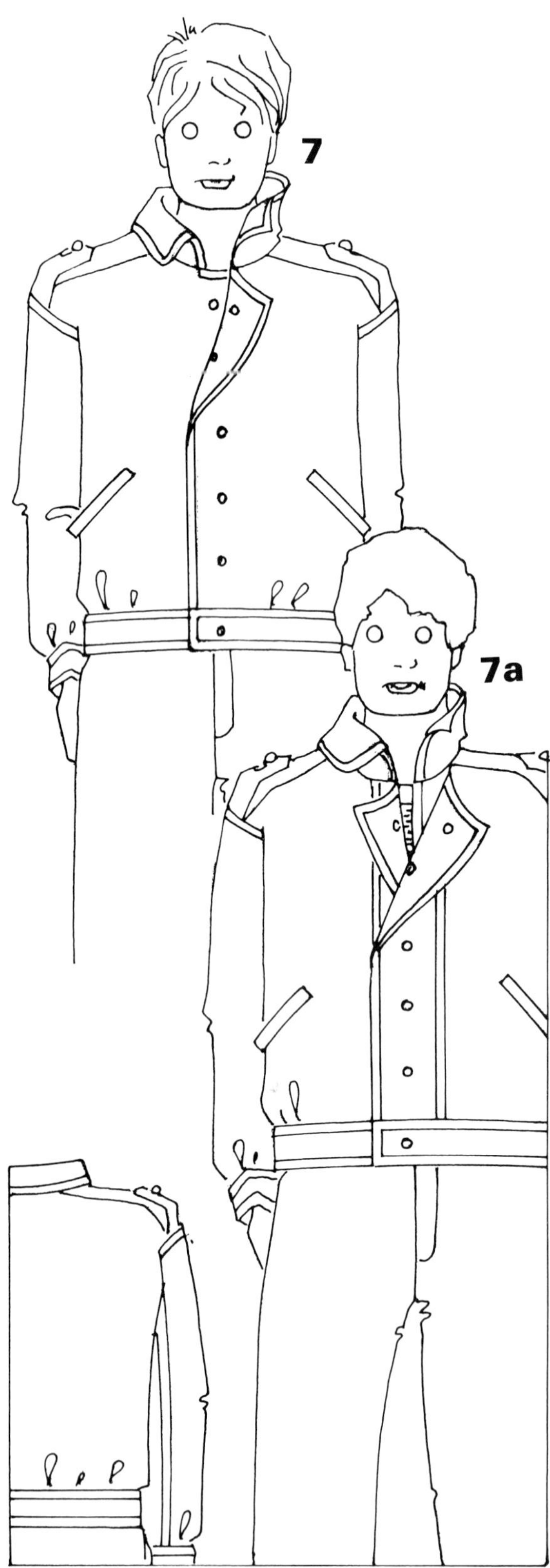

7 CASUAL JACKET

Trace off overgarment block and one-piece sleeve block.
Draw in finished length with straight hem line.
Complete adaptation for dropped shoulder with lowered armhole (ref. 13, page 42) on body and sleeve sections.
Extend shoulder 2.5cm with a straight line.

Body section Draw in shoulder strap lines.
Mark stud placings or buttonholes, add button stand.
Draw in line of lower band.
Draw in pocket opening:
92cm–122cm height length 11cm
128cm–152cm height length 13cm
158cm–170cm height length 15cm.
Draw in pocket bag.
Trace off back and front sections along strap lines.
Slope shoulders (2.5cm–3cm from outer edge) downwards 0.75cm.
Lower centre front 1cm, join to side seam.
Add extended facing to front.

Shoulder strap and tab Trace off shoulder straps on back and front. Place shoulder lines together, trace round pattern. Draw in tab line, trace off tab.

Lower band Trace off lower band, reduce length by 4cm at centre back. Make band twice depth, mark fold line through centre of band.

Pocket bag Trace off pocket bag.

Collar Construct a convertible collar (ref. 2, page 54).

Sleeve Shorten adapted sleeve by the measurement of the cuff depth.
Mark A at back pitch point, square down to B and C on front sleeve. C–D 1.5cm; trace off back and front sleeve. Curve line from A–B outwards 0.5cm.

Cuff Construct shirt cuff (ref. 1, page 50).
Add 4cm–5cm to cuff size measurement for shirts before commencing adaptation.

7a ALTERNATIVE FRONT FASTENING

Front Measure width of zip to be exposed. Mark in from centre front half this distance. Mark this line 'front edge line'.
Draw in facing line.
Draw in front flap line approx. 3.5cm each side of centre line.
Trace off front along front edge line.
Complete adaptation as for casual jacket.

Facing Trace off facing along facing line and front edge line.

Flap Trace off flap. Mark stud positions on centre front line.

Note The flap is made up separately and top-stitched to front section.

7 Casual jacket

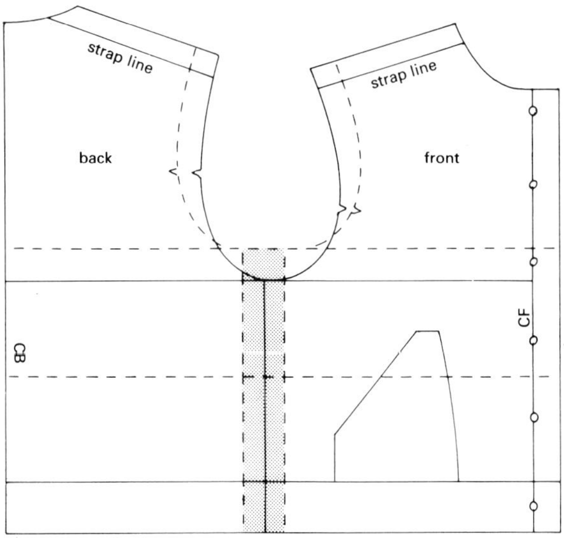

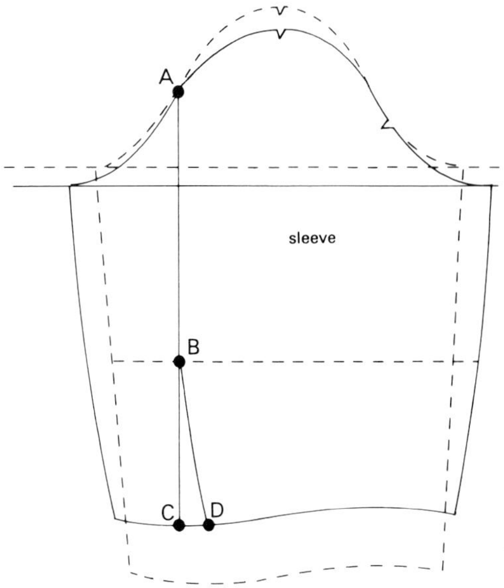

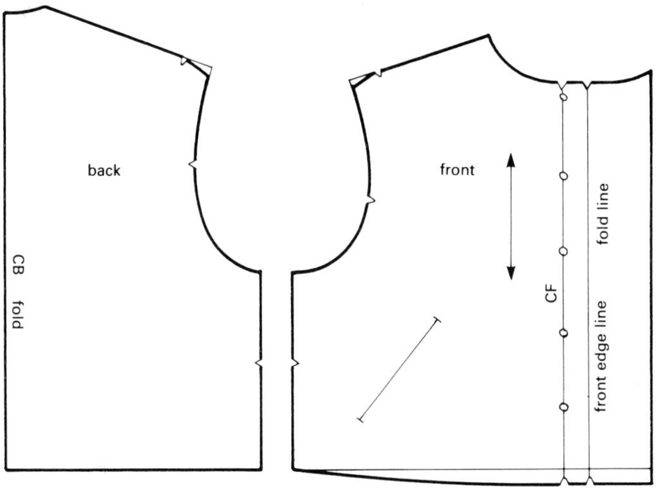

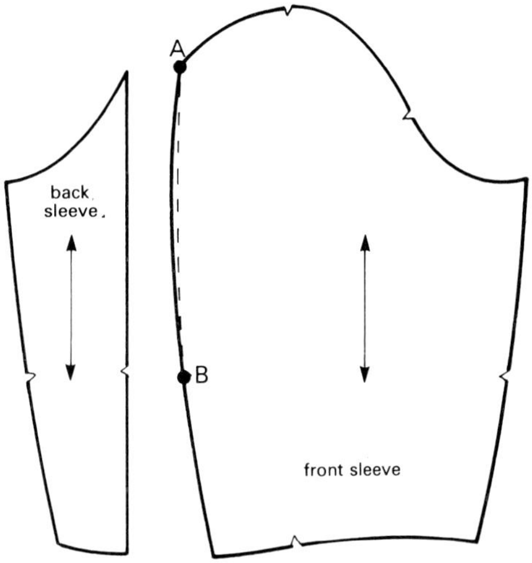

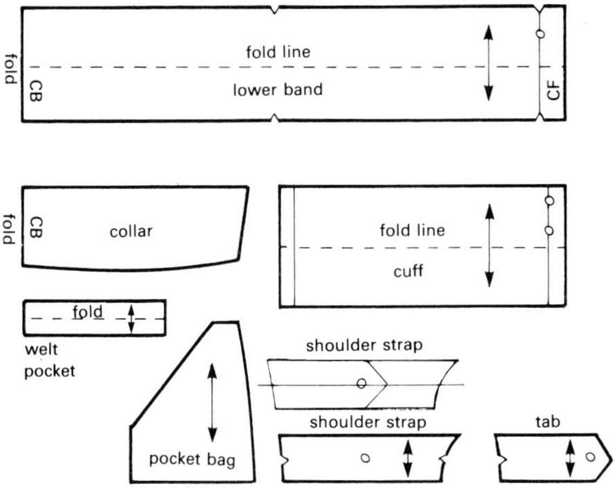

strap line
strap line
back
front
CB
CF
sleeve
A
B
C
D
back
front
CB fold
CF
fold line
front edge line
back sleeve
front sleeve
A
B

fold
CB
fold line
lower band
CF
fold
CB
collar
fold line
cuff
fold
welt pocket
pocket bag
shoulder strap
shoulder strap
tab

7a Alternative front fastening

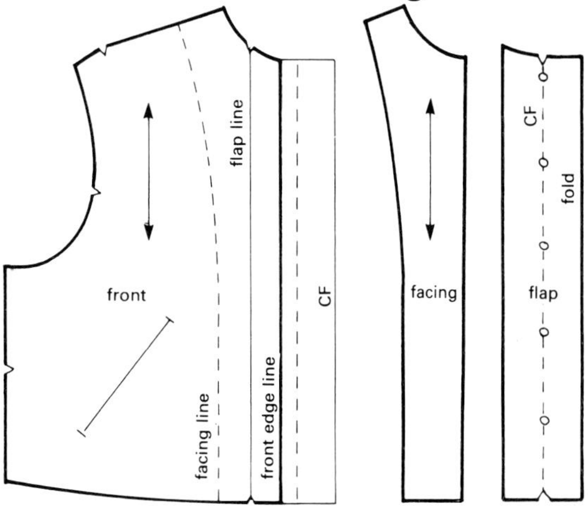

flap line
front
facing line
front edge line
CF
facing
CF
fold
flap

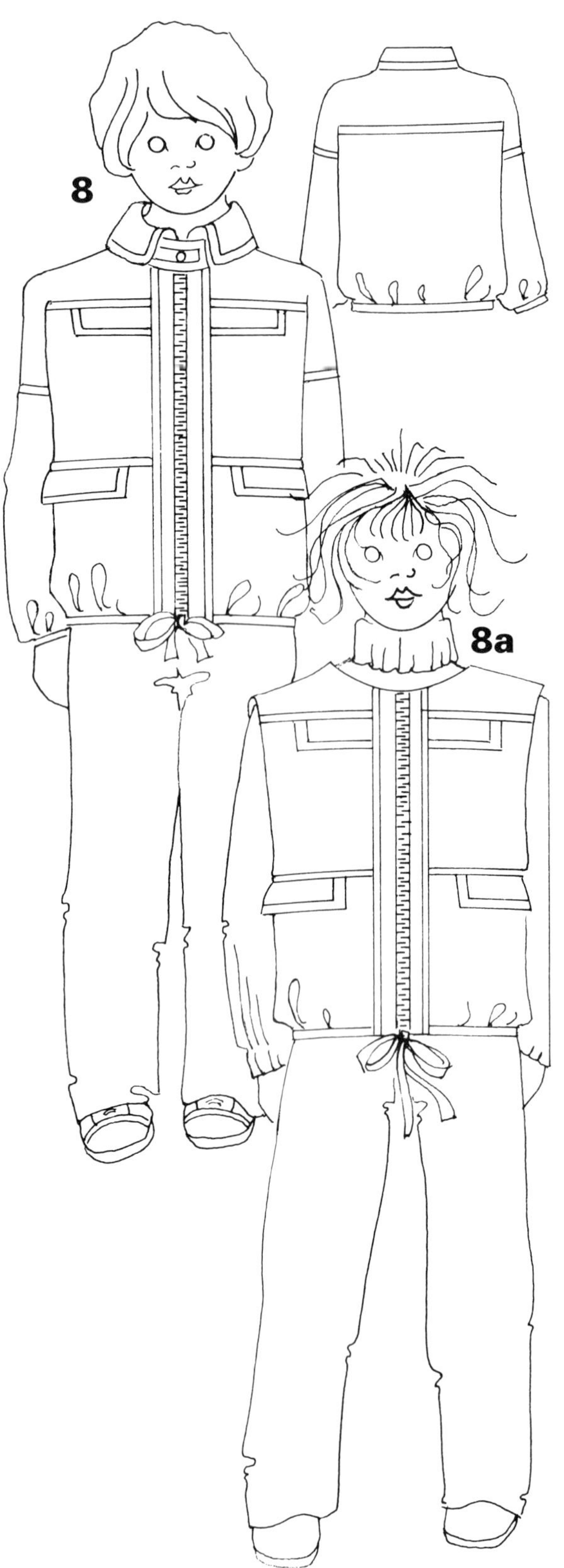

8 CASUAL JACKET

Trace off overgarment block and one-piece sleeve block.
Draw in finished length with straight hem.

Body sections Measure width of zip to be exposed. Mark in from centre front half this distance and mark this line front edge line. Mark strap line 2.5cm in from front edge line.
Draw in yoke line. Move side seam 2.5cm forward.
Draw in pocket flaps and pocket bags on yoke line and waist line.
Trace off back along yoke line. Trace off front along yoke and waistline. Trace off lower front along waistline. Add 5cm to hem line of back and lower front.
Trace off front strap.

Pocket flaps and bags Trace off pocket bags.
Trace off pocket flaps. Make flaps twice depth, mark fold line at centre of flap.

Collar Construct a shirt collar with band (ref. 3a, page 54). Square end of collar band.

Sleeve Mark A and B at underarm points.
A–C Approx. 6cm; square across. Square down from sleeve head pitch point.
Trace off lower section. Add 5cm to hem line for casing.
Complete adaptation for upper sections of sleeve. See extended sleeve with yoke (ref. 11, page 42).

8a SLEEVELESS ALTERNATIVE

Body section Draw in yoke lines, strap line and pockets as above.
Lower armhole 2cm. Draw in armhole facings.
Trace off armhole facings.
Complete body sections as for casual jacket without sleeve adaptation.

8 Casual jacket

8a Sleeveless alternative

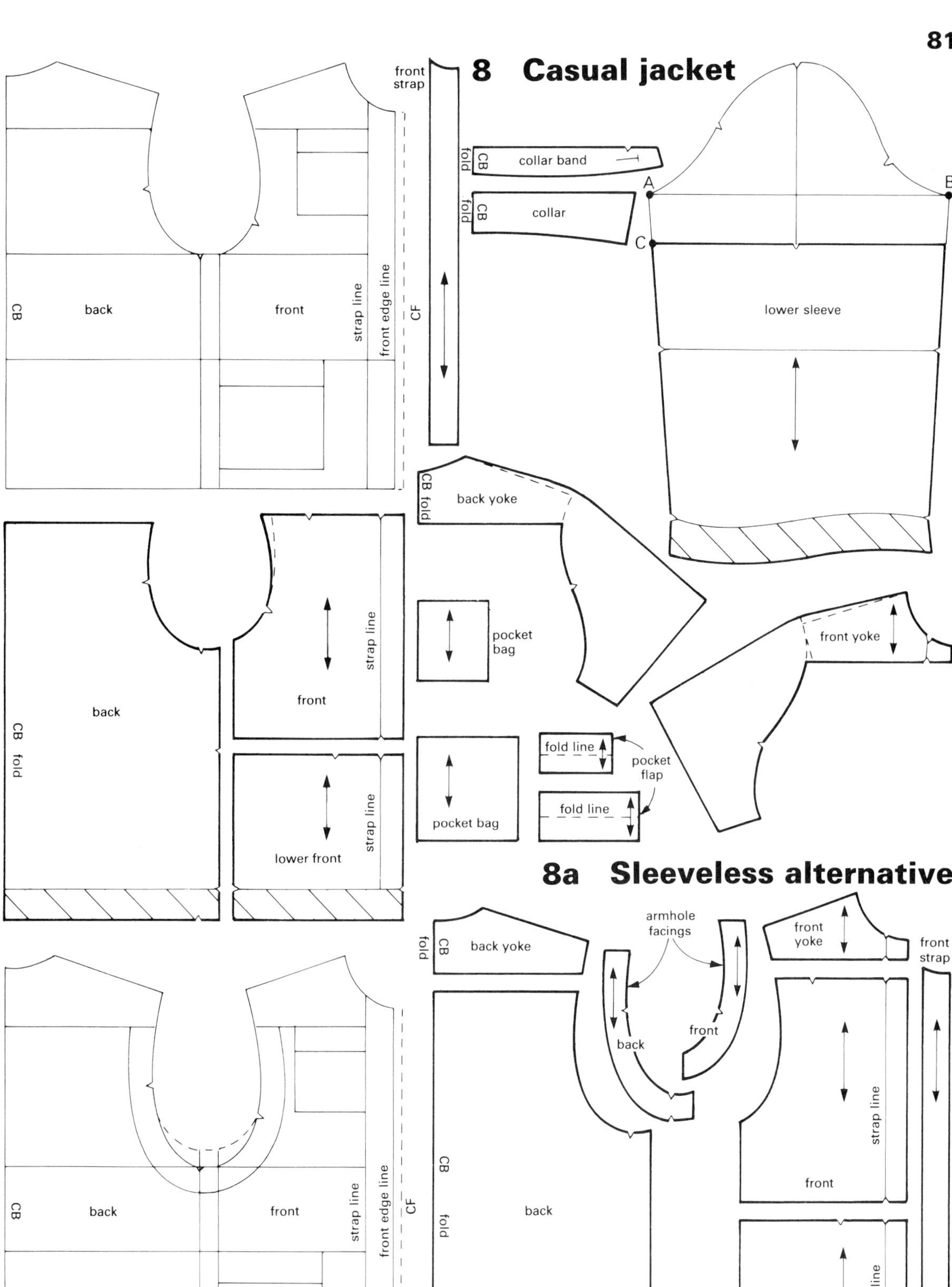

9 FASHION RAINCOAT
Trace off formal coat block and one-piece sleeve block.
Body sections Mark points A and B at underarm, C and D at hem line, E and F at shoulder. Join A–C and B–D.
Back Draw in yoke line, divide into three sections. Square down. Trace off back cut up lines, open required amount (example shows 3cm at top, 5cm at hem line).
Front Draw in yoke line. Mark buttonholes, button stand and facing line. Mark points G and H on yoke line, J at centre front hem line. Mark FP at front pitch point. Trace off yoke.
G–K ⅙ measurement G–H: square down to L.
Trace off front and side front; add 3cm flare to hem line at L on front, 2cm at L on side front.
Mark pocket opening and pocket bag on front.
Pocket and pocket bag Construct welt pocket length required and twice width. Mark fold line at centre.
Trace off pocket bag.
Collar and facing Construct convertible collar (ref. 2, page 54). Trace off facing.
Sleeve Mark points M, N, P, Q on underarm of sleeve.
Mark notches at sleeve head for position of gathers.
Mark R at front pitch point, M–S equals N–R.
P–T and Q–U ¼ measurement P–Q minus 2cm. Join S–T and R–U. Trace off middle section of sleeve, cut up centre line and open approx. 5cm. Raise sleeve head 1.5cm.
Trace off side sections of sleeve; place underarm seams to a vertical line. Trace round pattern.
Oversleeve On back mark new back pitch point BP.
A–BP The measurement M–S on sleeve.
Square up and across from V. V–W 1.5cm.
W–X The measurement E–BP on back plus 0.5cm; square down.
W–Y The measurement F–FP on front plus 0.5cm; square down.
Curve the lines W–X and W–Y. X–Z 3cm; square across.

10 CLASSIC RAINCOAT
Trace off overgarment block and one piece sleeve block.
Draw in finished length with curved front hem line.
Complete adaptation for raglan sleeve (ref. 14, page 44).
Body sections Complete adaptation for double breasted reefer collar (ref. 12, page 58).
Draw in back yoke line. Draw in welt pocket, pocket bag.
Trace off yoke section. Trace off back section.
Mark A and B on side seam.
B–C 2cm; join A–C.
Add a 4cm–6cm vent pleat at centre back from hipline.
Trace off front section. Mark D and E on side seam.
E–F 3.5cm; join D–F.
Collar and facing Trace off collar, widen the style line (ref. 11, page 58). Trace off facing, add approx. 0.5cm to rever from break point to collar point.
Pocket and pocket bag Trace off welt, double its depth, mark fold line at centre. Trace off pocket bag.
Sleeves Trace off adapted sleeves, mark in strap line.
Trace off strap, double its depth, mark fold line.
Belt Construct belt; G–H ½ waist measurement plus 20cm. G–J twice belt depth required; mark fold line.

9 Fashion raincoat

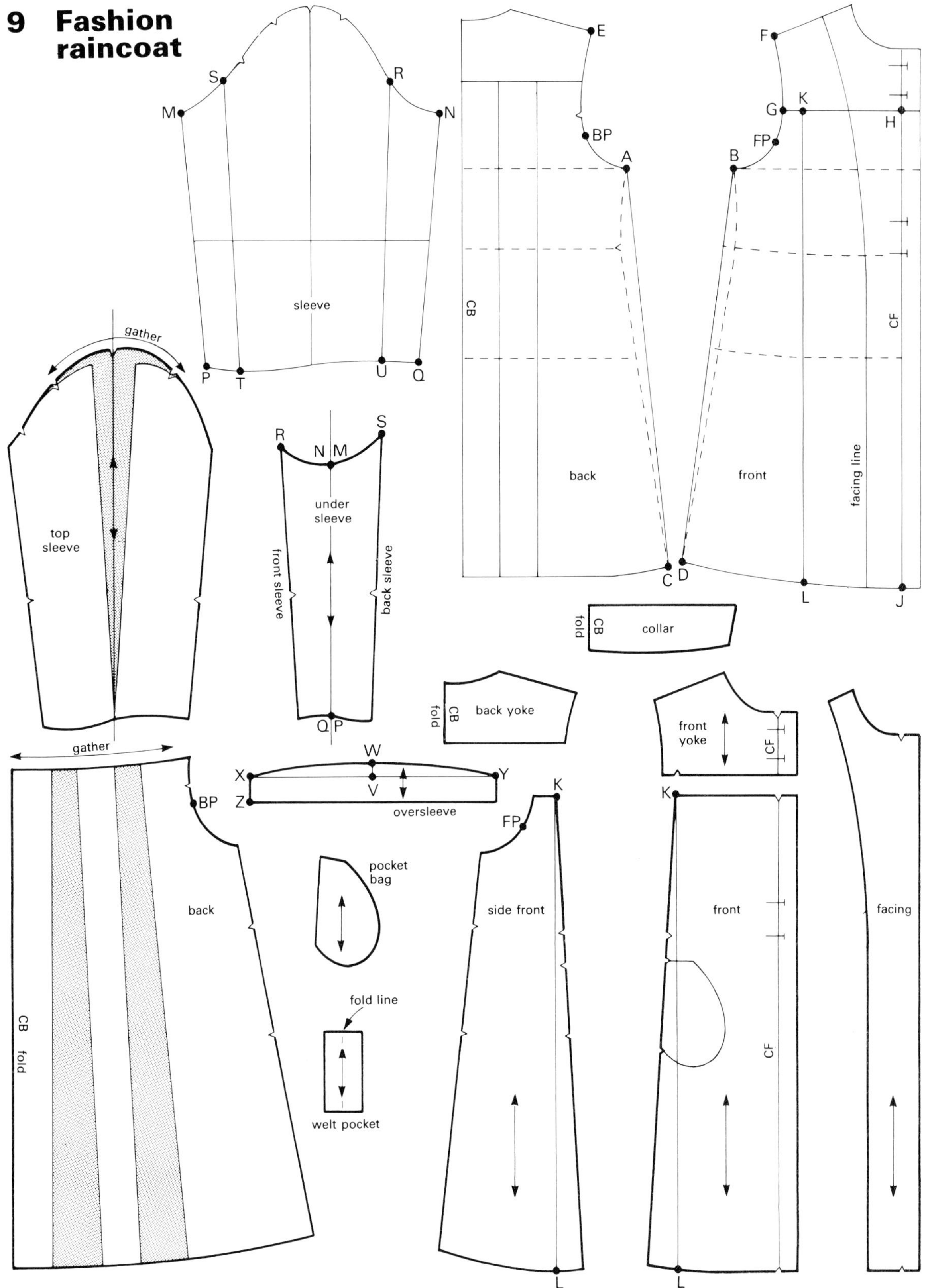

10 Classic raincoat

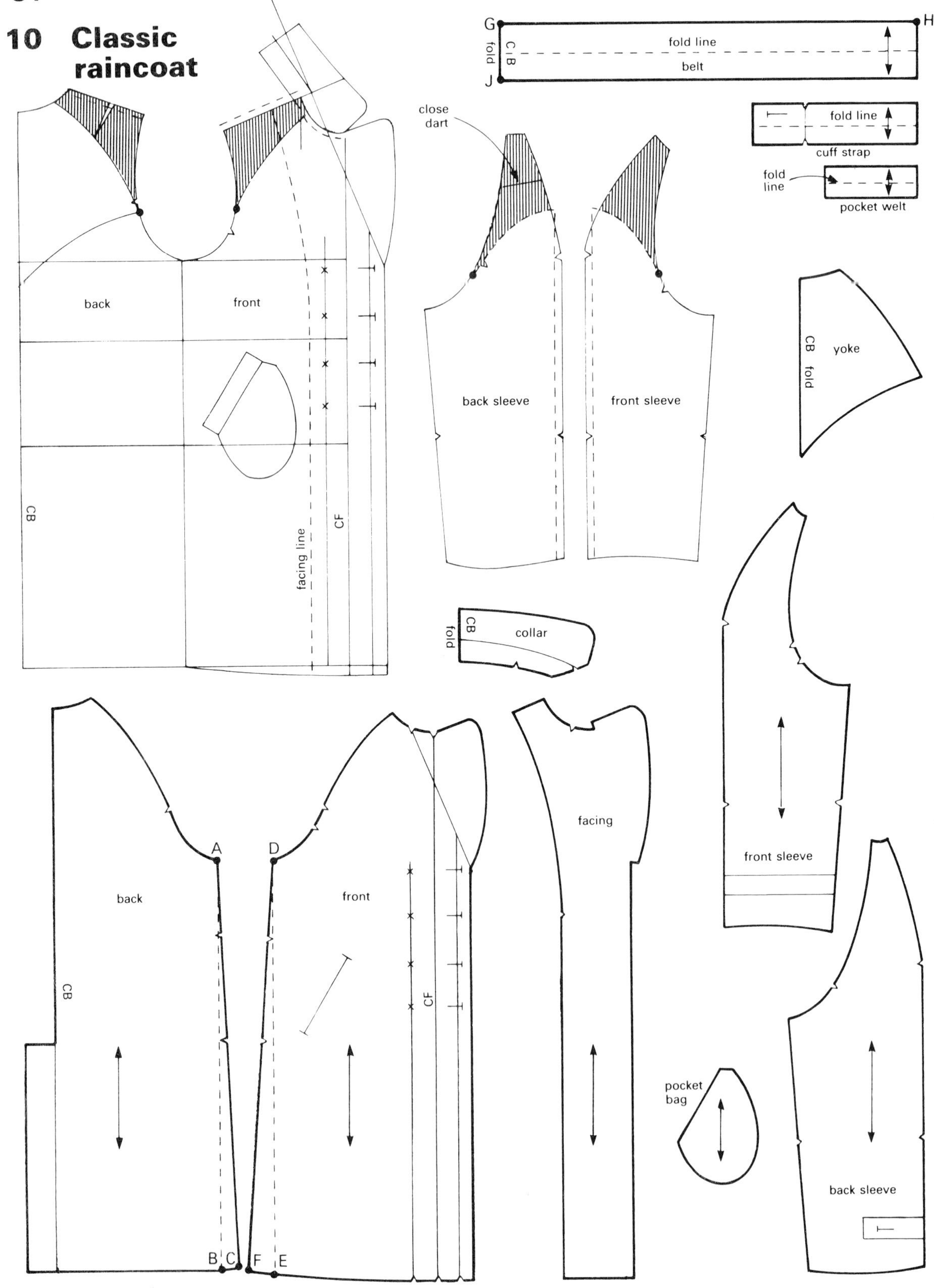

G
H
J
fold
C B
fold line
belt
fold line
cuff strap
fold line
pocket welt
close dart
back
front
back sleeve
front sleeve
yoke
CB
fold
facing line
CF
collar
A
D
B
C
F
E
facing
front sleeve
pocket bag
back sleeve

6 SKIRTS AND TROUSERS

The Skirt Block

For girls, sizes 92cm–140cm height
For girls above 140cm height the skirt block which has more waist shaping should be used (see page 138)

SKIRTS WITHOUT DARTS (92cm–104cm height)
Girls up to 104cm height have little waist shaping therefore a basic skirt is not a suitable garment for this group. The skirt block without darting has an easy-fitting waistline (5cm ease). It is usually developed into designs with straps, bib fronts or camisole tops.

MEASUREMENTS REQUIRED TO DRAFT THE BLOCK
(e.g. size 98cm height)
Refer to the size chart (page 18) for standard measurements.

Waist	54cm
Hip/seat	58cm
Waist to hip	12cm
Waist to knee	33cm

Back
Square both ways from 0.

0 – 1 Skirt length plus 1cm; square across.
0 – 2 Waist to hip plus 1cm; square across.
2 – 3 ¼ hip plus 1.5cm; square up to 4 and down to 5.
0 – 6 ¼ waist plus 1cm.
0 – 7 1cm; join 6–7 with a curve.
5 – 8 2.5cm; draw in side seam 6, 3, 8; curve hipline outwards 0.25cm, curve hem line up 0.25cm at 8.

Front
Square both ways from 9.

9 –10 Skirt length plus 1cm; square across.
9 –11 Waist to hip plus 1cm; square across.
11–12 ¼ hip plus 2cm; square up to 13, down to 14.
9 –15 ¼ waist plus 1.5cm.
9 –16 0.5cm; join 15–16 with a curve.
14–17 2.5cm; draw in side seam 15,12,17; curve hipline outwards 0.25cm, curve hem line 0.25cm at 17.

Note ELASTICATED WAISTS
Many skirts of all sizes have elasticated waistbands. This adaptation which allows for the growth of the child is shown in ref. 3 on page 88.

SKIRTS WITH DARTS (110cm–140cm height)
Skirts with darts have 1cm ease in the waistline of the skirt. The waistline of the skirt should be eased onto the skirt waistband.

MEASUREMENTS REQUIRED TO DRAFT THE BLOCK
(e.g. size 110cm height)
Refer to the size charts (pages 18 and 19) for standard measurements.

Waist	56cm
Hip	62cm
Waist to hip	13.2cm
Waist to knee	37cm

Back
Square both ways from 0.

0 – 1 Skirt length plus 1cm; square across.
0 – 2 Waist to hip plus 1cm; square across.
2 – 3 ¼ hip plus 1.5cm; square up to 4 and down to 5.
0 – 6 ¼ waist:
sizes 110cm–122cm height plus 1.2cm
128cm–140cm height plus 1.7cm.
0 – 7 1cm; join 6–7 with a curve.
5 – 8 2.5cm; draw in side seam 6, 3, 8; curve hipline outwards 0.25cm, curve hem line 0.25cm at 8.
9 Mid-way between 6 and 7; square down from the line 6–7.

Construct a dart on this line:
sizes 110cm–122cm height length 8cm, width 1cm
128cm–140cm height length 9cm, width 1.5cm.

Front
Square both ways from 10.

10–11 Skirt length plus 1cm; square across.
10–12 Waist to hip plus 1cm; square across.
12–13 ¼ hip plus 1.5cm; square up to 14, down to 15.
10–16 ¼ waist:
sizes 110cm–122cm height plus 1.3cm
128cm–140cm height plus 1.8cm.
10–17 0.5cm; join 16–17 with a curve.
15–18 2.5cm; draw in side seam 16, 13, 18; curve hipline outwards 0.25cm, curve hem line 0.25cm at 18.
19 Mid-way between 16 and 17; square down from the line 16–17.

Construct a dart on this line:
sizes 110cm–122cm height length 6.5cm, width 1cm.
128cm–140cm height length 7.5cm, width 1.5cm.

Skirt block without darts 92cm–104cm height

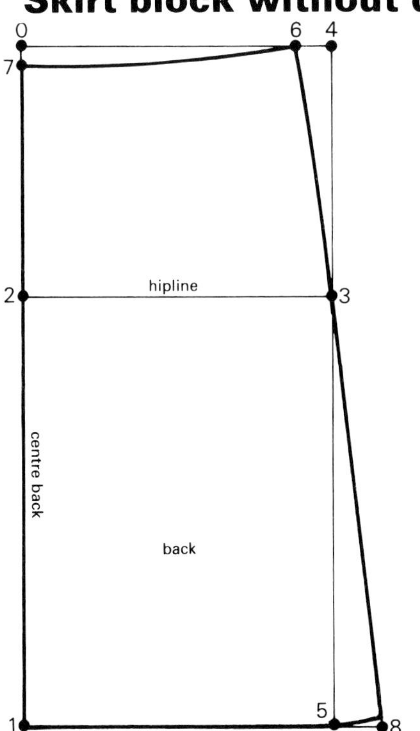

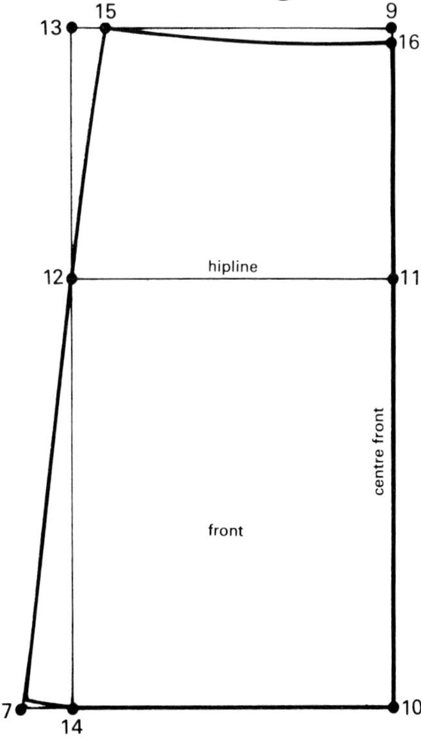

Skirt block with darts 110cm–140cm height

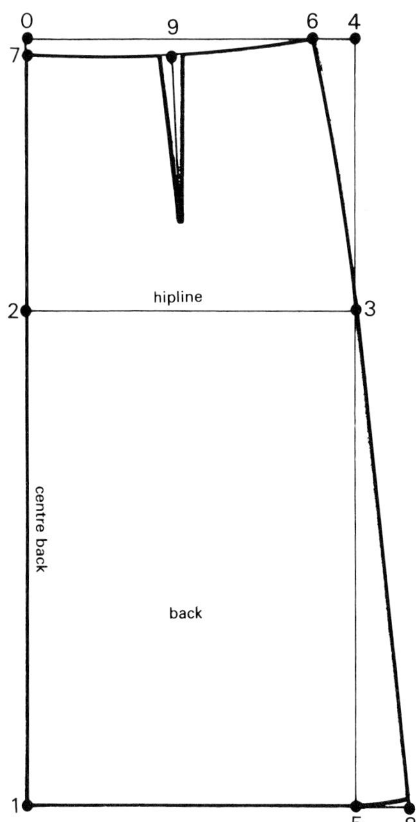

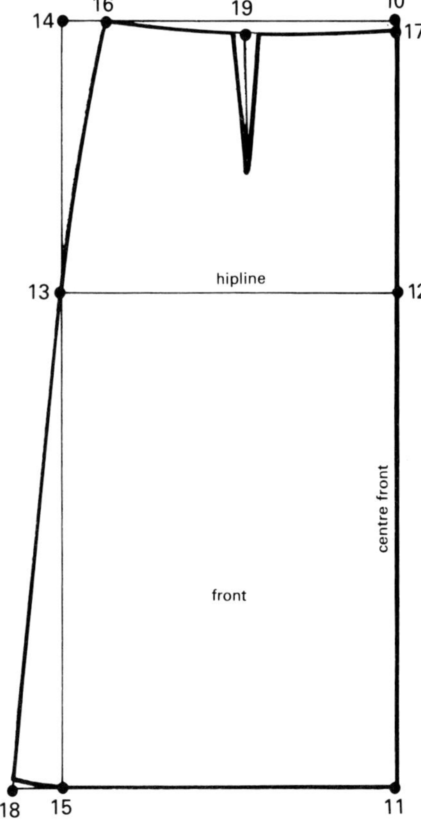

1 CAMISOLE TOP
This type of skirt is suitable for young children (up to approx. 110cm height) who have little waist shaping.
Bodice Trace round sleeveless dress block to waistline. Erase side seam, square down from underarm points, shape in side seam 0.5cm if required. Mark A, B, C and D at neckline. E and F at shoulders.
A–G 1cm. B–H, C–J, D–K 2.5cm. E–L, F–M 1cm. Draw in new neck and armhole curves.
Skirt Trace round skirt block, erase any darts. Make back and front waistline measurements equal those of front and back bodice. Mark points N and P. Join N and P to hem line.
The skirt can then be adapted to different styles.

Note The bodice requires an opening at centre back.

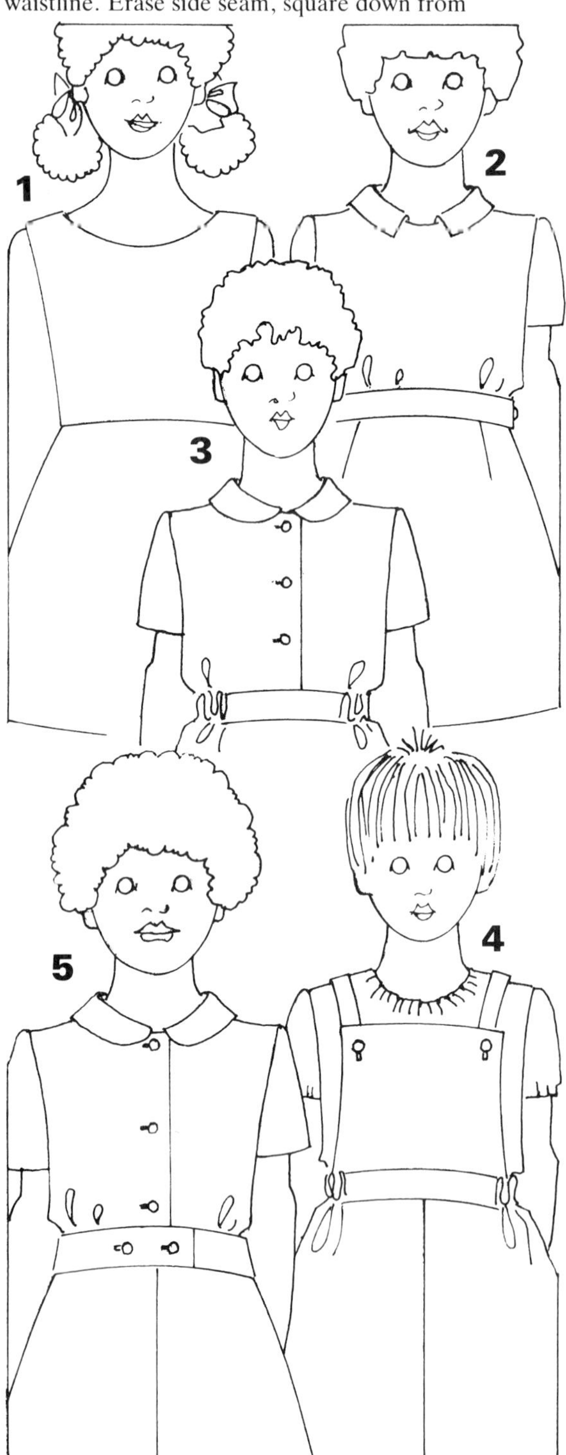

WAISTBANDS
Children up to 122cm height often require straps on skirts to hold them in position. Many skirts in all sizes have an elasticated waistband. They hold the skirt in position and they allow for the child's growth.

2 STANDARD WAISTBAND
Skirt without darts A–B ½ waist measurement plus 2.5cm (easy-fitting waistband). B–C 3cm–4cm button extension. Square down from A, B and C.
A–D Twice waistband depth; mark fold line down centre.
Skirt with darts A–B ½ waist measurement. B–C 3cm–4cm button extension, square down from A,B and C.
A–D Twice waistband depth; mark fold line down centre.
Note For a 'straight' finish at the seam opening the extension is added to only one end of the waistband.

3 ELASTICATED WAISTBAND
Skirts Mark A and B at centre front and back waist. Square up from the hipline to points C and D. Extend waistline curve to C and D. Join C and D to hem line.
Waistband E–F the measurement of A–C and B–D; square down from E and F. E–G twice waistband depth, square across to H. Mark fold line down centre.
On front waistline of skirt B–J ⅔ measurement B–D.
On waistband E–K the measurement A–C and D–J; square down. E–K is the length of waistband to be elasticated.

Note Skirts with elasticated waistbands do not require an opening. Openings are added only as style features. They are usually placed between B and J on front. Skirts with openings require a button extension on waistband.

4 BIB FRONT
Bib fronts can be added to most skirt styles.
Trace off bodice block. Draw in bib shape required.
Measure the length of strap (A–B plus C–D) required and construct straps the required width.

5 SHAPED WAISTBAND
On skirt block draw lines parallel to waistline; depth 4cm. Cut off back and front sections. Close darts. Place front section to back section. Trace round pattern; add 4cm button extension at centre front.

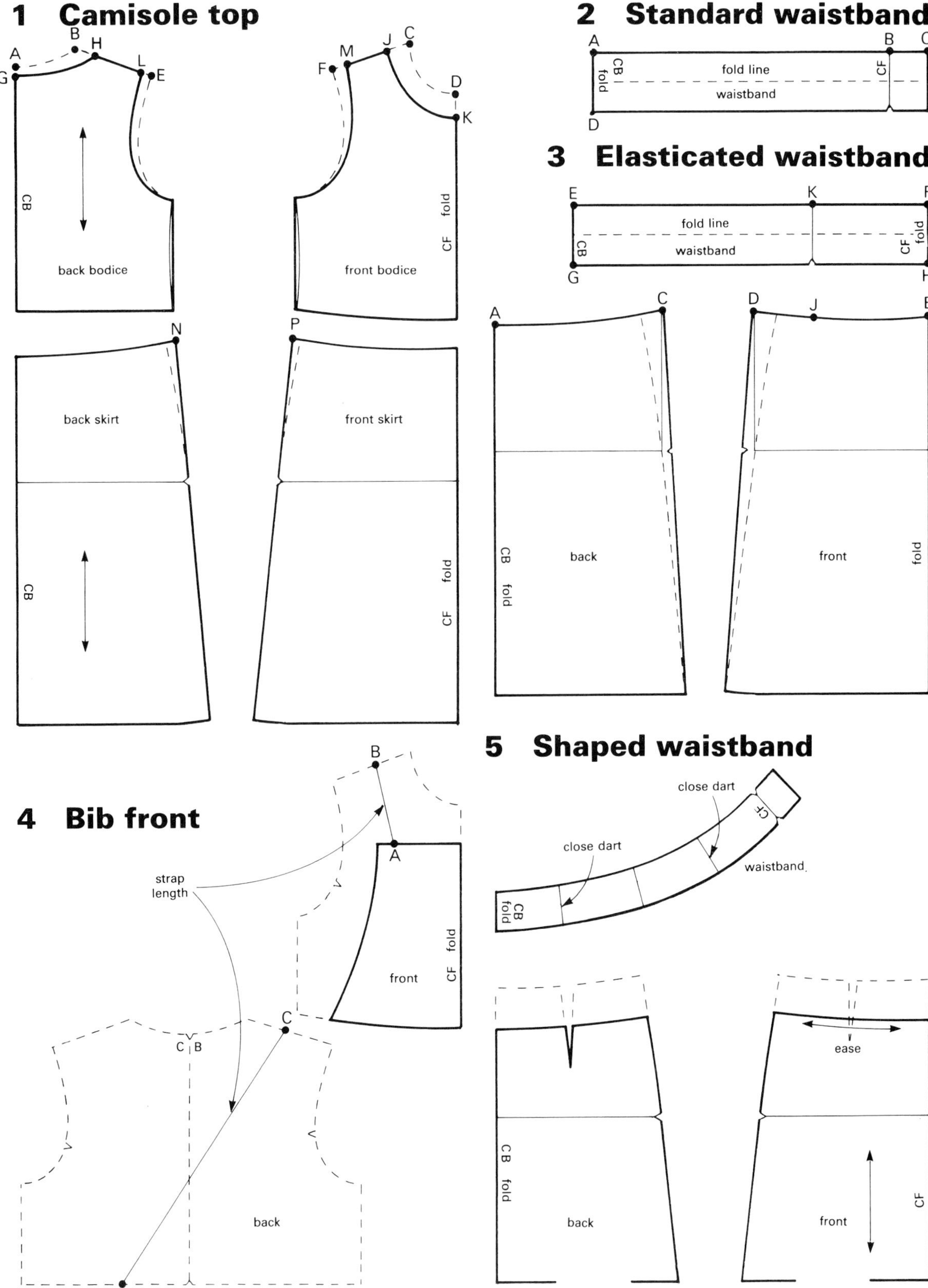
1 Camisole top
A
B
H
G
L
E
CB
back bodice
F
M
J
C
D
K
fold
CF
front bodice
N
back skirt
CB
P
front skirt
fold
CF
2 Standard waistband
A
B
C
CB
fold
fold line
waistband
CF
D
3 Elasticated waistband
E
K
F
fold line
CB
waistband
CF
fold
G
H
A
C
CB
fold
back
D
J
B
front
fold
4 Bib front
B
A
strap length
fold
CF
front
C
C B
back
D
5 Shaped waistband
close dart
CF
close dart
waistband
CB
fold
ease
CB
fold
back
front
CF

6 KILT – WORK DIRECTLY ON CLOTH
Square both ways from A.

A–B	Skirt length plus hem.	
A–C	92cm–122cm height	12cm
	128cm–152cm height	16cm
	158cm–164cm height	20cm.

A–D ½ measurement A–C; square down, mark centre front.

C–E	3 times (hip measurement minus A–C).	
E–F	92cm–122cm height	12cm
	128cm–152cm height	16cm
	158cm–164cm height	20cm; square down to G.

E–H ½ measurement E–F; square down, mark centre front.

Add 2cm to A–B and F–G for facings.
Pleat section C–E. Decide number of pleats (e.g. 20). Divide C–E into 20 sections. Divide each section into three and mark with pin lines as shown.

Waist shaping Fold pleats and tack to hipline. To shape waist take the edge of each pleat and lap it over the amount required to obtain a correct waist measurement.

Method Hip meas. minus waist meas. divided by pleat number. E.g. size 110cm: hips 62cm minus waist 56cm divided by number of pleats, (62 − 56) ÷ 20 = 0.3cm lap.

7a SLIGHTLY GATHERED SKIRT
Trace skirt block, erase any darts. Divide waistline into three sections, mark points A and B; square down. Cut up lines and open sections required amount. Trace round pattern.

7b VERY GATHERED SKIRT
Back Square both ways from A.
A–B Three times half hip measurement; square down;
A–C Skirt length; square across.
A–D Mid-way A–B; square down. Mark the line centre back.
Front Construct pattern as for back.

8a CIRCULAR SKIRT
The construction of a circular skirt is based on a circle. Make the waist measurement the circumference. Calculate radius from the circumference, see page 16.
A–B is the radius. A–C is the radius.
Draw a quarter circle from B–C.
C–D is skirt length. With a metre stick mark out edge of circle as shown.

8b HALF CIRCULAR SKIRT
The construction of a half circular skirt is based on a circle. Make the waist measurement the circumference. Calculate the radius from the circumference, see page 16.
A–B is twice the radius. A–C is twice the radius.
Draw a quarter circle from B–C.
C–D is skirt length. With a metre stick mark out edge of circle as shown.

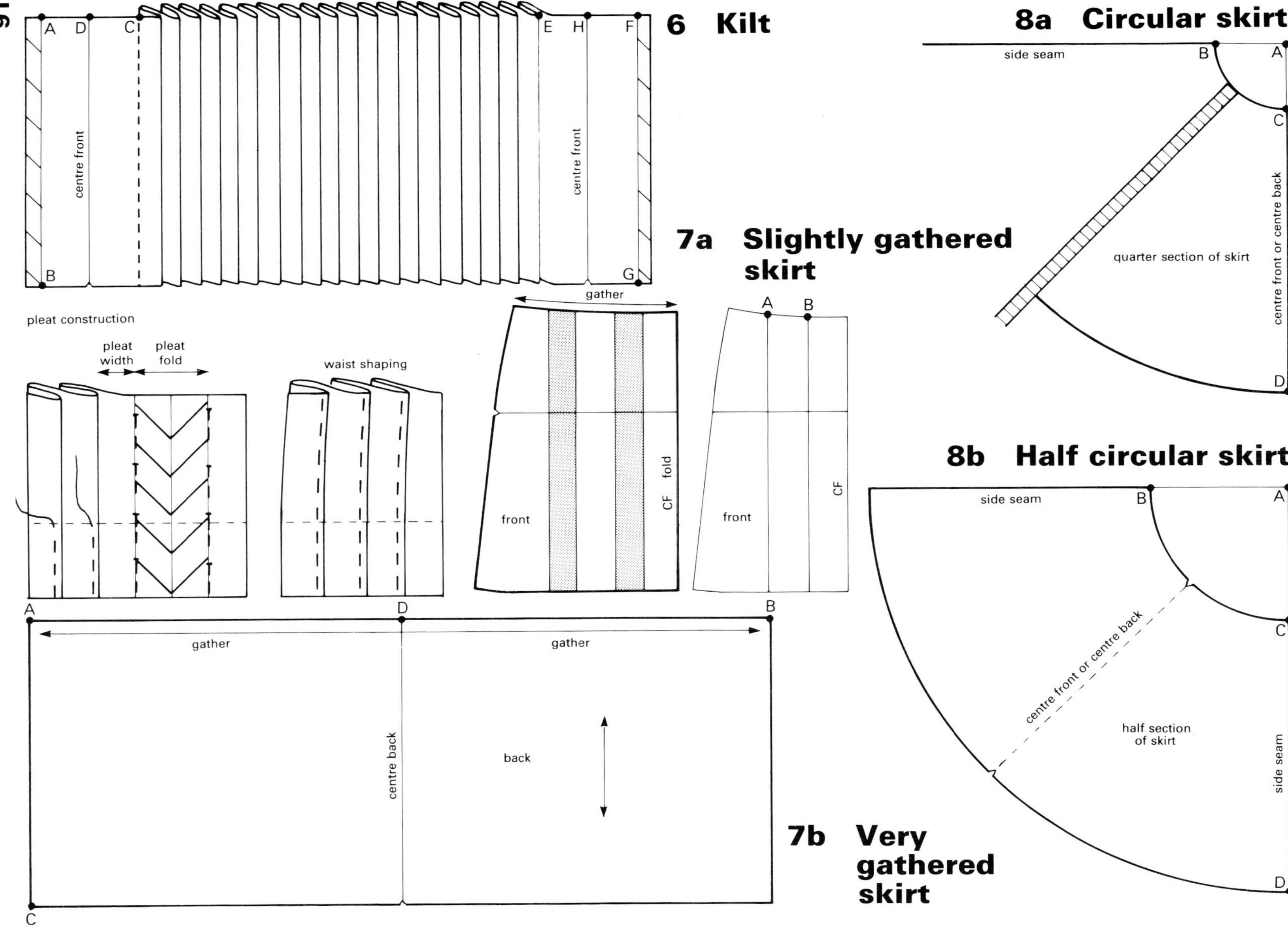

6 Kilt

7a Slightly gathered skirt

7b Very gathered skirt

8a Circular skirt

8b Half circular skirt

Note If an elasticated waistband is required, make the adaptation (ref. 3, page 88) before commencing the design.

9 FLARED SKIRTS

Skirts without darts Trace round back and front sections of the skirt block. Divide waistline into four sections.

Mark points A, B and C; square down. Cut up lines and open at hem line required amount. Trace round pattern.

Skirts with darts Trace round back and front sections of the skirt block. Measure the darts then erase them.

Divide waistlines into four sections. Mark points A, B and C; square down.

Construct three darts at A, B and C; the measurement of each dart is one third the dart allowance for that pattern piece.

Cut up lines, close darts, open at hem line the required amount. Trace round pattern.

10 FOUR GORED SKIRT

A four gored skirt is constructed from a flared skirt. It has centre back and front seams. This skirt hangs well on the figure because it can be cut with the grain line down the centre of each panel.

Back and front Mark in hipline, mark points A and B at hipline, C and D at hem line. D–E 2.5cm, join B–E. F is mid-way A–B, G is mid-way C–E; join F–G.

This becomes the grain line.

11 SECTIONED SKIRTS

Extra flare can be added to sections of skirts.

Trace off skirt block or flared skirt pattern (e.g. flared skirt).

Mark A at centre of waistline, B at centre of hem line. Join A–B. Draw curved style lines at required depth. Divide each curved lower section into four equal parts.

Flared section Cut up lines, open at hem line the required amount. Trace round pattern.

Flared and gathered section Cut up lines, open sections 3cm at top 6cm at hem line (extra or less can be inserted). Trace round pattern as shown.

Note It is necessary to ensure that when curved pattern pieces are opened at the top that each section is laid on a line squared out from the line of previous section (e.g. line C–D).

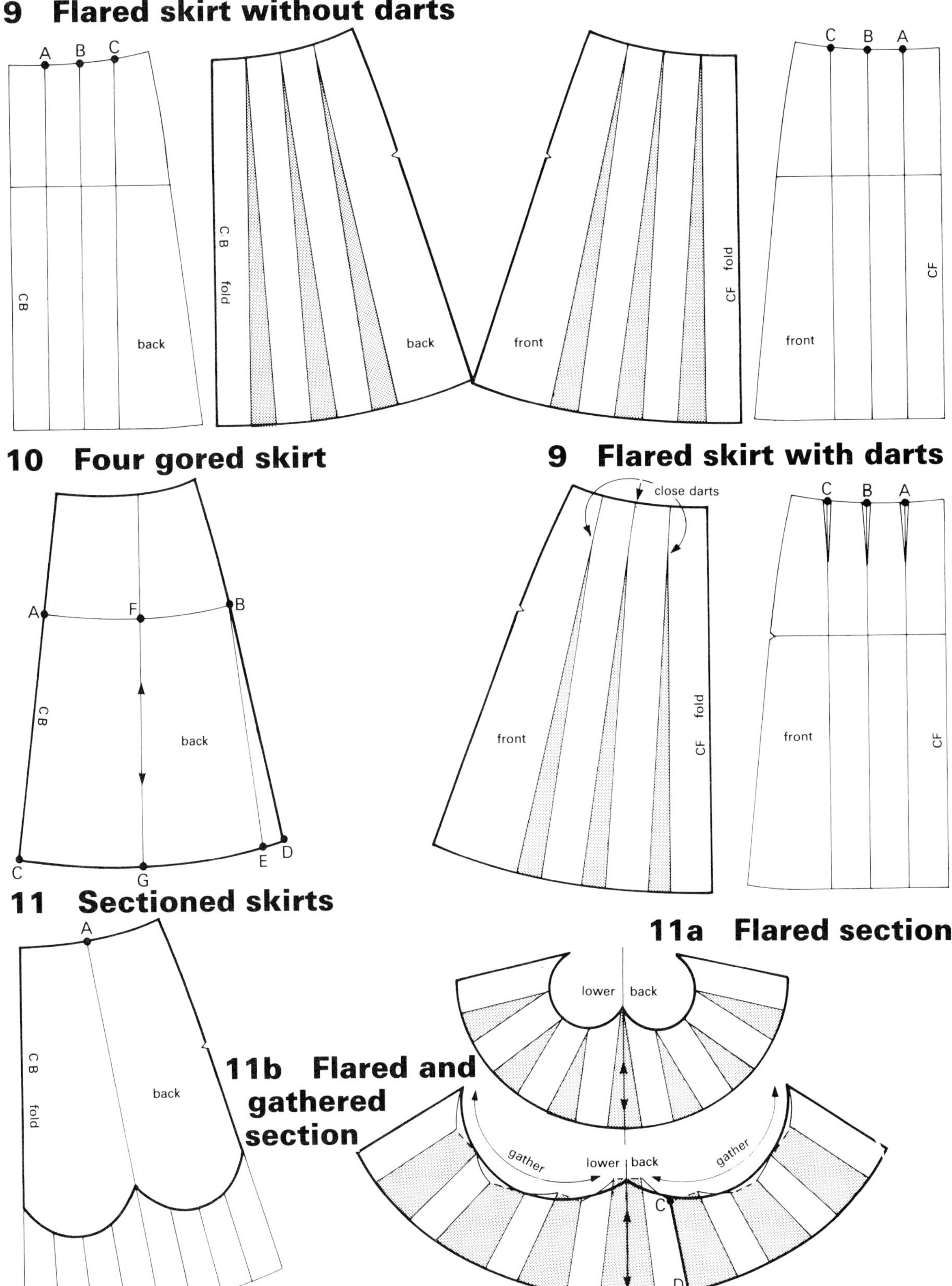
9 Flared skirt without darts
A B C
CB
back
C.B fold
back
front
CF fold
C B A
CF
front
10 Four gored skirt
A F B
CB
back
C G E D
9 Flared skirt with darts
close darts
front
CF fold
C B A
front
CF
11 Sectioned skirts
A
CB fold
back
B
11a Flared section
lower back
11b Flared and gathered section
gather
lower back
gather
C
D

Note If the elasticated waistband is required, make the adaptation (ref. 3, page 88) before commencing the design.

12 SKIRT WITH VENT PLEAT – BOX PLEAT
Trace off skirt block.
Back Mark centre back the pleat stitch line.
Add a pleat to this line width approx.:
92cm–122cm height 4cm
128cm–152cm height 5cm
158cm–164cm height 6cm.
Fold pleat into finished position; cut out pattern.
Front Mark A at pleat position on waistline; square down, cut up line and open twice back pleat width.
Mark fold line down centre. Fold pleat into finished position. Cut out pattern.

13 SKIRT WITH INVERTED PLEATS
Trace off skirt block.
Back Mark A at centre back waistline, square out.
A–B twice pleat width approx.:
92cm–122cm height 8cm
128cm–152cm height 10cm
158cm–164cm height 12cm; square down.
Mark fold line down centre. Fold pleat into finished position. Cut out pattern.
Front Mark C at pleat position on waistline; square down.
Cut up line. C–D four times pleat width approx.:
92cm–122cm height 16cm
128cm–152cm height 20cm
158cm–164cm height 24cm.
Divide C–D into four sections; square down from E, F, G.
Mark lines from E and G fold lines.
Fold pleat into finished position. Cut out pattern.

14 SKIRT WITH BACK AND FRONT PLEATS
Trace off skirt block.
Back Mark A and B at pleat positions on waistline; square down.
Cut up lines. A–C and B–D twice the measurement A–B.
Mark fold line down centre of each opening.
Fold pleats into finished position. Cut out pattern.
Front Construct front as for back.

SKIRTS WITH DARTS
Trace off skirt block.
Measure dart allowance, erase darts. Construct pleats.
Skirts with one pleat Draw in dart on pleat line; complete pattern.
Skirts with two pleats Draw a dart (half dart allowance) on each pleat line; complete pattern.

12 Skirt with vent pleat – box pleat

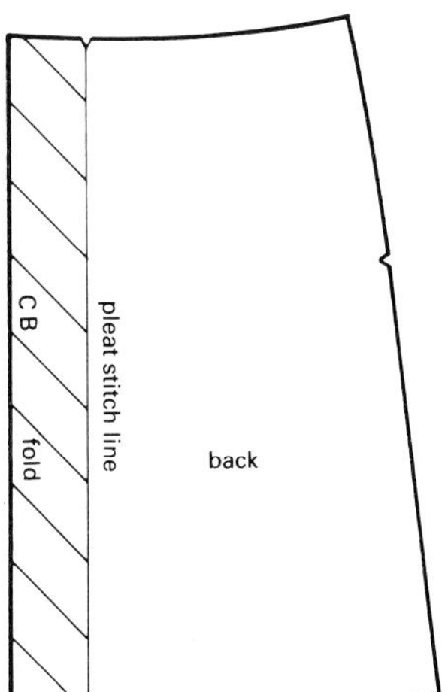

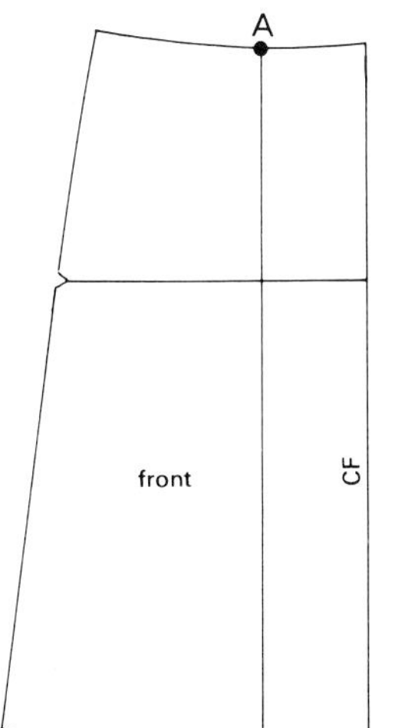

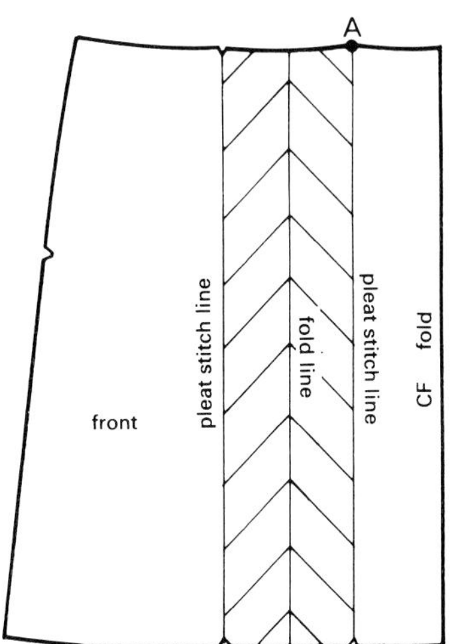

13 Skirt with inverted pleats

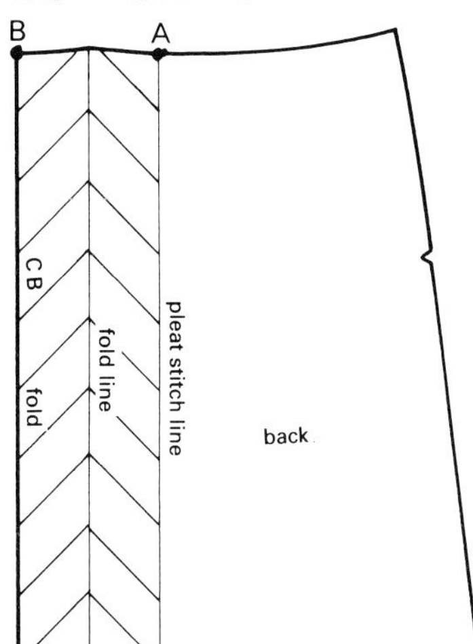

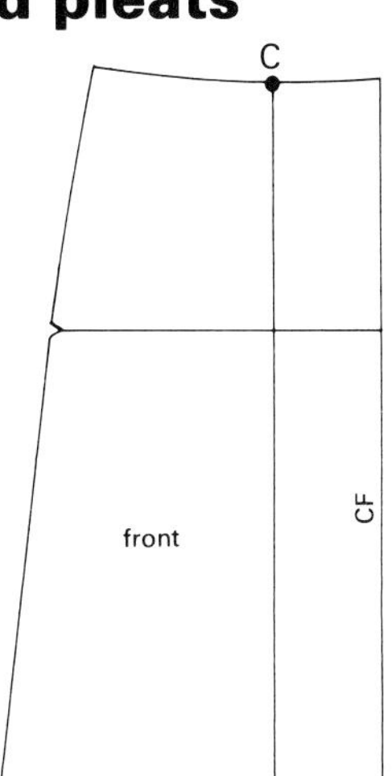

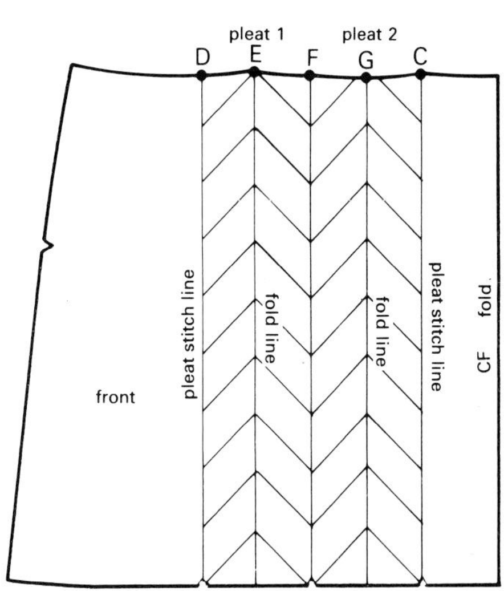

14 Skirt with back and front pleats

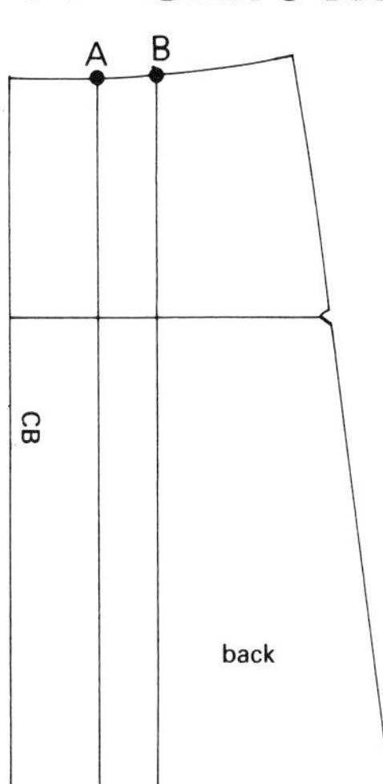

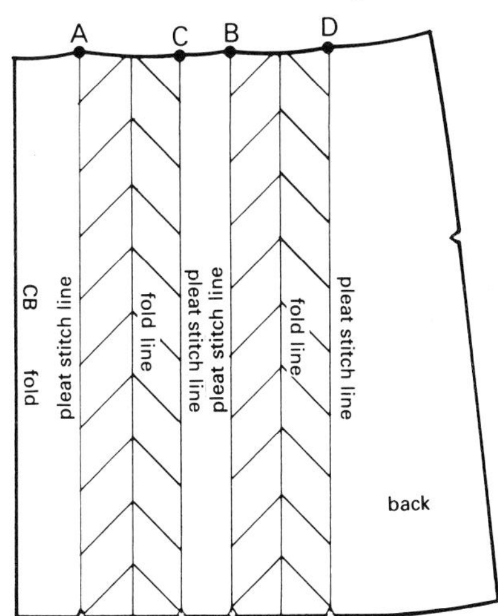

Skirt with darts

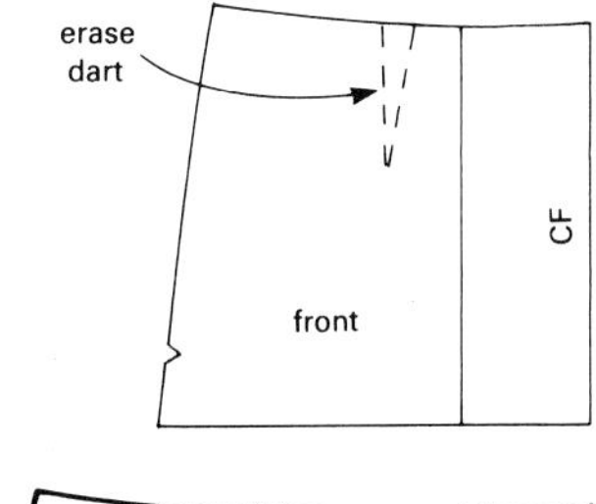

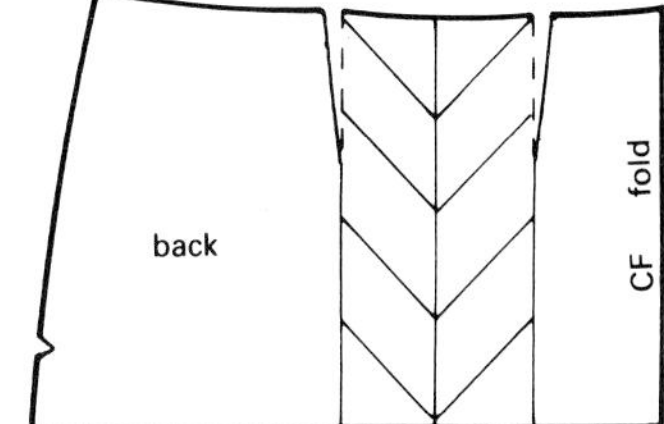

The Basic Trouser Block

For children, 92cm–122cm height, and boys 128cm–170cm height
For girls, 128cm–140cm height

The earliest figure difference that occurs between boys and girls is that of waist/hip relationship. For girls above 140cm height use the girls' trouser block on page 136 as this block has more waist shaping. Sizes up to 122cm height require more ease in the front of the trousers, this front–back proportion is systematically reduced as the size is increased.

Note 1 There is 1cm ease in the waistline of the trousers. The waistline of trousers should always be eased onto the waistband.

Note 2 The top of the waistband of the basic trouser block for children up to 122cm height and boys, sits on the waistline. For girls above 122cm height the bottom of the waistband sits on the waistline.

MEASUREMENTS REQUIRED TO DRAFT THE BLOCK
(e.g. boys and girls size 134cm height)
Refer to the size charts (pages 18 and 19) for standard measurements.

	Girls	Boys
Hip/seat	74cm	73cm
Waist	61cm	63cm
Body rise	22.4cm	22cm
Inside leg	61cm	61cm
Trouser bottom width	19cm	19cm
Waist to hip	15.6cm	15.6cm
Waist band depth	3cm	3cm

Front
Square down and across from 0.

Children, 92cm–122cm height; boys, 128cm–170cm height

0 – 1 Body rise plus 1cm, minus waistband depth; square across.
0 – 2 Waist to hip plus 1cm, minus waistband depth; square across.

Girls, 128cm–140cm height

0 – 1 Body rise; square across.
0 – 2 Waist to hip; square across.

1 – 3 Inside leg; square across.
1 – 4 ½ measurement 1–3:
sizes 92cm–122cm height minus 3cm
128cm–152cm height minus 3.5cm
158cm–170cm height minus 4cm;
square across.
1 – 5 1/12 hip/seat plus 1.5cm; square up to 6 and 7.
6 – 8 ¼ hip/seat:
sizes 92cm–122cm height plus 1.5cm
128cm–152cm height plus 1cm
158cm–170cm height plus 0.5cm.
5 – 9 1/16 hip/seat plus 0.5cm. 7–10 1cm.

Join 10–6; join 6–9 with a curve touching a point:
sizes 92cm–122cm height 2.25cm from 5
128cm–152cm height 2.5cm from 5
158cm–170cm height 2.75cm from 5.

Children, 92cm–122cm height; boys, 128cm–170cm height

10–11 ¼ waist:
sizes 92cm–122cm height plus 0.75cm
128cm–170cm height plus 0.25cm.

Girls, 128cm–140cm height

10–11 ¼ waist plus 1.25cm.
Construct a dart on line from 0; length 8cm, width 1cm.

3 –12 ½ trouser bottom width minus 0.5cm.
4 –13 The measurement 3–12 plus 1cm.
3 –14 ½ trouser bottom width minus 0.5cm.
4 –15 The measurement 3–14 plus 1cm.
Draw in side seam through points 11, 8, 13, 12; curve hipline outwards 0.25cm.
Draw inside leg seam 9, 15, 14; curve 9–15 in 0.75cm.

Back

5 –16 ¼ measurement 1–5; square up to 17 on hip/seat line, 18 on waistline.
16–19 ½ measurement 16–18.
18–20 1.5cm. 20–21 1.5cm.
21–22 ¼ waist:
sizes 92cm–122cm height plus 1.25cm
128cm–152cm height plus 2.25cm
158cm–170cm height plus 2.75cm.
Join 21–22 to touch the horizontal line from 0.
9 –23 ½ measurement 5–9. 23–24 0.25cm.
Join 21–19, join 19–24 with a curve touching a point:
sizes 92cm–122cm height 3.5cm from 16
128cm–152cm height 3.75cm from 16.
158cm–170cm height 4cm from 16.
17–25 ¼ hip/seat:
sizes 92cm–122cm height plus 1cm
128cm–170cm height plus 1.25cm.
12–26 1cm. 13–27 1cm. 14–28 1cm. 15–29 1cm.
Draw in side seam through points 22, 25, 27, 26; curve hipline outwards 0.25cm, 25–27 inwards 0.25cm.
Draw inside leg seam 24, 29, 28; curve 24–29 in 1.25cm.
21–30 ½ measurement 21–22; square down from the line 21–22.
Construct a dart on this line:
Sizes 92cm–122cm height length 7.5cm, width 1.5cm
128cm–152cm height length 9cm, width 2cm
158cm–170cm height length 11cm, width 2.5cm.
Curve hem line down 1cm at 3.

Trouser block

Children 92cm–122cm height
Boys 128cm–170cm height

Girls 128cm–140cm height

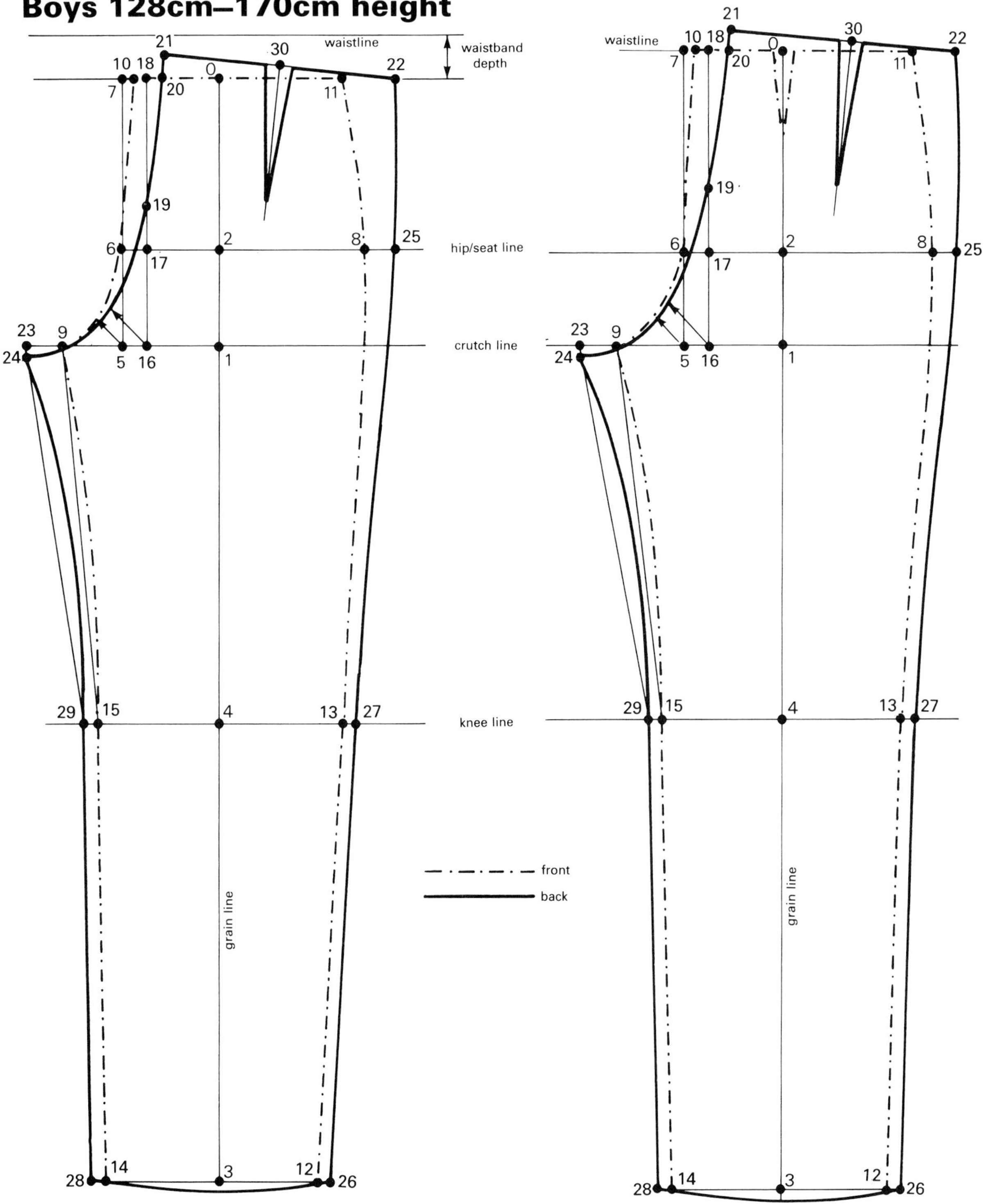

The Children's Easy-fitting Trouser Block

For boys and girls, sizes 92cm–170cm height

The block is suitable for easy-fitting trousers with an elasticated waist for infants and for 'baggy' dungaree-type trousers for older children.

MEASUREMENTS REQUIRED TO DRAFT THE BLOCK
(e.g. size 110cm height)
Refer to size charts (pages 18, 19 and 129) for standard measurements.

Hip	62cm
Waist	56cm
Body rise	18.9cm
Inside leg	48cm
Waist to hip	13.2cm
Trouser bottom width	17cm

Front

Square down and across from 0.

0 – 1 Body rise plus 1cm; square across.

1 – 2 Inside leg; square across.

1 – 3 ½ measurement 1–2:
sizes 92cm–122cm height minus 3cm
128cm–152cm height minus 3.5cm
158cm–170cm height minus 4cm;
square across.

1 – 4 1/12 hip plus 2cm; square up to 5.

4 – 6 ¼ hip:
sizes 92cm–122cm height plus 2.5cm
128cm–152cm height plus 2cm
158cm–170cm height plus 1cm;
square up.

5 – 7 Waist to hip; square across to 8.

4 – 9 ½ measurement 1–4 plus 0.5cm.

5 –10 1cm.

Join 10–7 and 7–9 with a curve touching a point:
sizes 92cm–122cm height 2.25cm from 4
128cm–152cm height 2.5cm from 4
158cm–170cm height 2.75cm from 4.

10–11 ¼ waist:
sizes 92cm–122cm height plus 2cm
128cm–152cm height plus 3cm
158cm–170cm height plus 4cm

2 –12 ½ trouser bottom width minus 0.5cm; join 6–12.

Mark 13 on knee line; join 8–11 with a slight curve.

2 –14 ½ trouser bottom width minus 0.5cm.

3 –15 The measurement 3–13; join 14–15.

Complete inside leg seam 9, 15, 14; curve the line 9–15 inwards 0.5cm

Back

4 –16 ¼ measurement 1–4; square up to 17.

16–18 ½ measurement 16–17.

17–19 1.5cm.

19–20 1.5cm.

20–21 ¼ waist:
sizes 92cm–122cm height plus 2.5cm
128cm–152cm height plus 3.5cm
158cm–170cm height plus 4.5cm.

Join 20–21 to touch a horizontal line from 0.

16–22 ¼ hip:
sizes 92cm–122cm height plus 2cm
128cm–152cm height plus 2.25cm
158cm–170cm height plus 2.5cm.

9 –23 ½ measurement 4–9.

23–24 0.25cm.

Join 20–18; join 18–24 with a curve touching a point:
sizes 92cm–122cm height 3.5cm from 16
128cm–152cm height 3.75cm from 16
158cm–170cm height 4cm from 16.

12–25 1cm; draw in side seam 21, 22, 25. Mark point 26 on knee line.

14–27 1cm.

15–28 The measurement 13–26.

Draw inside leg seam 24, 28, 27; curve the line 28–24 inwards 0.75cm.

Note More ease can be inserted in the back crutch line by opening a wedge at the seat line. See the adaptation for basic trousers (ref. 1, page 102).

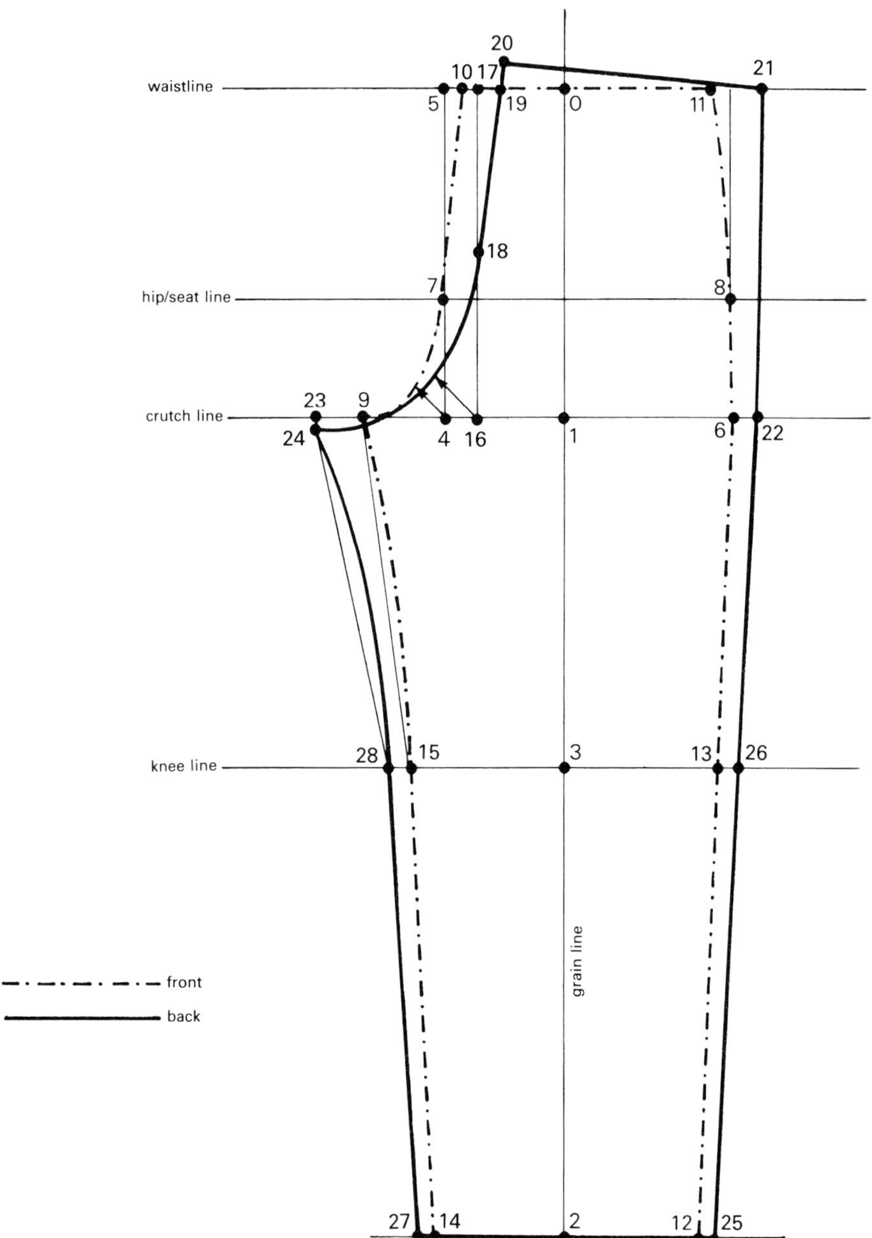

20
21
10
17
waistline
5
19
0
11
18
7
8
hip/seat line
23
9
crutch line
24
4
16
1
6
22
28
15
3
13
26
knee line
grain line
front
back
27
14
2
12
25

The Jeans Block – Close-fitting

For girls and boys, sizes 92cm–170cm height

Note There is 1cm ease in the waistline of the jeans. The waistline is eased onto the waistband.

MEASUREMENTS REQUIRED TO DRAFT THE BLOCK
(e.g. boys, size 134cm height)
Refer to the size charts (pages 18, 19 and 129) for standard measurements.

Hip/seat	73cm		
Low waist	66cm	Inside leg	61cm
(92cm–122cm height use the waist measurement)		Jeans bottom width	17cm
		Waist to hip	15.6cm
Body rise	22cm	Waistband depth, e.g.	3cm

Front
Square down and across from 0.

0 – 1 Body rise minus 1.5cm and waistband depth; square across.
0 – 2 Waist to hip minus 1.5cm and waistband depth; square across.
1 – 3 Inside leg; square across.
1 – 4 ½ measurement 1–3:
sizes 92cm–122cm height minus 3cm
128cm–152cm height minus 3.5cm
158cm–170cm height minus 4cm;
square across.
1 – 5 1/12 hip/seat plus 1cm; square up to 6 and 7.
5 – 8 ¼ hip/seat plus 0.5cm.
5 – 9 1/16 hip/seat.
7 –10 Sizes 92cm–134cm height 1cm
140cm–170cm height 1.5cm.

Join 10–6 and 6–9 with a curve touching a point:
sizes 92cm–122cm height 2.5cm from 5
128cm–152cm height 2.75cm from 5
158cm–170cm height 3cm from 5.

10–11 ¼ low waist plus 0.5cm.
3 –12 ½ jeans bottom width minus 0.5cm.
4 –13 The measurement 3–12 plus 1cm.
3 –14 ½ jeans bottom width minus 0.5cm.
4 –15 The measurement 3–14 plus 1cm.

Draw side seam 11, 8, 13,12; curve 8–11 out 0.25cm.
Draw inside leg seam 9, 15, 14. Curve in 9–15 0.5cm.

Back
5 –16 ¼ measurement 1–5; square up to 17 on hip/seat line, 18 on waistline.
16–19 ½ measurement 16–18. 18–20 1.5cm. 20–21 1.5cm.
21–22 ¼ low waist:
sizes 92cm–122cm height plus 0.75cm
128cm–152cm height plus 1cm
158cm–170cm height plus 1.25cm;
join 21–22 to touch the line squared out from 0.
9 –23 ½ measurement 5–9 less 0.5cm. 23–24 0.25cm.

Join 21–19 and 19–24 with a curve touching a point:
sizes 92cm–122cm height 3.25cm from 16
128cm–152cm height 3.5cm from 16
158cm–170cm height 3.75cm from 16.

17–25 ¼ hip/seat plus 0.5cm.
12–26 1cm. 13–27 1cm. 14–28 1cm. 15–29 1cm.

Draw side seam 22, 25, 27,26; curve 22–25 out 0.25cm, 25–27 in 0.25cm.
Draw inside leg seam 24, 29, 28; curve 24–29 in 1cm.

21–30 ½ measurement 21–22; square down from the line 21–22. Construct a dart on this line:
sizes 92cm–122cm height length 4cm, width 0.75cm
128cm–152cm height length 5cm, width 1cm
158cm–170cm height length 6cm, width 1.25cm.

To complete front sections
Trace off front section; mark point 6.
Draw in curved pocket line A–B and pocket bag.
Cut off side piece along line A–B; add 3.5cm from A–B.
Draw in fly piece shape to point C 5cm below 6.
Fly piece width 3.5cm–4cm.
Trace off fly piece and pocket bag.

To complete back sections
Trace off back section; mark points 16, 17, 21, 22, 24, 25.
Cut along hip/seat line, open a wedge at 17:
sizes 92cm–122cm height 2cm
128cm–152cm height 2.5cm
158cm–170cm height 3cm.

17–D 0.5cm; draw in new crutch line from 21–24.
Draw in pocket design.
21–E ⅓ measurement 21–16. 22–F ⅓ measurement 22–25.
Cut off yoke section along line E–F; close dart.
Join 21–22 and E–F with straight lines.
Patch pocket Trace back pocket.
Waistband G–H twice waistband depth; H–J low waist measurement; J–K fly width.
Mark centre back ½ measurement H–J; mark fold line.

JEANS SHORTS
For jeans shorts cut across draft at length required.

Jeans block

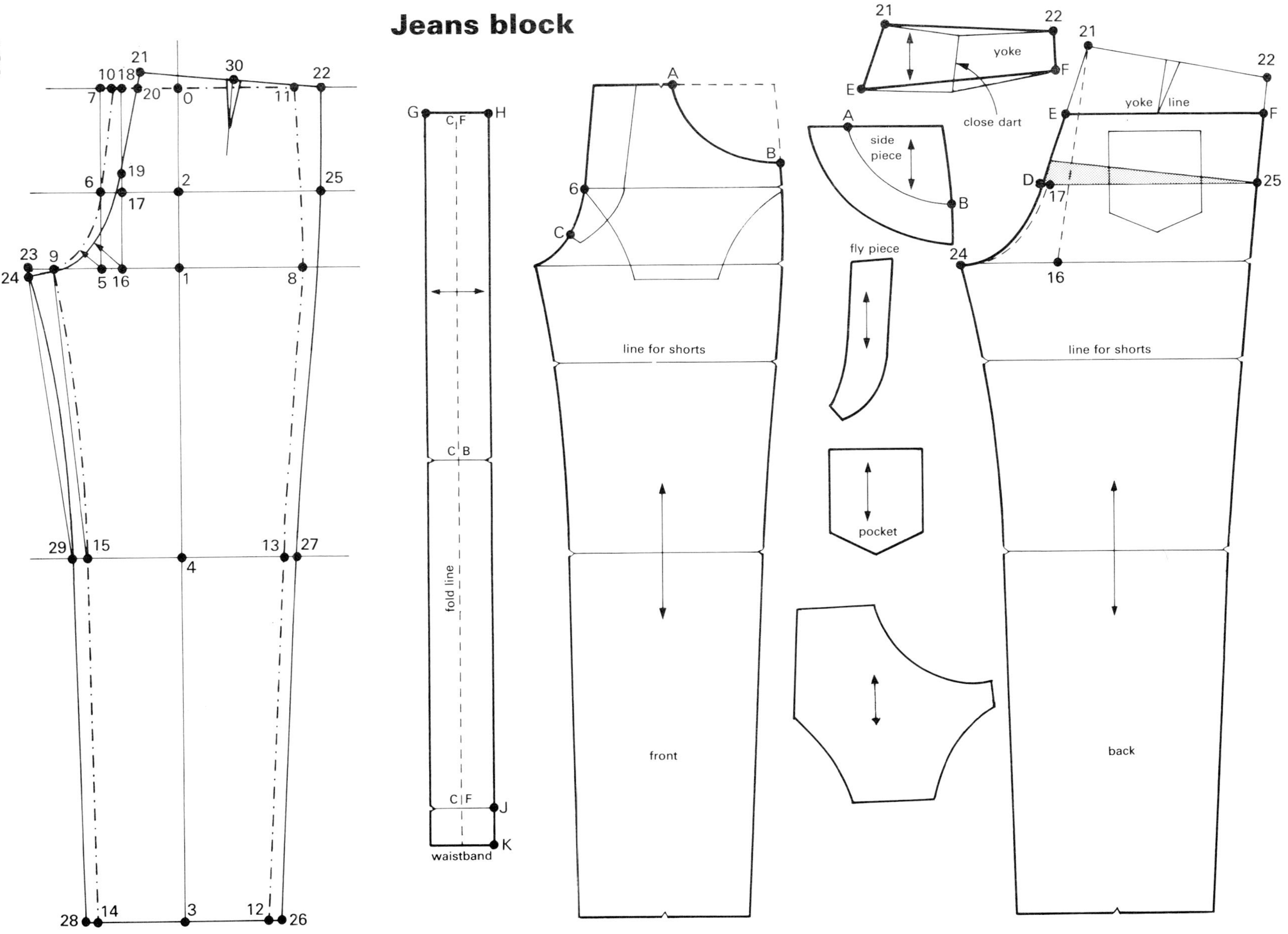

C F
C B
fold line
C F
waistband
line for shorts
front
side piece
fly piece
pocket
yoke
close dart
yoke line
line for shorts
back

1 BOYS' BASIC TROUSERS (adjustable waistband)

Boys' basic trousers are worn mainly for school wear. The waistband has 5cm ease and it is adjustable to allow for growth.

Adaptation 1 Simple elasticated double cloth waistband.

Adaptation 2 Single cloth waistband, tailored finish with elasticated straps.

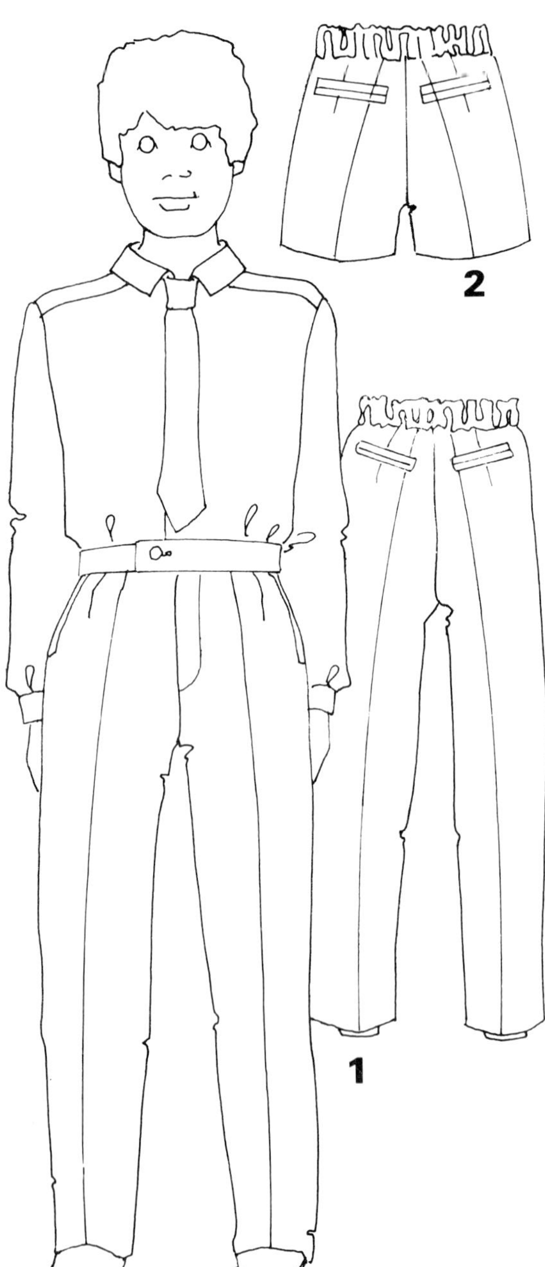

Front Trace off front section of trousers.
Mark points 0, 4, 9, 10, 11.
Cut along knee line and along grain line from 0–4.
Open at waistline: 92cm–122cm height 2cm
128cm–152cm height 3cm
158cm–170cm height 4cm.
11–A 2cm. Draw in new side seam line from A.
Erase old line from 11
Trace round pattern.
A–B ⅙ measurement 10–A minus 0.5cm.
A–C ⅕ waist measurement plus 1cm.
Join B–C for pocket line. C–D 2cm.
B–E and D–F: 92cm–122cm height 3cm
128cm–152cm height 3.5cm
158cm–170cm height 4cm.
Join E–F and F–D for pocket facing.
10–G ⅔ measurement 9–10.
10–H 92cm–122cm height 3cm
128cm–152cm height 3.5cm
158cm–170cm height 4cm.
Draw in fly piece as shown. Draw in pocket bag.
B–J ½ measurement B–0. Mark tuck at 0 1cm less than amount trousers have been opened. Mark 2cm tuck at J. Trace off frontside piece.

Back Trace off back section of trousers.
Mark in points 17, 21, 22, 24, 25, 30.
Cut along seat line and open a wedge at 17.
17–K 92cm–122cm height 1.5cm
128cm–152cm height 2cm
158cm–170cm height 2.5cm.
17–L 0.5cm; draw in new crutch line from 21–24.
22–M 1.5cm; draw new side seam from M to crutch line.
30–N ¼ measurement 21–M minus 1cm. Draw in pocket mouth and pocket bag as shown.

Fly piece, pocket facing and pocket bags Trace off these pattern pieces from front and back sections.

Waistband, double cloth
P–Q ½ waist measurement plus 2.5cm; square down.
Q–R Width of fly piece; square down.
P–S Twice waistband depth; square across. Mark fold line down centre.
P–T ⅔ measurement P–Q; square down. P–T is the length of waistband to be elasticated.

Waistband, single cloth
P–Q ½ waist measurement plus 2.5cm; square down.
Q–R Width of fly piece; square down.
P–S Waistband depth; square across.
P–T ⅓ measurement P–Q plus 3cm; square down to U.
Cut up line T–U. Add 2.5cm facing pieces to each section. Construct small strap.
Cut cloth facing for front waistband, length 5cm.

2 SHORT TROUSERS

For short trousers cut across trouser draft at length required. Curve hem line down 1cm at centre back.

1 Boys' basic trousers

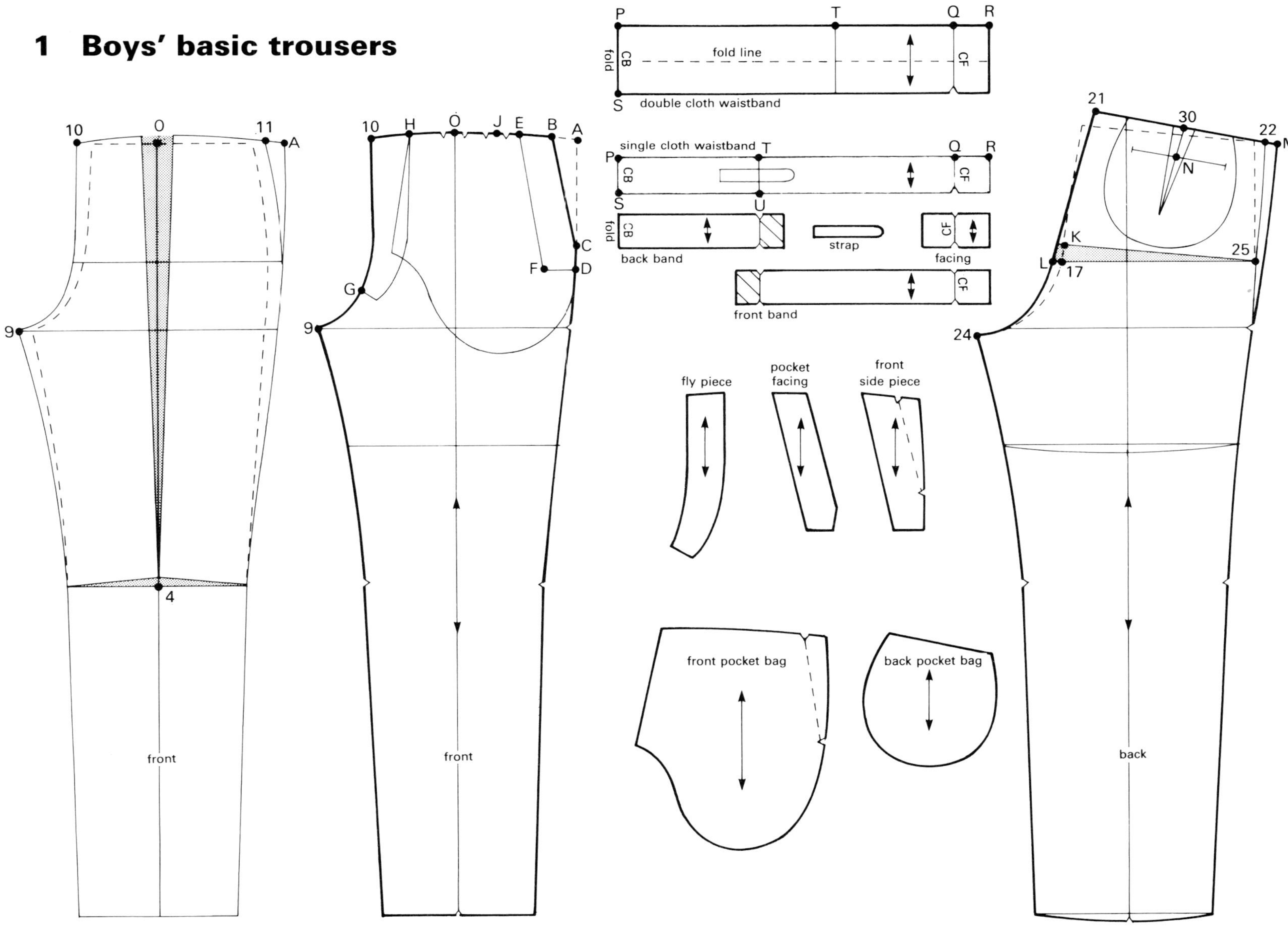

FASHION TROUSERS FOR BOYS AND GIRLS
Simple adaptations can be made to the trouser block. Trouser legs can be widened or narrowed (ref. 2, this page). Extra ease can be added for elasticated waists (ref. 3, this page). Tucks can be added (ref. 1, page 102). The designs illustrated are based on the girls' trouser block, but the adaptations can also be used with the boys' block.

2 TROUSERS – SLIMLINE
Trace off basic trouser block, reverse front section.
Front Mark points 0, 8, 9, 10, 11, 12, 13, 14, 15.
0–A ½ measurement 0–11.
11–B ½ measurement 8–11; join A–B with a curve.
Draw in pocket bag as shown.
10–C ½ measurement 9–10 plus 1cm; square out.
Square out from 10. 10–D 3cm; square down.
12–E 1cm; 14–F 1cm; join 13–E and 15–F.
Trace off side piece, add 3cm from A–B.
Trace off pocket bags as shown.
Back Mark points 17, 24, 25, 26, 27, 28, 29.
Cut across seat line; open a wedge at 17 1cm–1.5cm.
17–G 0.5cm; draw in new crutch line from 21–24.
26–H 1cm; 28–J 1cm; join 27–H and 29–J.
Waistband Square both ways from K.
K–L Waist measurement; L–M 3cm; K–N ½ measurement K–L.
Square down from K, L, M, N.
K–P Twice waistband depth; square across.
Mark fold line through centre.

3 FASHION TROUSERS
Trace off basic trouser block, reverse front section.
Front Mark points 0, 8, 9, 10, 11, erase any darts.
11–A 4cm; join A to crutch line.
0–B ⅕ measurement 0–A.
9–C ¼ measurement 9–10; join B–C.
B–D ¼ measurement B–C.
A–E ½ measurement A–8; join D–E. Draw in pocket bag.
10–F ½ measurement 9–10 plus 1cm.
Square out from 10; 10–G 3cm; square down.
Trace off front, yoke, side piece and pocket bag.
Back Mark points 17, 21, 22, 24, 25, 27.
Cut across seat line; open a wedge at 17 1.5cm–2cm.
17–H 0.5cm; draw in new crutch line from 21–24.
22–J 3cm; join J–27. Mark K on hipline.
J–L ½ measurement J–21; join K–L.
Trace off back and back side piece.
Waistband M–N The measurement 21–J on back.
N–P The measurement A–10 on front, P–Q 3cm.
Square down from M, N, P, Q.
M–R Twice waistband depth; square across. Mark fold line down centre.
Strap Construct strap twice width required and length required. (Measure from back waist to front waist plus 5cm ease.) Mark fold line down centre.

2 Trousers – slimline

3 Fashion trousers

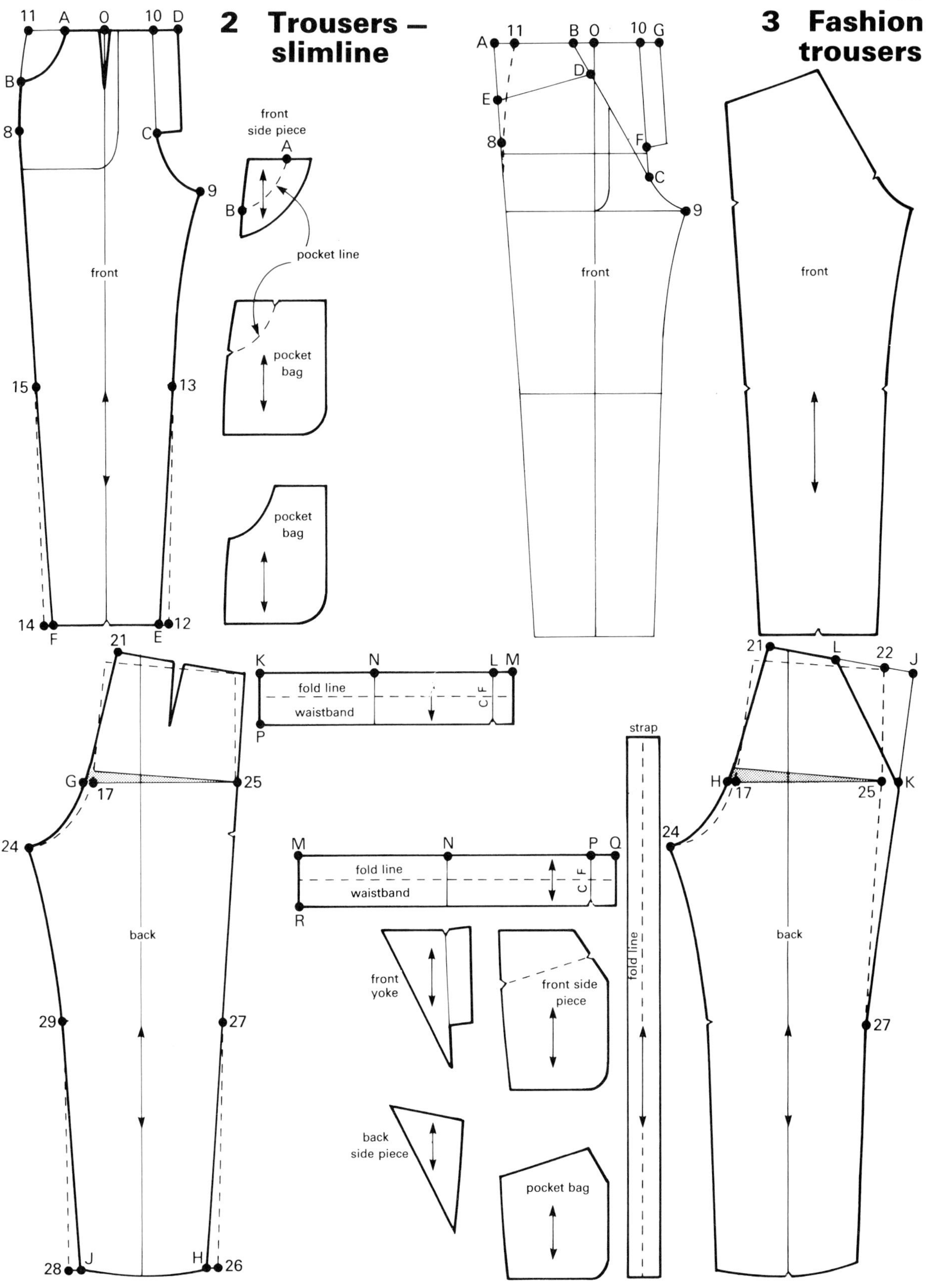

4 CULOTTES

Trace off skirt block to required culotte length.

Back Mark A at centre back waistline.

A–B body rise: 92cm–134cm height plus 1cm
140cm–164cm height plus 1.5cm;
square across.

A–C Finished length; square across.

A–D ½ measurement A–B minus 1cm.

B–E ⅛ hip: 92cm–134cm height plus 1cm
140cm–164cm height plus 1.5cm;
square down to hem line.

B–F 92cm–134cm height 2.5cm
140cm–164cm height 3cm.

Join D E with a curved line touching point F.

Front Mark G at centre front waistline.

G–H Finished length; square across.

G–J body rise: 92cm–134cm height plus 1cm
140cm–164cm height plus 1.5cm;
square across.

G–K ½ measurement G–J.

J–L ⅛ hip: 92cm–134cm height minus 2.25cm
140cm–164cm height minus 2cm;
square down to hem line.

J–M 92cm–134cm height 3.5cm
140cm–164cm height 4cm.

Join K–L with a curved line touching point 11.

Waistband Construct waistband required (page 88).

5 STANDARD DUNGAREES (CLOSE-FITTING)

Trace off basic trouser block, reverse front section. Erase any darts.

Back trousers Mark points 17, 21, 22, 24, 25, 27. Cut across seat line 17–25; open 1.5cm–2cm at 17.

17–A 0.5cm; draw in crutch line. 22–B 2cm; join B–27.

Front trousers Mark points 0, 1, 8, 9, 10, 11.

11–C 3cm; join C–8. 0–D ⅓ measurement 0–C.

C –E ⅔ measurement C–8; join D–E (pocket line).

Draw in pocket bag. Trace off pocket bags and side piece. Add 3cm extension to side piece from D–E.

Front bib Trace off bodice block. Mark points G and F on front waistline. G–H ¼ measurement G–F. Draw in bib front and pocket shape required. Trace bib and pocket. On front trousers, 10–J the measurement H–F on bodice.

Waistband K–L the measurement 21–B on back trousers; square up. L–M the measurement C–J on front trousers. K–N twice waistband depth; square across. Mark fold line. From M draw shape of bib for 3cm up from H to P, reverse shape to top of waistband.

Strap Measure strap length on back and front. Add 5cm ease. Draw strap; length required, twice width required, mark fold line. Add shaping at centre back.

Note 1 For easy-fitting dungarees use easy-fitting trouser block. Note that the point numbers on the blocks differ slightly.

Note 2 A fly front can be added for boys (ref. 1, page 102).

4 Culottes

5 Standard dungarees

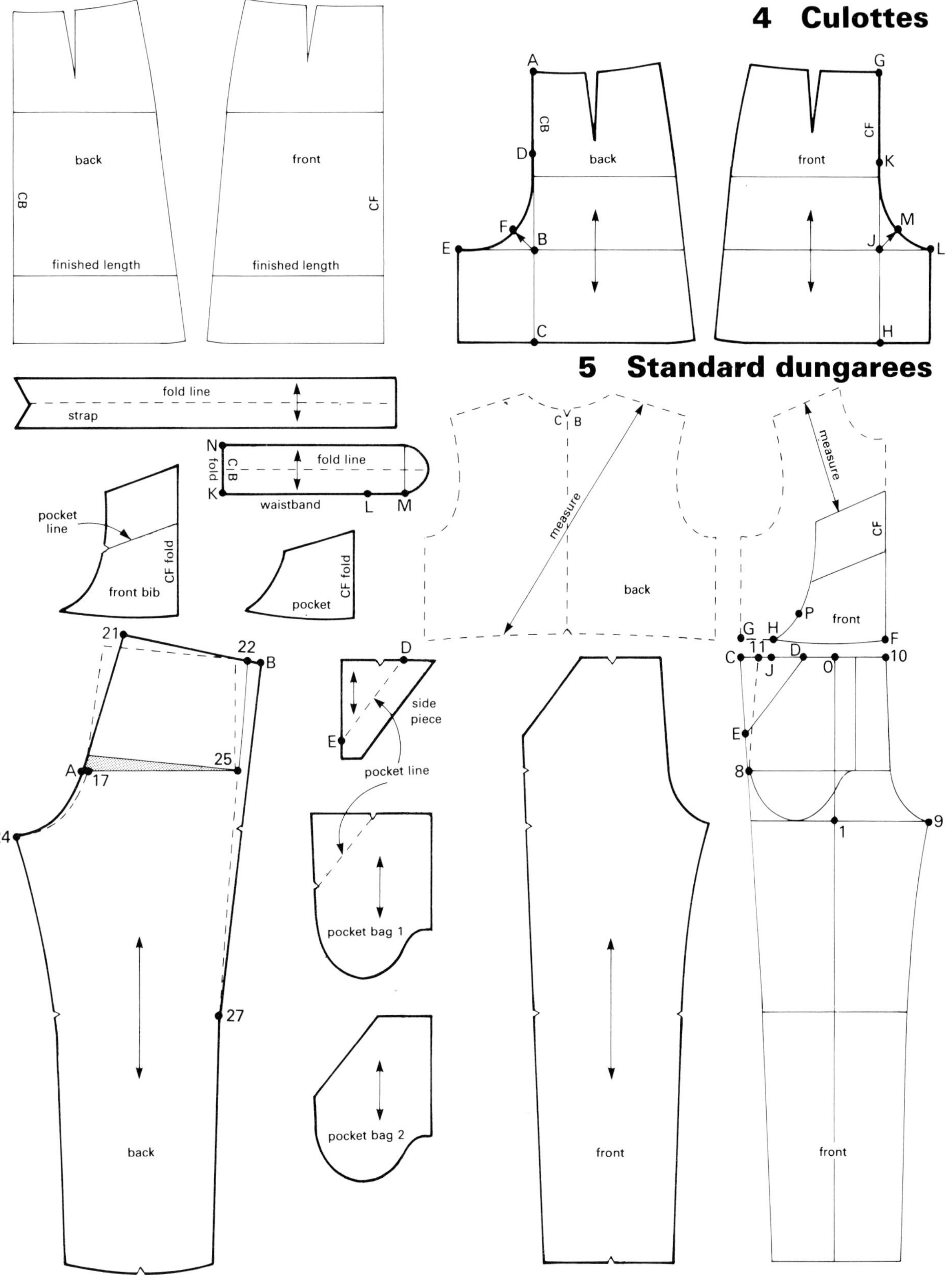

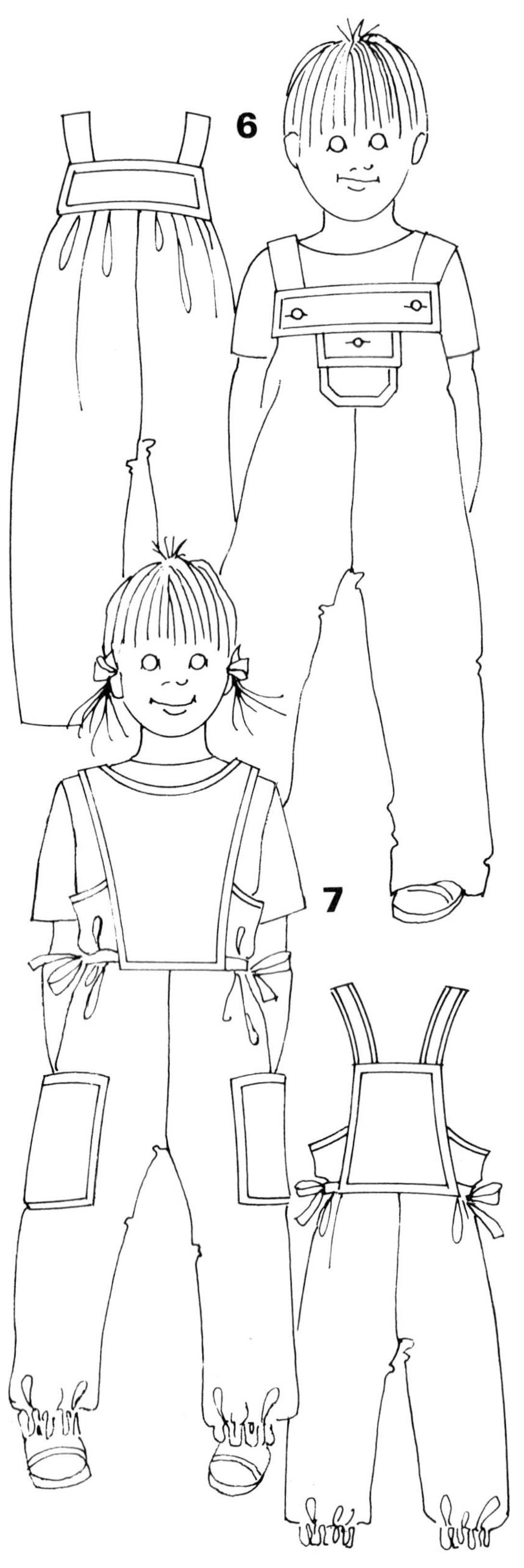

6 DUNGAREES – EASY-FITTING

Trace off easy-fitting trouser block; reverse front section. Trace off front and back bodice.

Front Mark point A at front of trousers; square up. Place front bodice to the line touching trousers at A. Draw a line from underarm point to hipline. Mark point B at neck, C at underarm. B–D 2.5cm, square across to E. E–F ¼ measurement D–E. C–G 2.5cm; draw in bib shape. D–H ¼ measurement A–D; square across Draw in pocket shape on bib, pocket bag on trousers. Add facing for side pocket. Trace off yoke.

Pockets Trace off pocket bag. Trace off pocket, add 3cm facing, trace off pocket flap, double the depth; mark fold line.

Back On back bodice mark point L at neck.

L–M 4cm; square across to N.

N–P ⅕ measurement M–N; complete bib as front.

Trace off bib shape. Cut off yoke.

Mark points Q and R on trouser waistline; R–S the measurement J–K on front. Place bodice to trousers at Q and S. Draw a straight line from T at top of centre back to hip/seat line. Extend grain line to U. Trace round back. Cut along hip/seat line. Open a wedge (approx. 3cm) at V. Redraw crutch line. Draw straight line from U–W on knee line. Cut up line U–W and knee line. Open at U 8cm. Add facing for side pocket.

Strap Measure strap length on front and back, add 5cm ease and a 5cm button extension.

Facings Draw in back and front armhole facings. Trace off facings, join at side seam.

7 DUNGAREES – EASY-FITTING

Trace off easy-fitting trouser block; reverse front section. Trace off front and back bodice.

Front Mark points A and B on trouser waistline; square up from A. Place front bodice to the line touching trousers at A. Draw a line from underarm point to hipline. Mark point C on waistline. Mark D and E at neck. D–F 1cm, E–G 1.5cm.

G–H Strap width required. Draw panel line H–B.

B–J ¼ measurement B–H: C–K the measurement B–J minus 1.5cm.

Draw in pocket shape. Trace off trousers, bib and pocket; add 3cm facing to pocket, 5cm to trouser hem.

Back On back bodice mark points L, M and N.

L–P ½ measurement L–M: draw in bib as shown.

N–Q 1.5cm; draw back strap width G–H. Mark buttonhole.
Measurement C–K, P–S measurement B–J.

M–R Join S–R.

Mark T and U on hip/seat line, V on waistline. Open a wedge at T 2.5cm. T–W 0.5cm, draw new crutch line.

V–X The measurement L–P.

Place side section to point X on trousers. Join R to knee line. Trace round pattern. Add 5cm to trouser hem.

Bibs Trace off back bib. Trace off strap. Add 3cm ease to G and H on front bib; add back strap to bib.

Facing Trace off side sections; join at side seam.

Side ties Construct ties required length and width.

6 Dungarees – easy-fitting

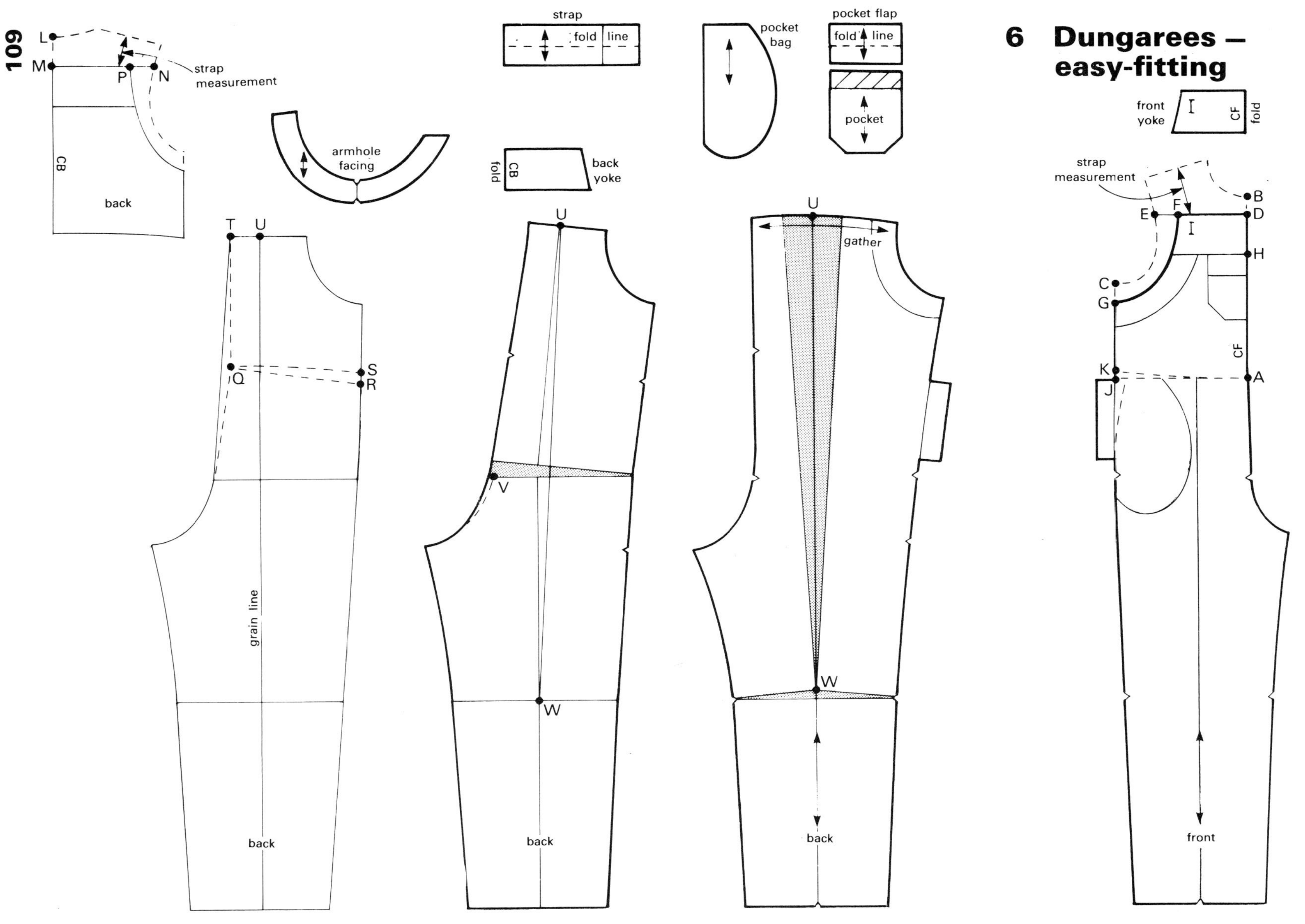

7 Dungarees – easy-fitting

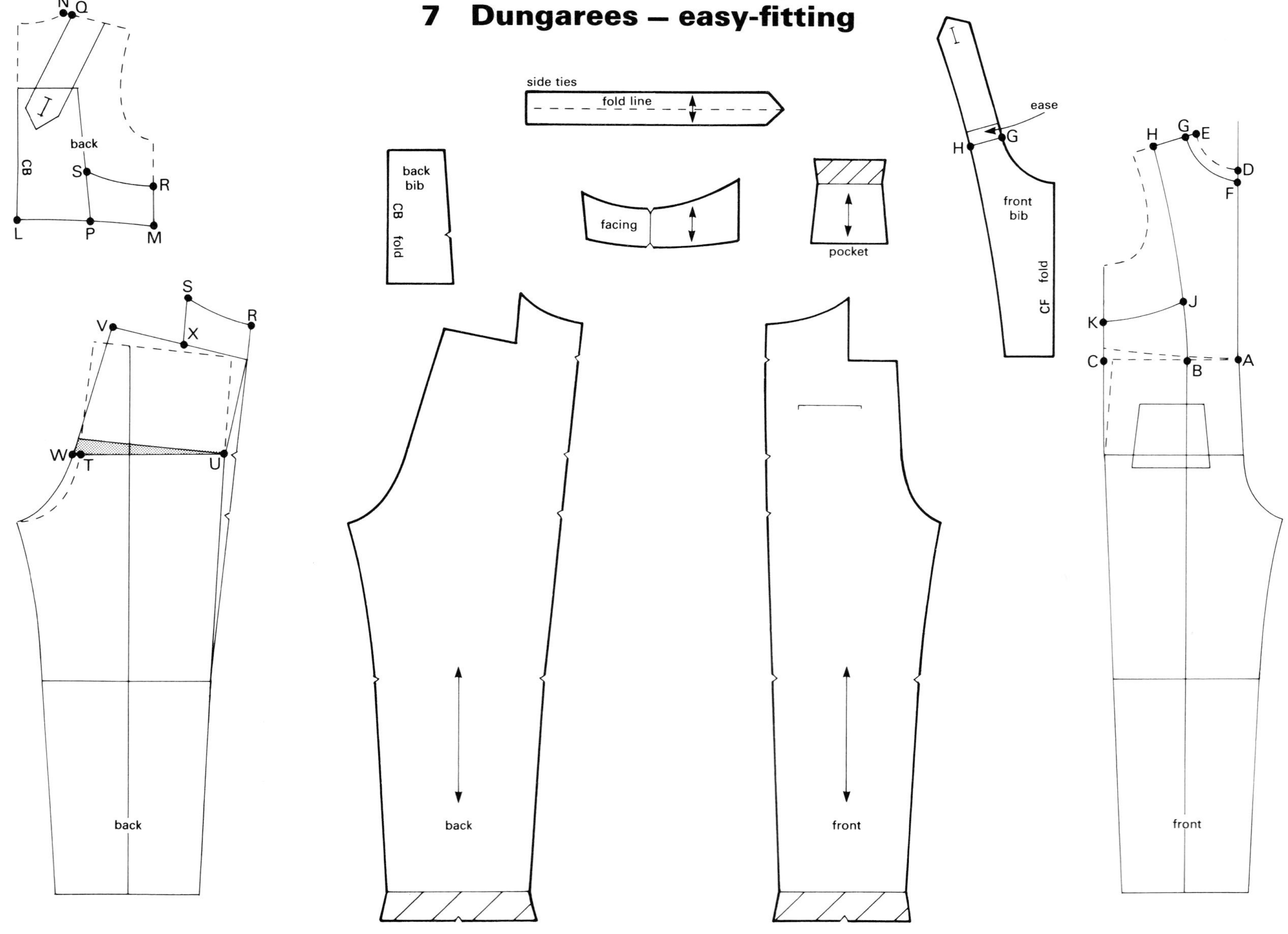

7 SHIRTS, JERSEY WEAR AND SPORTSWEAR

Shirts and sportswear are easy-fitting or stretch garments therefore these blocks can also be used for girls with developing figures.

The Shirt Block for Children and Girls

For children, sizes 92cm–122cm height
For girls, sizes 128cm–164cm height

MEASUREMENTS REQUIRED TO DRAFT THE BLOCK
(e.g. size 110cm height)
Refer to size charts (pages 18, 19 and 129) for standard measurements.

Chest	59cm	Neck size	28.2cm
Scye depth	14.4cm	Sleeve length	39.5cm
Neck to waist	25.6cm	Cuff size	16cm
Across back	24.4cm		

Body sections

Square up and down from 0; square across approx. 10cm.

0 – 1 Scye depth plus 2cm; square across.
0 – 2 Neck to waist; square across.
0 – 3 Shirt length required; square across.
1 – 4 ½ chest:
sizes 92cm–122cm height plus 8cm
128cm–152cm height plus 8.5cm
158cm–164cm height plus 9.5cm;
square up, square down to 5.
0 – 6 Sizes 92cm–122cm height plus 3cm
128cm–152cm height plus 3.25cm
158cm–164cm height plus 3.5cm;
square across to 7.
6 – 8 ⅕ neck plus 0.2cm; square down to 9.
0 –10 ⅓ measurement 0–9; draw a curve from 8–10.
6 –11 ⅕ scye depth minus 0.5cm; square out.
0 –12 ⅕ measurement 0–1 plus 1cm; square half-way across the block.
1 –13 ½ across back:
sizes 92cm–122cm height plus 2cm
128cm–152cm height plus 2.25cm
158cm–164cm height plus 2.5cm;
square up to 14 and 15.
15–16 0.75cm; join 8–16.
14–17 ½ measurement 12–14 minus 1.5cm.
14–18 0.5cm; join 17–18 with a curve.
7 –19 Sizes 92cm–122cm height plus 3.5cm
128cm–152cm height plus 4cm
158cm–164cm height plus 5cm;
square across.
19–20 ⅕ neck size minus 0.8cm.
19–21 ⅕ neck size:
sizes 92cm–122cm height minus 1.2cm
128cm–152cm height minus 1.4cm
158cm–164cm height minus 1.6cm;
draw in neck curve.
19–22 ⅕ scye depth plus 0.5cm; square out.
20–23 The measurement 8–16. Draw a line from 20 to touch the line from 22.
21–24 ½ measurement 4–21 plus 1cm; square across.
4 –25 The measurement 1–13:
sizes 92cm–122cm height minus 1cm
128cm–152cm height minus 0.8cm
158cm–164cm height minus 0.2cm;
square up to 26.
25–27 ½ measurement 13–25 plus 0.5cm; square down to 28 and 29. Draw armscye curve 16, 18, 27, 26, 23.
29–30 ¼ measurement 28–29.
29–31 ⅓ measurement 5–29. 29–32 ⅓ measurement. 3–29. Join 30–31 and 30–32 with curves.

Curve both side seams in 0.75cm at 28.

21–33 1.5cm button stand; square down.
33–34 3.5cm facing; square down. Shape neckline.
12–35 2cm (back pleat); square down.

Sleeve

Square down from 0.

0 – 1 ¼ armscye measurement (see measuring a curve on page 31); square across.
0 – 2 Sleeve length minus cuff depth plus 2cm ease; square across.
1 – 3 ½ measurement 1–2; square across.
0 – 4 ½ armscye measurement; square down to 5.
0 – 6 ½ armscye measurement; square down to 7.

Divide 0–4 into four sections, mark points 8, 9, 10.
Divide 0–6 into four sections, mark points 11, 12, 13.

8 – 0 Raise the curve:
sizes 92cm–122cm height 0.5cm at 9; 0.75cm at 10.
128cm–152cm height 0.75cm at 9; 1.25cm at 10.
158cm–164cm height 1cm at 9; 1.75cm at 10.

Raise the curve at 11:
sizes 92cm–122cm height 0.5cm
128cm–152cm height 0.75cm
158cm–164cm height 1cm.

Hollow the curve at 13:
sizes 92cm–122cm height 0.5cm
128cm–152cm height 0.75cm
158cm–164cm height 1cm.

5 –14 ¼ measurement 2–5 minus 0.5cm; join 4–14.
7 –15 ¼ measurement 2–7 minus 0.5cm; join 6–15.

Mark points 16 and 17 on the line from 3.

14–18 1cm; join 16–18 with a curve.
15–19 1cm; join 17–19 with a curve.
20 midway 2–18; square up to 21.
21–22 ⅓ measurement 20–21.
20–23 0.75cm; join 18–2 with a curve.

Cuff

Cuff length – cuff size plus 2cm.
Cuff depth – approx. size 4.5cm–7cm (ref. 1, page 50).

Collar

Construct a shirt collar (ref. 3, page 54).
Depth of shirt collar and stand approx. 6–8cm.

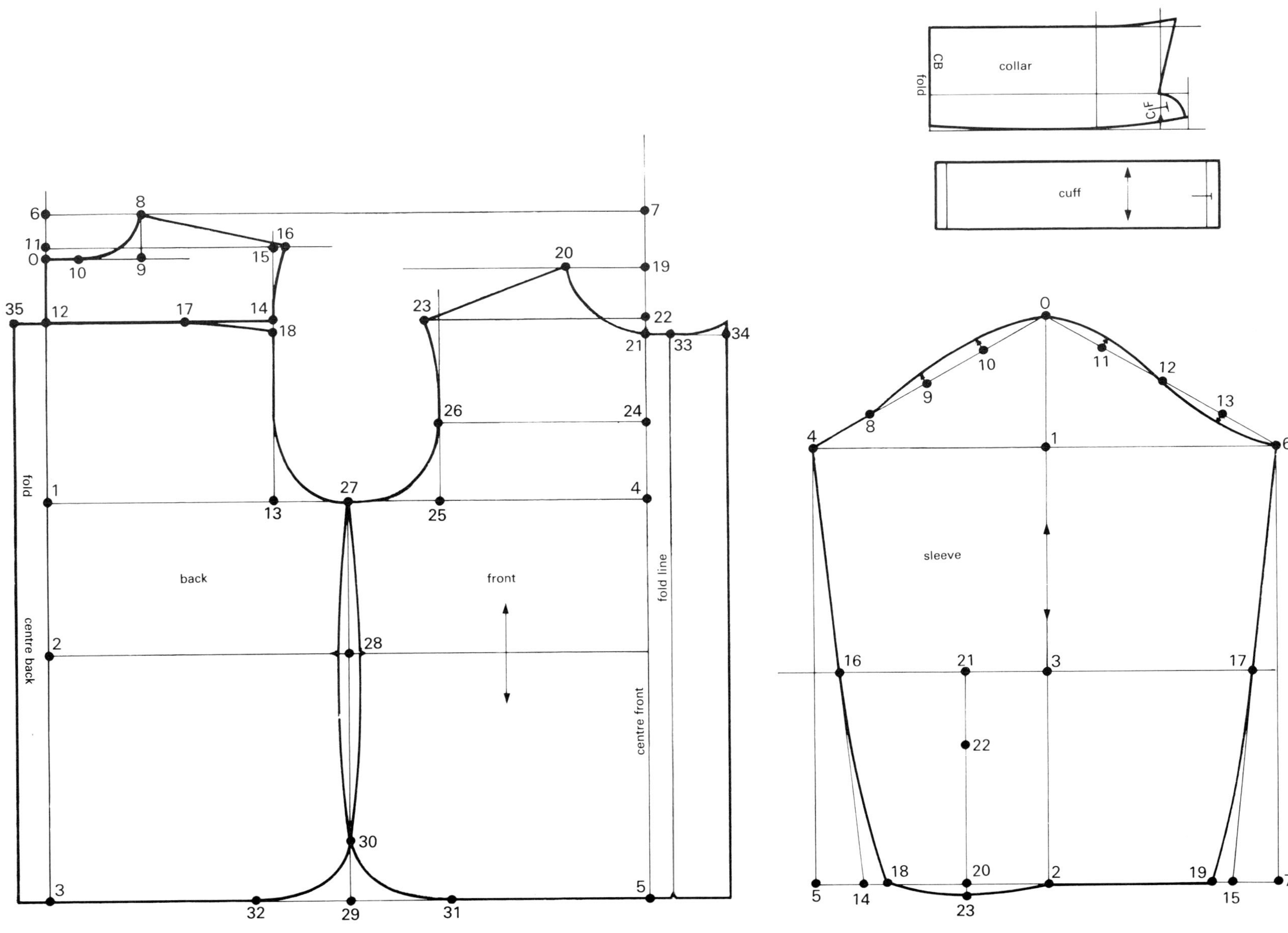
back
front
fold
centre back
centre front
fold line
sleeve
collar
CB
fold
C F
cuff

Shirt Block for Boys

Approximate age 8–14 years
For boys, size 128cm–170cm height

MEASUREMENTS REQUIRED TO DRAFT THE BLOCK
(e.g. size 134cm height)
Refer to size chart (page 19) for standard measurements.

Chest	70cm
Scye depth	17.4cm
Neck to waist	31.2cm
Across back	29.2cm
Neck size	31cm
Sleeve length	49cm
Cuff size	18cm

Body sections
Square down from 0; square across approx. 10cm.

0 – 1 Scye depth plus 2cm; square across.
0 – 2 Neck to waist; square across.
0 – 3 Shirt length required; square across.
1 – 4 ½ chest:
sizes 128cm–152cm height plus 9cm
158cm–170cm height plus 10cm;
square up, square down to 5.
0 – 6 Sizes 128cm–152cm height 3.5cm
158cm–170cm height 3.75cm;
square across to 7.
6 – 8 ⅕ neck plus 0.2cm; square down to 9.
0 –10 ⅓ measurement 0–9; draw a curve from 8–10.
6 –11 ⅕ scye depth minus 0.5cm; square half-way across the block.
0 –12 ⅕ measurement 0–1 plus 1cm; square half-way across block.
1 –13 ½ across back:
sizes 128cm–152cm height plus 2.25cm
158cm–170cm height plus 2.5cm;
square up to 14 and 15.
15–16 0.75cm; join 8–16.
14–17 ½ measurement 14–12 minus 1.5cm.
14–18 0.5cm; join 17–18 with a curve.
7 –19 Sizes 128cm–152cm height 5cm
158cm–170cm height 5.8cm.
19–20 ⅕ neck size minus 0.8cm.
19–21 ⅕ neck size:
sizes 128cm–152cm height minus 1.5cm
158cm–170cm height minus 1.2cm;
draw neck curve.
19–22 ⅕ scye depth plus 0.5cm; square out.
20–23 The measurement 8–16. Draw the line from 20 to touch the line from 22.
21–24 ½ measurement 4–21 plus 1cm; square across.
4 –25 The measurement 1–13:
sizes 128cm–152cm height minus 1cm
158cm–170cm height minus 1.5cm;
square up to 26.
25–27 ½ measurement 13–25 plus 0.5cm; square down to 28 and 29. Draw armhole curve 16, 18, 27, 26, 23.
29–30 ¼ measurement 28–29.
29–31 ⅓ measurement 5–29.
29–32 ⅓ measurement 3–29;
join 30–31 and 30–32 with a curve.
Curve both side seams inwards 0.75cm at 28.
21–33 1.5cm button stand; square down.
33–34 3.5cm facing; square down. Shape neckline.
12–35 2cm (back pleat); square down.

Sleeve
Square down from 0.

0 – 1 ¼ armscye measurement (see 'measuring a curve' on page 31); square across.
0 – 2 Sleeve length minus cuff depth plus 2cm ease; square across.
1 – 3 ½ measurement 1–2; square across.
0 – 4 ½ armscye measurement; square down to 5.
0 – 6 ½ armscye measurement; square down to 7.
Divide 0–4 into four sections, mark points 8, 9, 10.
Divide 0–6 into four sections, mark points 11, 12, 13.
8 – 0 Raise the curve:
sizes 128cm–152cm height 0.75cm at 9; 1.25cm at 10
158cm–170cm height 1cm at 9; 1.75cm at 10.
Raise the curve at 11:
sizes 128cm–152cm height 0.75cm
158cm–170cm height 1cm.
Hollow the curve at 13:
sizes 128cm–152cm height 0.75cm
158cm–170cm height 1cm.
5 –14 ¼ measurement 2–5 minus 0.5cm; join 4–14.
7 –15 ¼ measurement 2–7 minus 0.5cm; join 6–15.
Mark points 16 and 17 on the line from 3.
14–18 1cm; join 16–18 with a curve.
15–19 1cm; join 17–19 with a curve.
20 is mid-way 2–18; square up to 21.
21–22 ⅓ measurement 20–21.
20–23 0.5cm; join 18–2 with a curve.

Cuff
Cuff length – cuff size plus 2cm.
Cuff depth – approx. size 5.5cm–8cm. (ref. 1, page 50).

Collar
Construct a shirt collar, one-piece or collar with band (ref. 3, page 54).
Depth of classic shirt collar and stand:
sizes 128cm–152cm height 7cm
158cm–170cm height 8cm.

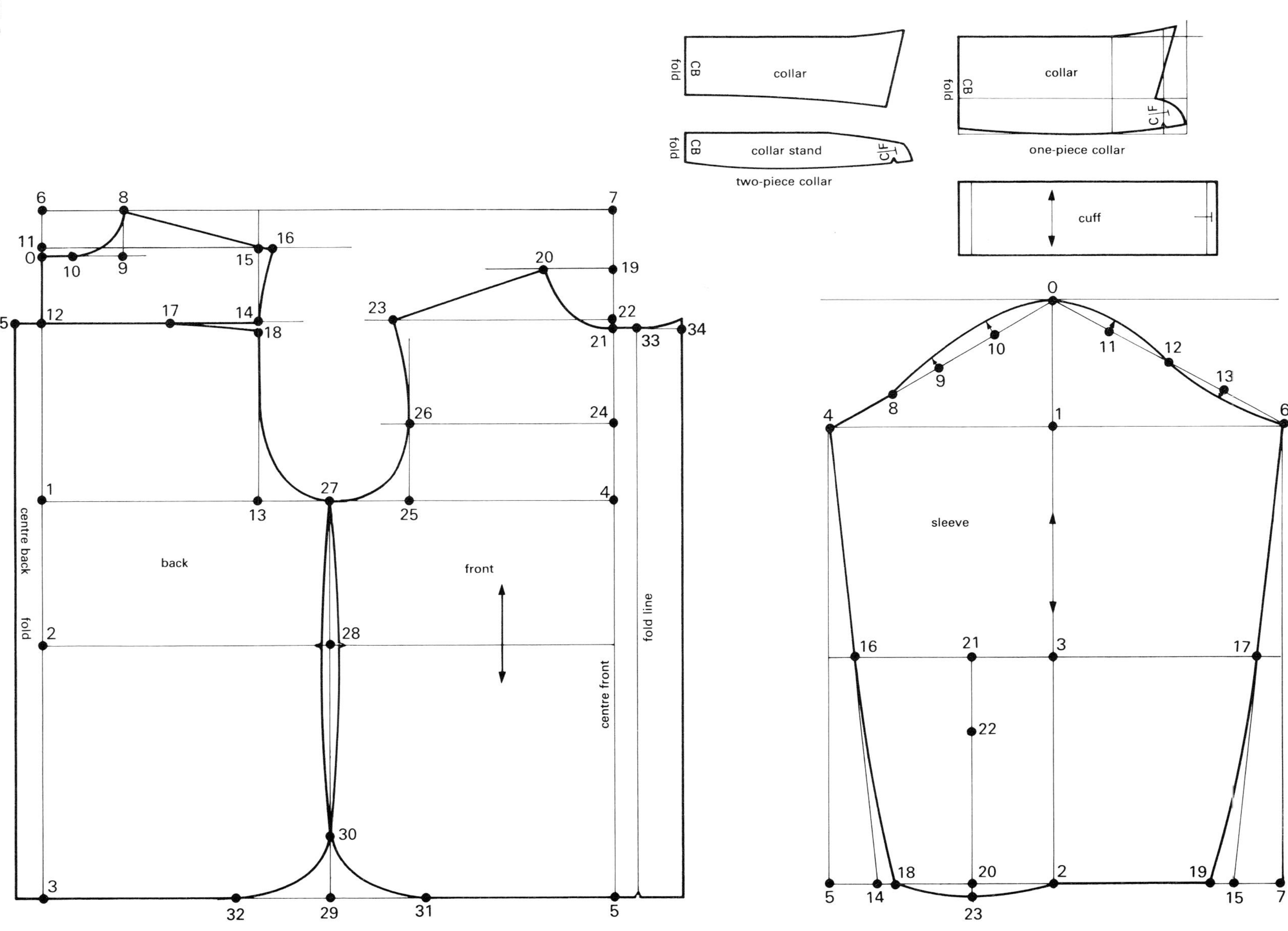
fold
CB
collar
fold
CB
collar stand
C F
two-piece collar
fold
CB
collar
C F
one-piece collar
cuff
centre back
fold
back
front
centre front
fold line
sleeve

Tee-shirt and Jersey Blocks

For boys and girls, sizes 92cm–170cm height

MEASUREMENTS REQUIRED TO DRAFT THE BLOCKS
(e.g. size 110cm height)
Refer to the size charts (pages 18, 19 and 129) for standard measurements.

Chest	59cm
Across back	24.4cm
Neck to waist	25.6
Scye depth	14.4cm
Neck size	28.2cm
Sleeve length from shoulder	39.5cm
Wrist	13.6cm

These blocks are drafted for jersey fabrics or to be used as base patterns for knitwear. The first instructions given are those necessary for a tee-shirt and the brackets show the extra measurements required to construct a block for knitwear.

Body sections
Square down and across from 0.

0 – 1 Neck to waist; square across.
0 – 2 Finished length; square across.
0 – 3 Scye depth:
sizes 92cm–134cm height plus 0.5cm (1cm)
140cm–170cm height plus 1cm (1.5cm);
square across.
0 – 4 ½ measurement 0–3; square across.
0 – 5 ¼ measurement 0–4; square across.
0 – 6 ⅕ neck size plus 0.25cm; square up.
6 – 7 Sizes 92cm–134cm height 1.25cm
140cm–170cm height 1.5cm;
Draw in neck curve.
3 – 8 ½ across back (plus 0.5cm); square up to 9 and 10.
10–11 0.5cm; join 7–11.
3 –12 ¼ chest:
sizes 92cm–134cm height plus 1cm (2.5cm);
140cm–170cm height plus 1.5cm (2.5cm);
square down to 13.
Draw in armscye curve from 11 through 9 to 12.
0 –14 ⅕ neck size minus 1cm; draw in front neck.
Back and front sections are the same shape except for the neck curve.

Sleeve
Square down from 15.

15–16 ½ measurement 0–3 plus 1cm; square across.
15–17 Sleeve length from shoulder; square across.
15–18 The measurement of diagonal line from 11–12 on body section plus 2cm; square down to 19.
18–20 ⅓ measurement 18–15.
Draw in sleeve head.
18–20 Hollow the curve:
sizes 92cm–134cm height 0.4cm
140cm–170cm height 0.6cm.
20–15 Raise the curve:
sizes 92cm–134cm height 1.25cm
140cm–170cm height 1.75cm.
17–21 ½ wrist:
sizes 92cm–134cm height plus 1.5cm
140cm–170cm height plus 2cm.

Short sleeve
15–22 Sleeve length required; square across to 23.
23–24 Sizes 92cm–134cm height 2.25cm
140cm–170cm height 2.5cm.

RAGLAN ADAPTATION
Trace off the block required. Mark points 9, 12, 15, 18, 20.
Delete the curve from 9–12.

Body sections
A–12 and B–12 are the measurements 18–20 on sleeve.
Curve the lines inwards: 92cm–134cm height 1cm
140cm–170cm height 1.5cm.
Mark points C and D at neck.
C–E and D–F: 92cm–122cm height 2cm
128cm–152cm height 2.5cm
158cm–170cm height 3cm.
Join A–E and B–F.

Sleeve
Trace off completed sleeve; extend centre line of sleeve. Draw parallel lines each side of the centre line; the measurement of each line from centre line:
sizes 92cm–122cm height 2cm
128cm–152cm height 2.5cm
158cm–170cm height 3cm.
20–G The measurement A–E on back.
20–H The measurement B–F on front.
Join G–H with a curve.

Tee shirt and jersey blocks

Raglan adaptation

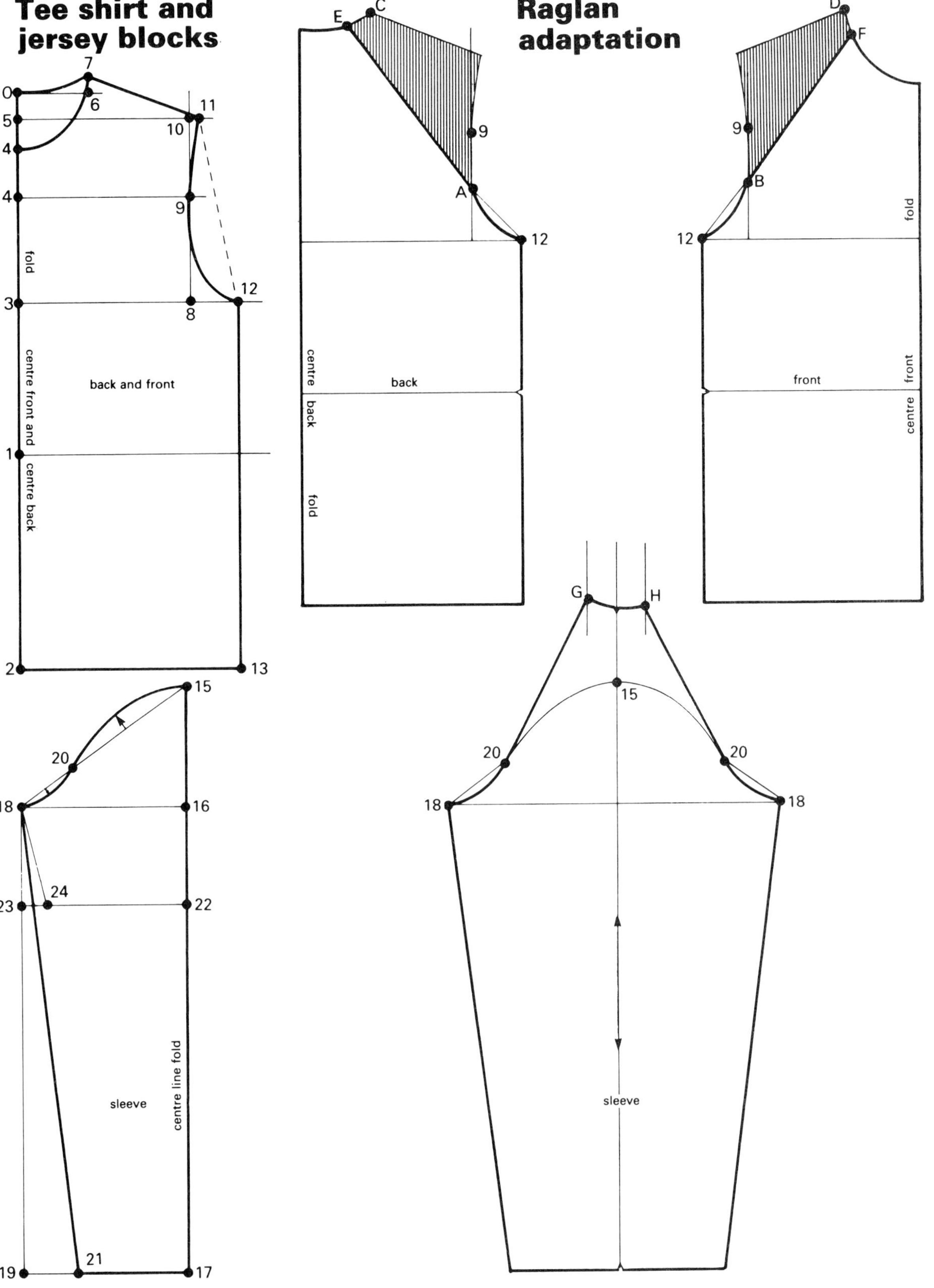

Track Suit Block

For boys and girls, sizes 92cm–170cm height

MEASUREMENTS REQUIRED TO DRAFT THE BLOCKS
(e.g. size 110cm height)
Refer to the size charts (pages 18, 19 and 129) for standard measurements.

Chest	59cm
Across back	24.4cm
Neck to waist	25.6cm
Scye depth	14.4cm
Neck size	28.2cm
Sleeve length from shoulder	39.5cm
Wrist	13.6cm

Stretch fabric should be used for track suits. The block is drafted for this type of fabric.

Body sections

Square down and across from 0.

0 – 1 Neck to waist; square across.
0 – 2 Finished length; square across.
0 – 3 Scye depth:
sizes 92cm–122cm height plus 2.5cm
128cm–152cm height plus 3cm
158cm–170cm height plus 3.5cm.
0 – 4 ½ measurement 0–3; square across.
0 – 5 ¼ measurement 0–4; square across.
0 – 6 ⅕ neck size plus 0.25cm; square up.
6 – 7 Sizes 92cm–134cm height 1.25cm
140cm–170cm height 1.5cm.
3 – 8 ½ across back plus 1.25cm; square up to 9 and 10.
10–11 0.75cm; join 7–11.
3 –12 ¼ chest:
sizes 92cm–134cm height plus 4cm
140cm–170cm height plus 4.5cm;
square down to 13.
Draw in armscye curve from 11 through 9 to 12.
0 –14 ⅕ neck size minus 1cm; draw in front neck.
Back and front are the same except for neck curves.

Sleeve

Square down from 15.
15–16 ½ measurement 0–3 plus 1cm; square across.
15–17 Sleeve length from shoulder; square across.
15–18 The measurement of diagonal line from 11–12 on body section plus 2cm; square down to 19.
18–20 ⅓ measurement 18–15.
Draw in sleeve head.
18–20 Hollow the curve:
sizes 92cm–134cm height 0.4cm
140cm–170cm height 0.6cm.
20–15 Raise the curve:
sizes 92cm–134cm height 1.25cm
140cm–170cm height 1.75cm.
17–21 ½ wrist:
sizes 92cm–134cm height plus 2cm
140cm–170cm height plus 3cm.

Note The raglan adaptation for tee-shirts and knitwear (page 116) can be used with the track suit block.

Trousers

Trace off back and front sections of basic trouser block. Mark points 0, 1, 3, 8, 9, 13, 15, 24, 27, 29.
Adjust body rise on back and front; 0–1 is body rise measurement plus 2cm (the trousers sit on the normal waistline with easy-fitting crutch).
Mark A, B and C, D on waistline. Erase waist darts.

Back

Mark points E and F on seat line.
24–G 1cm.
B–H 92cm–134cm height 2cm
140cm–170cm height 2.5cm.
F–J 92cm–134cm height 1.5cm
140cm–170cm height 2cm.
K and L: 92cm–134cm height 1cm in on hem line
140cm–170cm height 1.5cm in on hem line.
Draw inside leg seam G, 29, K.
Draw side seam H, J, 27, L.
Cut along seat line and open a wedge at E.
E–M 92cm–134cm height 2.5cm
140cm–170cm height 3cm.
E–N 0.5cm. Draw new crutch line A, N, G.
Add 4cm to hem and waistline for casings.

Front

C–P 1cm. 9–Q 1cm; draw new crutch line.
R and S: 92cm–134cm height 1cm in on hem line
140cm–170cm height 1.5cm in on hem line
Draw in inside leg seam Q, 15, R.
D–T 92cm–134cm height 3cm
140cm–170cm height 2.5cm.
8–U 92cm–134cm height 1cm
140cm–170cm height 1.5cm.
Draw side seam T, U, 13, S.
Add 4cm to hem and waistline for casings.

Note The trouser leg can be cut in one piece. Draw a vertical line. Place side seams of front and back trousers together at waist and hem.
Trace new pattern.

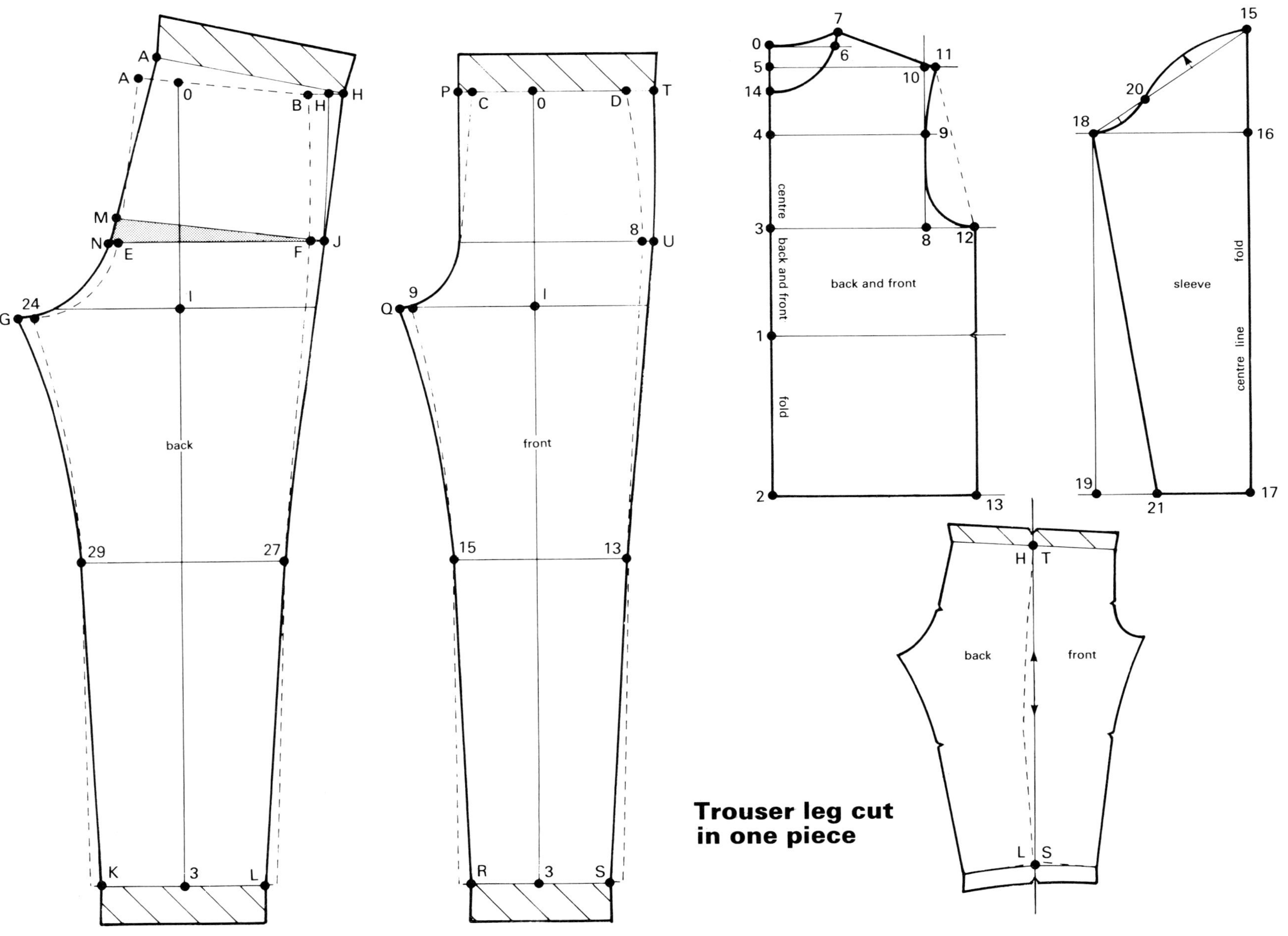

Trouser leg cut in one piece

PLAY OR GYM SHORTS
Trace back and front sections of basic trouser block:

92cm–122cm height	to 5cm below crutch line
128cm–152cm height	to 6cm below crutch line
158cm–170cm height	to 7cm below crutch line.

Mark points 0, 1, 9, 24.
Adjust body rise 0–1 on back and front; 0–1 body rise minus 1.5cm (the shorts sit below natural waistline).

Front Mark point A and B on waistline, C and D on hem line.

A–E	1cm; 9–F 1cm. Draw new crutch line E–F.	
C–G	2cm; join F–G with a curve.	

Mark H on side seam at seat line.

B–J	92cm–122cm height	2cm
	128cm–152cm height	4cm
	158cm–170cm height	5cm.
H–K	92cm–122cm height	1cm
	128cm–152cm height	2cm
	158cm–170cm height	2.5cm.
D–L	92cm–122cm height	0.25cm
	128cm–152cm height	0.5cm
	158cm–170cm height	0.75cm.

Draw new side seam J, K, L.
Draw hem line G–L with a curve. Draw in pocket shape. Add 4cm to waistline for casing.

Back Mark points M and N on waistline, P and Q on seat line, R and S on hem line.
Erase dart.

24–T	1cm; R–U 2cm; join T–U with a curved line.	
N–V	92cm–122cm height	1.5cm
	128cm–152cm height	2.5cm
	158cm–170cm height	3cm.
Q–W	92cm–122cm height	1cm
	128cm–152cm height	2cm
	158cm–170cm height	2.5cm.
S–X	92cm–122cm height	0.25cm
	128cm–152cm height	0.5cm
	158cm–170cm height	0.75cm.

Draw new side seam V, W, X. Draw hem line U–X with a curve.
Cut along seat line P–W and open a wedge at P.

P–Y	92cm–122cm height	2cm
	128cm–152cm height	2.5cm
	158cm–170cm height	3.5cm.
P–Z	0.5cm. Draw in new crutch line.	

Add 4cm to waistline for casing.

Pocket Trace off pocket shape, add 2.5cm to top edge for facing.

Play or gym shorts

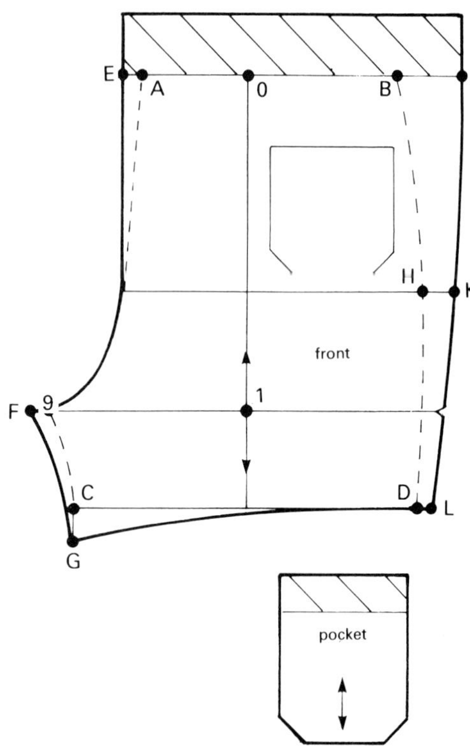

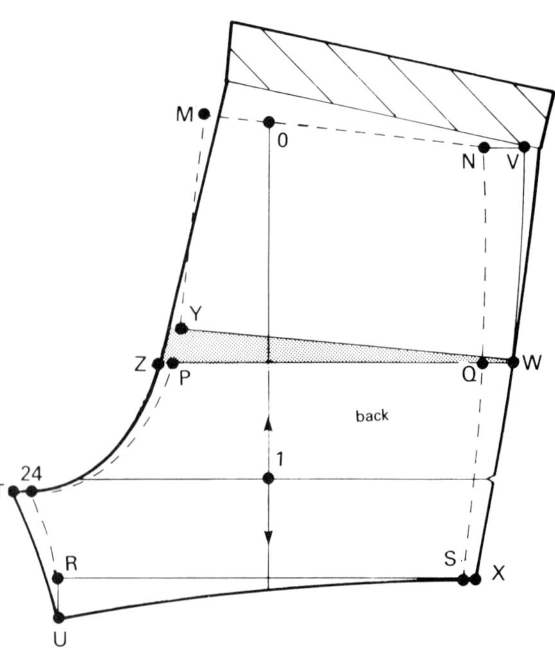

8 NIGHTWEAR

Classic Pyjama Block

For boys, sizes 128cm–170cm height

Pyjamas in stretch fabrics for younger children can be constructed using the track suit block (page 118).

MEASUREMENTS REQUIRED TO DRAFT THE BLOCK
(e.g. boys size 134cm height)
Refer to the size chart (page 19) for standard measurements.

Chest	70cm	Sleeve length	49cm
Scye depth	17.4cm	Hip/seat	73cm
Neck size	31cm	Waist	63cm
Across back	29.2cm	Body rise	22cm
Neck to waist	31.2cm	Inside leg	61cm

PYJAMA JACKET
Body section
Square down from 0.

0 – 1 Scye depth:
sizes 128cm–152cm height plus 2.5cm
158cm–170cm height plus 3cm;
square across.

0 – 2 Neck to waist; square across.

0 – 3 Pyjama jacket length; square across.

1 – 4 ½ chest:
sizes 128cm–152cm height plus 8.5cm
158cm–170cm height plus 9.5cm;
square down to 5. 5–6 1cm.

0 – 7 ¼ scye depth minus 2cm; square across.

0 – 8 Sizes 128cm–152cm height 1.75cm
158cm–170cm height 2cm; square across to 9.

8 –10 ⅕ neck size; draw in neck curve.

1 –11 ½ back:
sizes 128cm–152cm height plus 2cm
158cm–170cm height plus 2.5cm;
square up to 12.

12–13 0.75cm; join 10–13.

11–14 ½ measurement 11–12.

9 –15 Sizes 128cm–152cm height 1cm
158cm–170cm height 1.5cm; square across.

15–16 ⅕ neck size minus 0.3cm.

15–17 ⅕ neck size minus 0.5cm; draw in neck curve.

12–18 1.5cm; square across.

16–19 The measurement 10–13 minus 0.25cm.

17–20 ½ measurement 17–4 plus 1cm; square across.

4 –21 The measurement 1–11 minus 1cm; square up to 22.

21–23 ½ measurement 11–21; square down to 24 on waistline 25 at hem line. Join 6–25 with a curve.

Draw in armscye 13, 14, 23, 22, 19.

24–26 1cm; 24–27 1cm; square down; join 23 to 26 and 27 with curves.

17–28 2cm; square down. 28–29 6cm extended facing; square down. Draw in neck curve at top.

Draw in pocket. Trace pocket add 2.5cm facing.

Collar Construct convertible collar (ref. 2, page 54).

Sleeve
Square down from 0.

0 – 1 ¼ armscye measurement (see page 30 measuring a curve); square across.

0 – 2 Sleeve length; square across.

0 – 3 ½ armscye measurement plus 1cm; square down to 4.

0 – 5 ½ armscye measurement plus 1cm; square down to 6.

Divide 0–3 into four sections, mark points 7, 8, 9.
Divide 0–5 into four sections, mark points 10, 11, 12.
Raise the curve 7–0:
sizes 128cm–152cm height 0.75cm at 8; 1.25cm at 9
158cm–170cm height 1cm at 8; 1.75cm at 9.
Raise the curve at 10:
sizes 128cm–152cm height 0.75cm
158cm–170cm height 1cm.
Hollow the curve at 12:
sizes 128cm–152cm height 0.75cm
158cm–170cm height 1cm.

4 –13 ⅓ measurement 2–4 minus 1cm; join 3–13.

6 –14 ⅓ measurement 2–6 minus 1cm; join 5–14.

PYJAMA TROUSERS
Front
Square down and across from 0.

0 – 1 Body rise plus 1cm; square across.

1 – 2 Inside leg; square across.

1 – 3 ½ measurement 1–2 minus 4cm; square across.

1 – 4 ¼ seat:
sizes 128cm–152cm height plus 3cm
158cm–170cm height plus 4cm
square up to 5, down to 6 and 7.

4 – 8 ¼ measurement 4–5.

4 – 9 1/12 seat minus 0.5cm; draw in front fork through points 9, 8, 5.

7 –10 Sizes 128cm–152cm height 3cm
158cm–170cm height 3.5cm.

Draw inside leg seam 9, 6, 10; curve in 9–6 1.5cm.

Back

5 –11 2.5cm.

11–12 Sizes 128cm–152cm height 3cm
158cm–170cm height 3.5cm;
join 12–0 with a curve.

4 –13 ½ measurement 4–5.

9 –14 1/12 seat minus 0.5cm.

14–15 0.5cm. Join 12–13; join 13–15 with a curve.

6 –16 Sizes 128cm–152cm height 2.5cm
158cm–170cm height 3.5cm.

10–17 Sizes 128cm–152cm height 1.5cm
158cm–170cm height 2.5cm.

Draw inside leg seam 15, 16, 17; curve in 15–16 1.75cm.

2 –18 2cm.

5 –19 7cm. Add 4cm to top of waistline and front crutch line from 19–8.

Note Front and back of pyjama trousers can be cut in one piece; side seam line 0–18 becomes grain line.

Pyjama jacket

Pyjama trousers

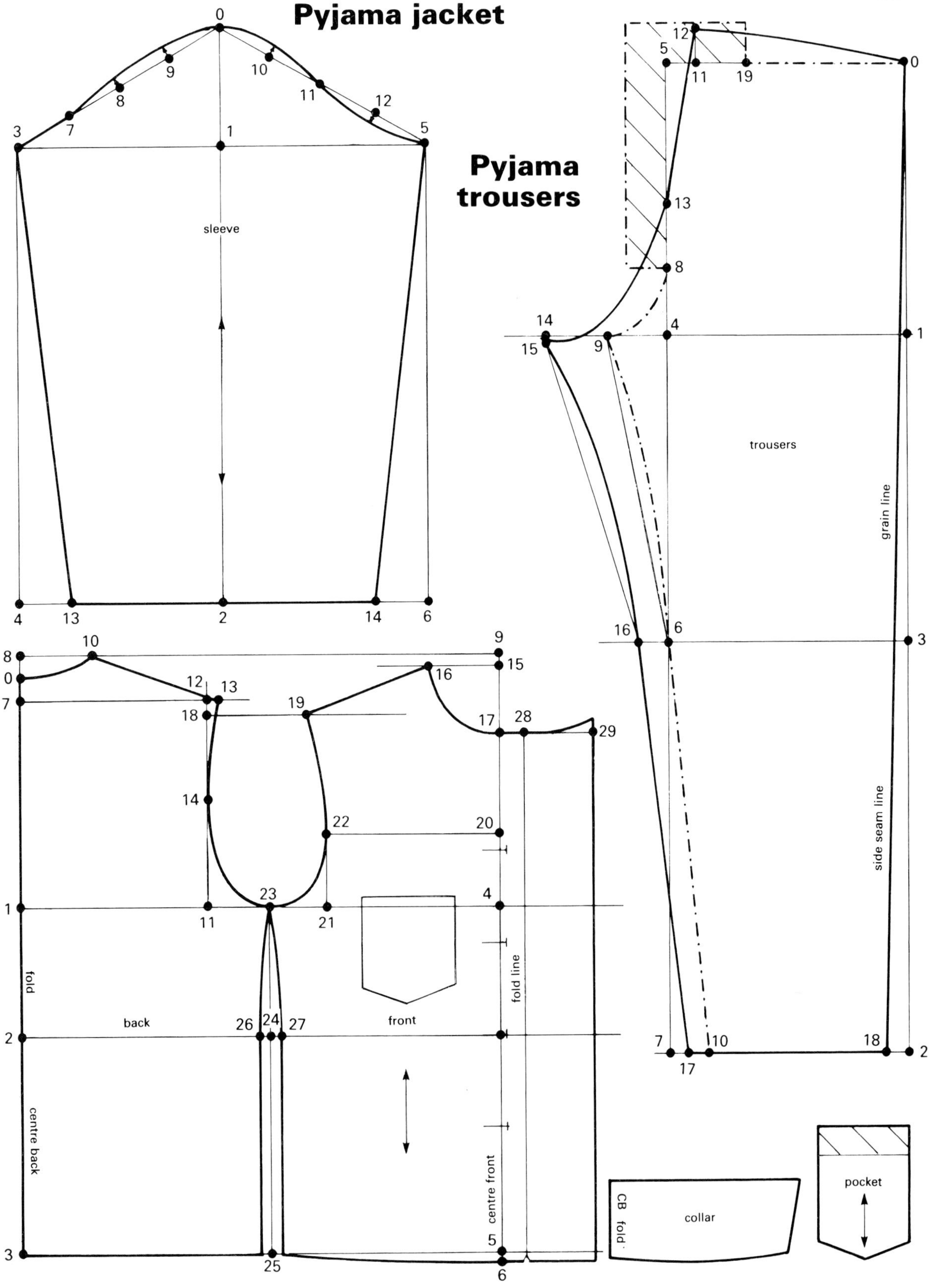

NIGHTWEAR An increasing amount of nightwear is made in jersey fabrics, particularly designs with the track suit or extended tee-shirt look. However the classic nightdress made in woven fabric is still popular. This type of nightwear must be designed to include extra fullness in the body.

1 CLASSIC NIGHTDRESS WITH YOKE (BOUND NECKLINE)

Trace off dress block and one-piece sleeve block. Extend body sections to required length. Mark points A, B, C, D at neck points, E and F at sleeve pitch points, G and H at position of sleeve gathers. Mark J and K at underarm. Join J and K to hem line.

Back A–L the measurement A–B minus 2cm; square down.

Front Draw in yoke shape. Trace off lower section. Mark point M on centre front. M–N is position of gathers.

M–P The measurement M–N; square down.

Front yoke Trace off front yoke. Mark buttonholes, button stand. Mark fold line (yoke is self-faced).

Sleeve Mark Q and R at pitch points on sleeve.

Q–S The measurement E–G on back section.

R–T The measurement F–H on front section.

Mark U and V at underarm points. Cut up centre line of sleeve and open 4cm–6cm at sleeve head, 2cm–3cm at hem line. Raise sleeve head 1cm.

Trace round pattern. Add 4cm to hem line for casing.

2 SLEEVELESS ADAPTATION (BOUND NECKLINE)

Body sections Construct body sections of classic nightdress to the knee line.

Front yoke Trace off front yoke. Mark fold line at centre front (yoke is self-faced).

Neck tie Extend neck binding to make the ties.

Note This design is often decorated with lace or narrow frilling made from same or contrasting fabric.

BATHROBE OR EASY-FITTING DRESSING GOWN

Trace off overgarment block and one-piece sleeve. Draw in finished length with curved front hem line.

Back and front Construct the basic kimono block (ref. 17, page 46).

Construct deep dolman sleeve (ref. 19, page 46).

Square down from new underarm point.

Add 2.5cm flare to hem on both side seams.

Facing and collar The design has a wrap over front. Add 5cm to centre front line instead of button stand.

Mark A at break point.

Complete the instructions for a simple roll collar (ref. 9, page 56).

Pocket Draw in pocket shape on front body section.

Trace off pocket; add 3cm to top edge for facing.

Belt Construct belt; B–C twice width required; C–D ½ waist measurement plus 35cm. Mark fold line.

1 Classic nightdress with yoke

2 Yoke for sleeveless adaptation

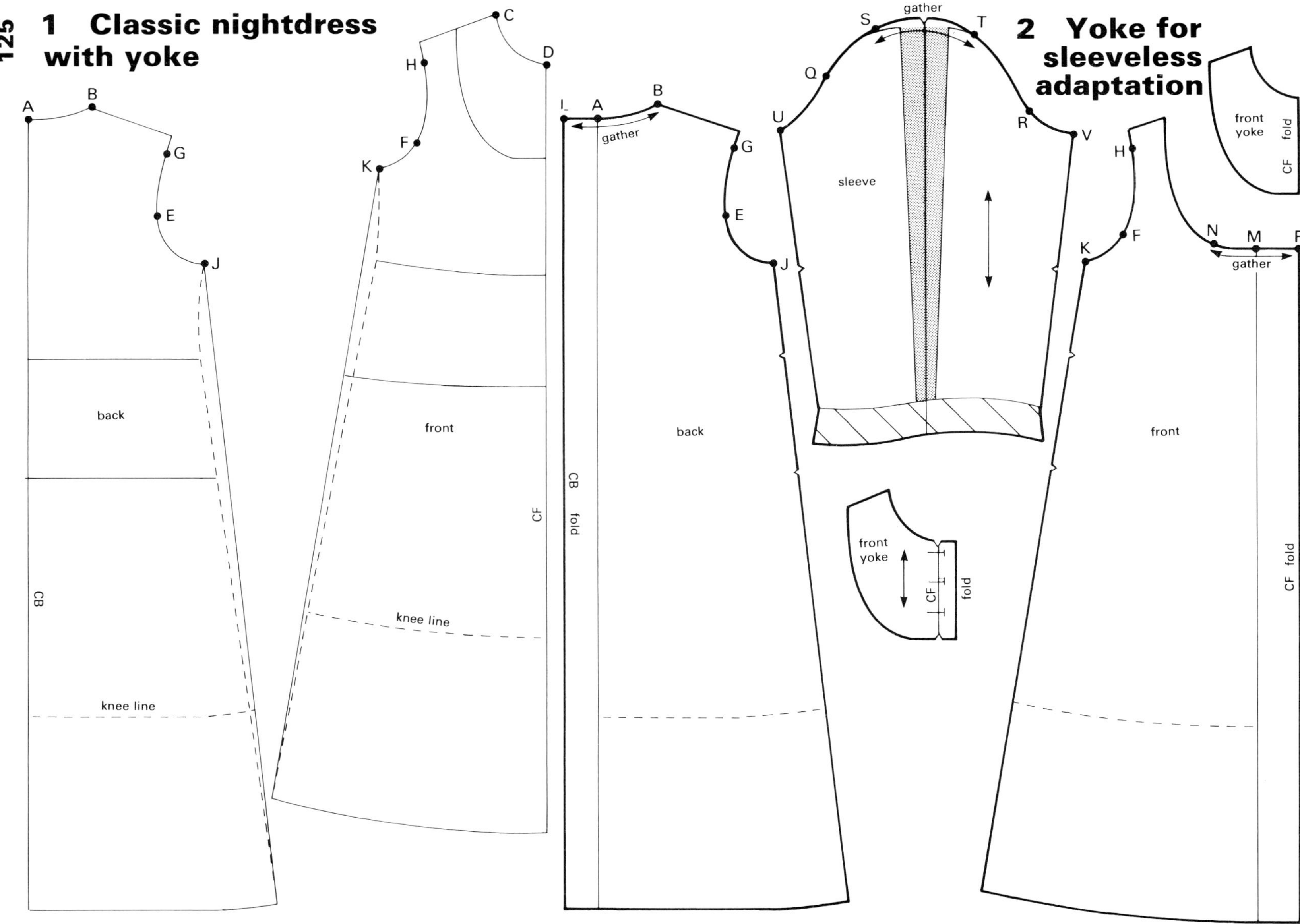

Bathrobe or easy-fitting dressing gown

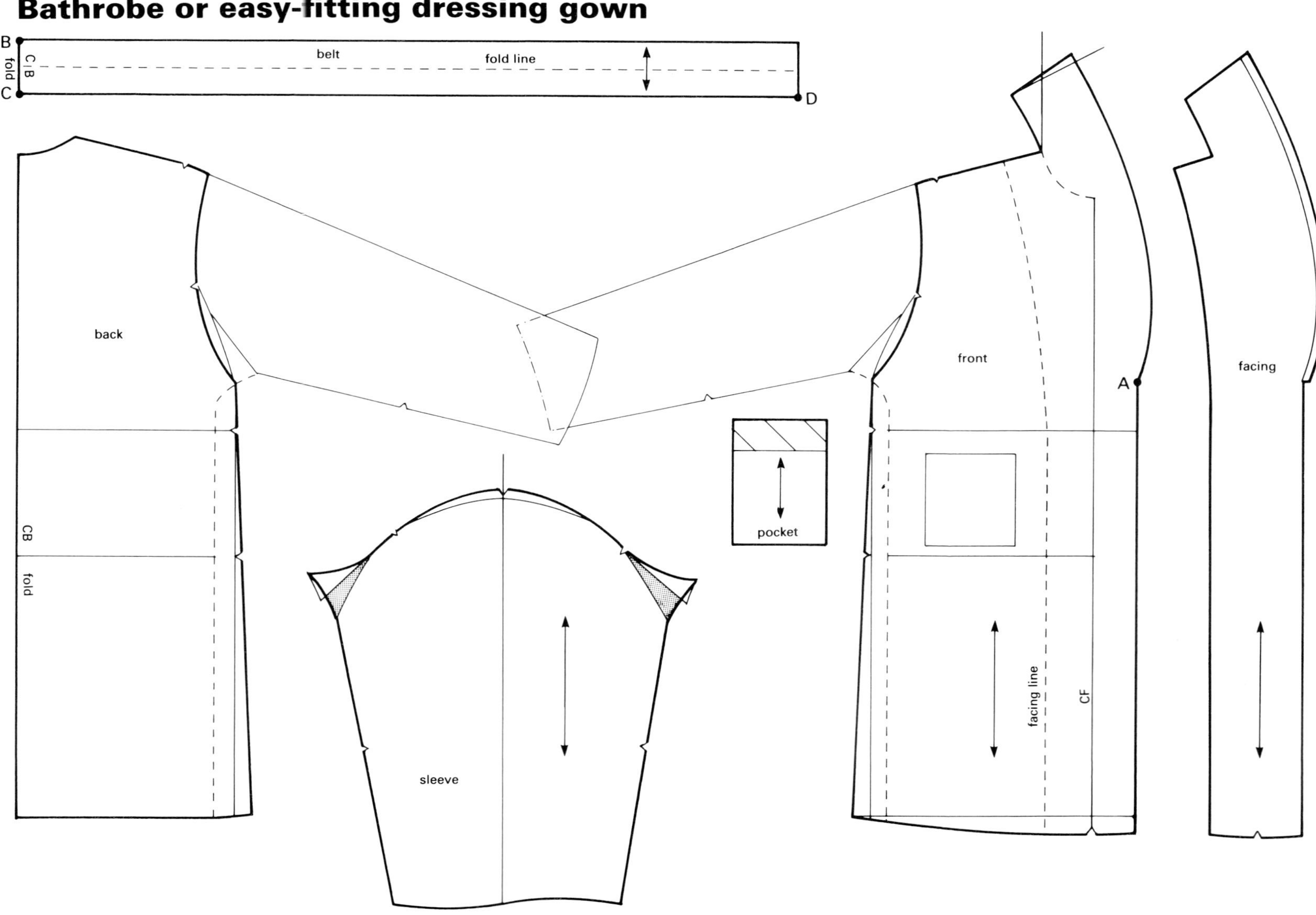

9 THE BASIC BLOCKS AND SIZE CHARTS – GIRLS (DEVELOPING FIGURES)

Approximate age 11–14 years

Body measurements

Girls (developing figures) 146cm–164cm height
Approximate age 11–14 years

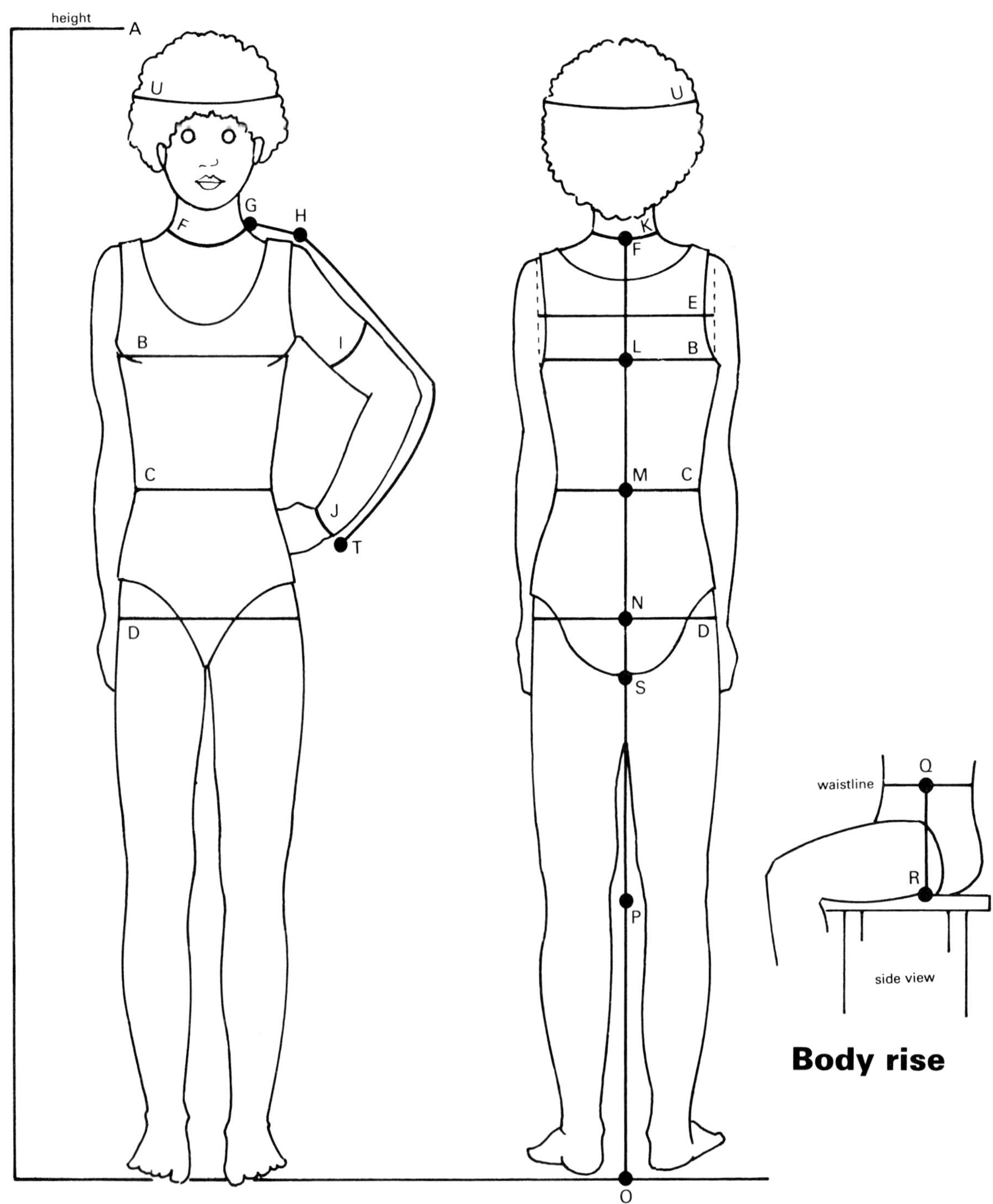

Body rise

Standard Body Measurements

Girls (developing figures), 146cm–164cm height: approx. age 11–14 years

The size charts and blocks in this section are constructed for girls who are in the process of figure development. They are usually growing fast and experiencing quite rapid changes in their measurements. The blocks are particularly concerned with the size of the bust; they are constructed for bust shapes A and B (girls who have reached mature size C require blocks constructed for women).

At this period of development the increasing variance in the bust sizes of girls in a height group means that the customer needs to refer to bust and hip sizes as well as height. Most manufacturers include this additional information on the labels from 146cm height.

INDIVIDUAL BLOCKS
Read the section on methods of measuring body dimensions and drafting the blocks for individual figures, page 12.

The dart size should relate to the shape of the bust:
Stage A – use a dart size of 2cm–3cm;
Stage B – use a dart size of 4cm–5cm;
Stage C – the blocks in this book are unsuitable for mature figures (use blocks constructed for women).

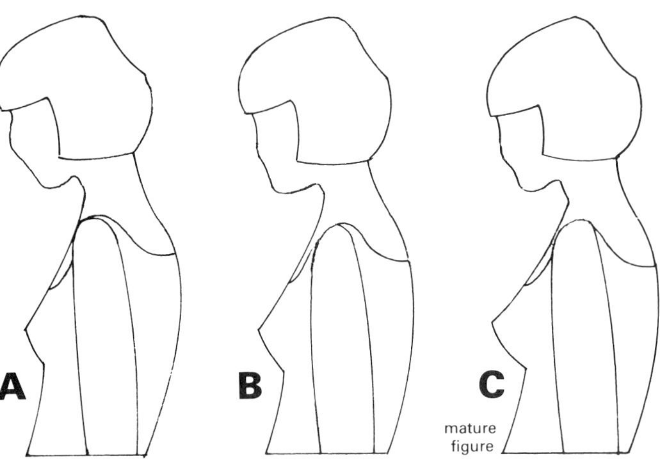

A	HEIGHT	146	152	158	164
APPROXIMATE AGE		11 –	– – –	– – –	– 14
B	BUST	78	81	84	87
C	WAIST	65	66	67	68
D	HIP	83	86	89	92
E	ACROSS BACK	31	32.2	33.4	34.6
F	NECK SIZE	33	34	35	36
G–H	SHOULDER	11	11.4	11.8	12.2
	DART	2	3	4	5
I	UPPER ARM	23.2	24	24.8	25.6
J	WRIST	15.2	15.6	16	16.4
K–L	SCYE DEPTH	18.4	19	19.6	20.2
K–M	NECK TO WAIST	33.8	35.2	36.6	38
M–N	WAIST TO HIP	17.6	18.4	19.2	20
K–O	CERVICAL HEIGHT	123.6	129	134.4	139.8
M–P	WAIST TO KNEE	50	52	54	56
Q–R	BODY RISE	24	25	26	27
S–O	INSIDE LEG	68	71	74	76
H–T	SLEEVE LENGTH	54	56	58	59
U	HEAD CIRCUMFERENCE	55.2	55.6	56	56.4
Extra measurements (garments)					
CUFF SIZE, TWO-PIECE SLEEVE		13	13.3	13.6	13.9
CUFF SIZE, SHIRTS		19	20	20.5	21
TROUSER BOTTOM WIDTH		20	20.5	21	21.5
JEANS BOTTOM WIDTH		18	18.5	19	19.5

The Bodice Block

For girls, sizes 146cm–164cm height

The relationship between height and bust development can vary considerably during puberty, therefore the dart size is only a general guide to the average figure.
When drafting for individual figures the dart size which relates to the correct stage of development should be chosen. If a girl has a fully developed figure an adult block will be required.

MEASUREMENTS REQUIRED TO DRAFT THE BLOCK
(e.g. size 158cm height)
Refer to the size chart (page 129) for standard measurements.

Bust	84cm
Across back	33.4cm
Neck size	35cm
Shoulder	11.8cm
Neck to waist	36.6cm
Scye depth	19.6cm
Dart	4cm
Waist to hip	19.2cm

Body sections
Square both ways from 0.

0 – 1 Neck to waist plus 1.5cm; square across.
1 – 2 Waist to hip; square across.
0 – 3 ½ bust plus 5cm; square down to 4 and 5 (e.g. 158cm height (84 ÷ 2) + 5 = 47).
0 – 6 1.5cm.
6 – 7 Scye depth plus 1cm; square across to 8.
6 – 9 ½ measurement 6–7; square out.
6 –10 ¼ scye depth minus 2cm; square out.
0 –11 ⅕ neck size minus 0.2cm; draw in neck curve.
7 –12 ½ across back plus 0.5cm; square up, mark point 13.
11–14 Shoulder measurement plus 0.8cm ease.
3 –15 ⅕ neck size minus 0.7cm.
3 –16 ⅕ neck size minus 0.2cm; draw in neck curve.
16–17 ½ measurement 8–16;
sizes 146cm–152cm height plus 1.5cm
158cm–164cm height plus 1.75cm;
square across.
8 –18 The measurement 7–12 plus 0.5cm, plus ¼ dart measurement; square up to 19.
14–20 Sizes 146cm–152cm height 1cm
158cm–164cm height 1.25cm;
square across.
15–21 The measurement of the dart.
21–22 Shoulder measurement; draw front shoulder line to touch the line from 20.
8 –23 ½ measurement 8–18.
23–24 1.5cm; join 15–24 and 21–24 to form dart.
18–25 ½ measurement 12–18; square down to 26 and 27.

Draw in armscye shape as shown; measurement of curve: from 12 2.5cm; from 18 2cm.
There is 0.8cm ease on back shoulder, this can be eased into front shoulder during making-up or a dart can be constructed.

11–28 ½ measurement 11–14; square down 5cm from the line 11–14. Construct a dart 0.8cm wide on this line.

Waisted dresses
4 –29 1cm; join 1–29 with a curve.

Sleeve
Draft a one-piece sleeve (page 30) or a two-piece sleeve (page 32) to fit armscye measurement.

THE DART
The bodice block for developing figures can be used for most children's wear styles. The dart position has to be changed depending on the style. For most designs the dart can be swung to the underarm position.
Method Draw a line from the centre of the side seam to the bust point. Cut up the line. Close the original dart and secure with tape. Shorten the dart by 2cm. For more advanced methods of changing the dart position read the section on dart manipulation in *Metric Pattern Cutting* or other books concerned with women's wear. Because the blocks for girls with developing figures have bust darts they can be adapted easily into the more mature designs shown in these books.

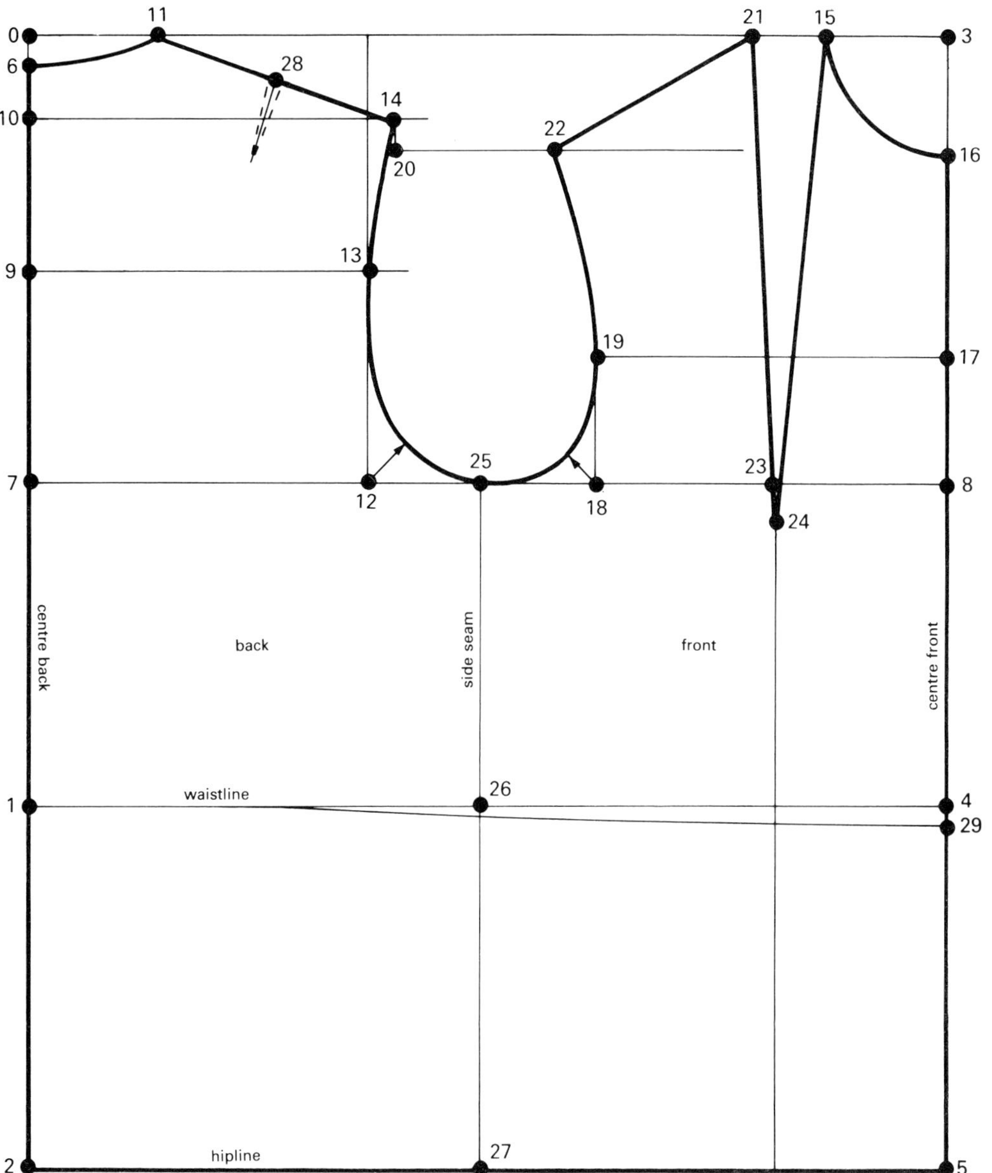
0
11
21
15
3
6
28
10
14
22
20
16
9
13
19
17
7
12
25
18
23
24
8
centre back
back
side seam
front
centre front
1
waistline
26
4
29
2
hipline
27
5

Shaping the Bodice Block

Note Standard ease allowed on a shaped waisted dress is 6cm.

SHAPED BODICE BLOCK TO WAISTLINE

Trace off bodice block to waistline.
Mark points 1, 7, 8, 12, 18, 24, 25, 29 on the bodice block.

7–A ½ measurement 7–12; square down to B.
Square down from 24–C. A–D and 24–E 2cm.

1–F ¼ waist:
sizes 146cm–152cm height plus 4cm
158cm–164cm height plus 4.5cm.

29–G ¼ waist:
sizes 146cm–152cm height plus 4.5cm
158cm–164cm height plus 5cm.

Draw in curved side seams from 25–F and 25–G.
Construct back dart on the line D–B:
sizes 146cm–152cm height 2.5cm dart
158cm–164cm height 3cm dart.

Construct front dart on the line E–C:
sizes 146cm–152cm height 3cm dart
158cm–164cm height 3.5cm dart.

SHAPED BODICE BLOCK TO HIPLINE

Trace off bodice block to hipline, omit point 29 and the line 26–27.
Complete instructions above for shaped bodice block.
Extend the line A–B to H. H–J 5cm.
Extend the line 24–C to K. K–L 7cm.
Complete darts as shown.
M is mid-way between 2–5.
Complete back side seam 25, F, M and front side seam 25, G, M with slightly curved hiplines.

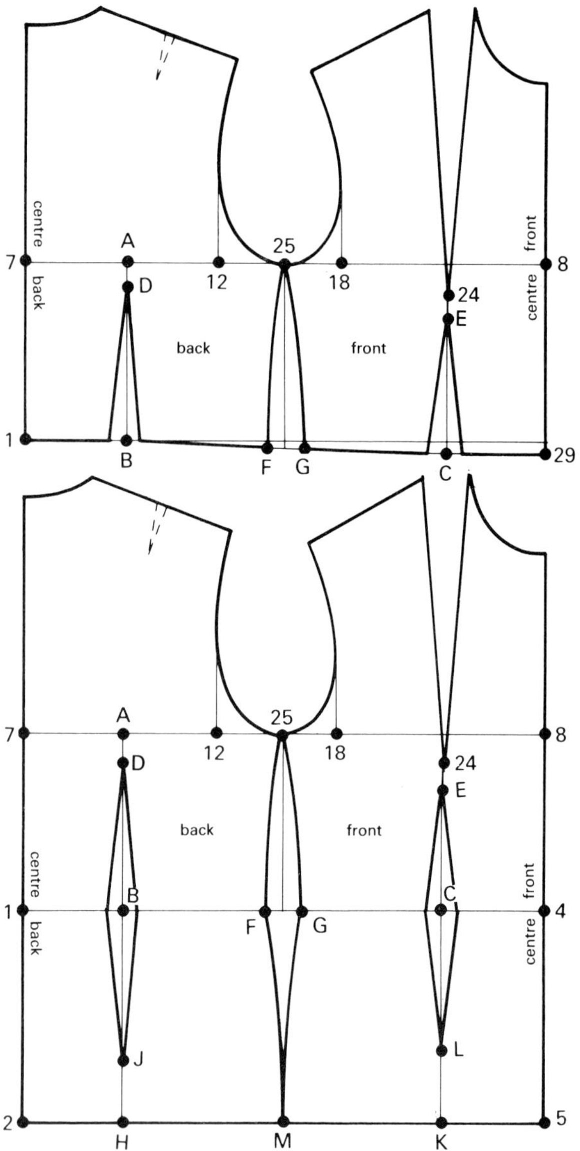

The Dress Block

Trace round standard bodice block to hipline.
Mark side seam to waistline only. Mark points 2, 5, 7, 8, 12, 18, 25, 26.

5–A ½ measurement 2–5; square down to B.
26–C 1.5cm; B–D 3cm. Draw in back side seam 25, C, A, D.

Curve 25–C inwards 0.25cm, curve C–A outwards slightly.

26–E 2cm; B–F 3cm. Draw in front side seam 25, E, A, F.

Curve 25–E inwards 0.25cm. Curve E–A outwards slightly.
Shape up hem line 0.25cm at D and F.

Extra waist shaping

Construct back and front darts as shown on this page – 'Shaped bodice block to hipline'.

Extra flare

Drop perpendicular lines from the base of back and front darts on shoulder. Cut up lines.
Open block at hem line the required amount.
It is usual to include more flare in the front section of the block.

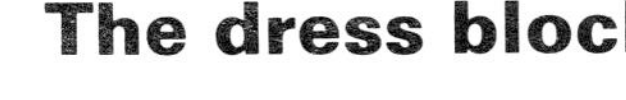

The dress block

7
12
25
18
8
C
E
26
back
front
2
A
5
centre back
centre front
F
B
D

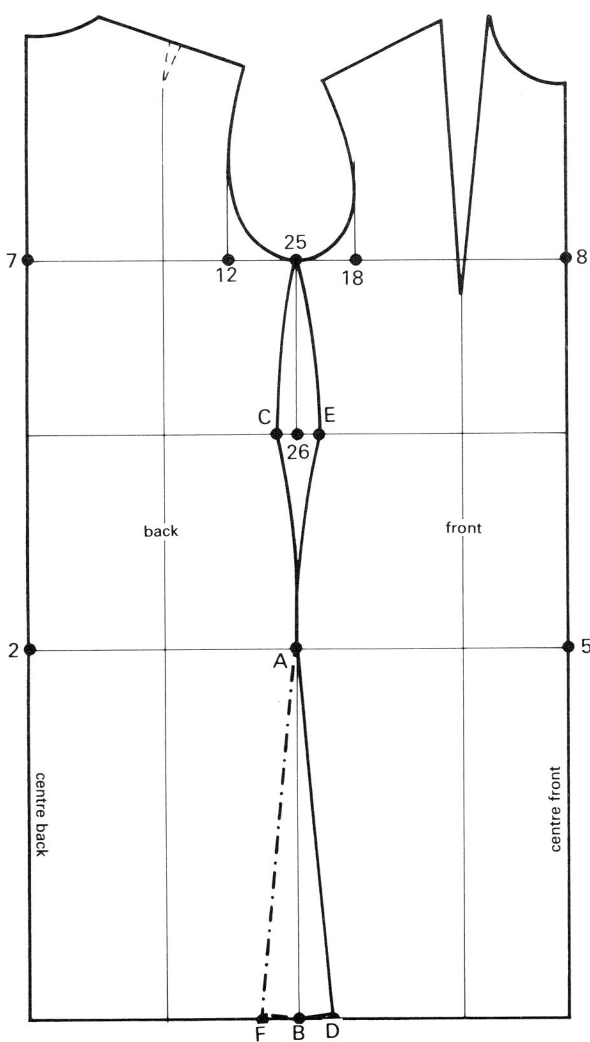

The dress block with extra flare

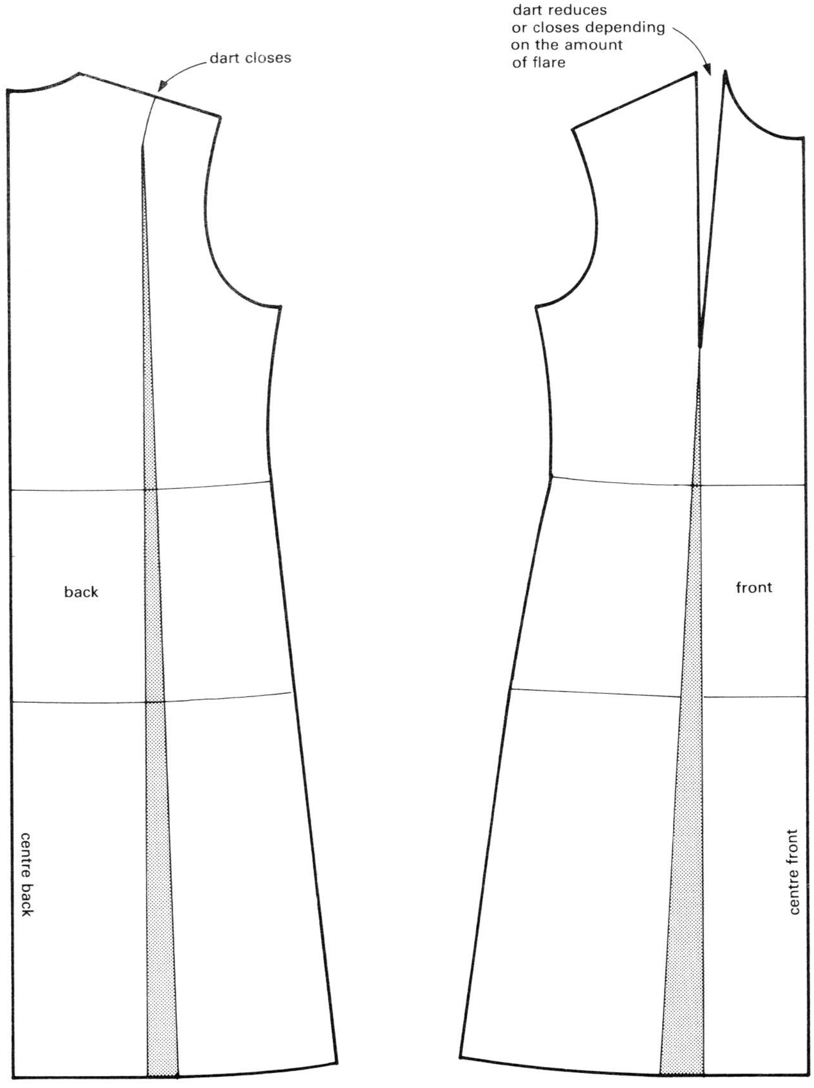

dart closes
dart reduces
or closes depending
on the amount
of flare
back
front
centre back
centre front

The Overgarment Block

For girls, sizes 146cm–164cm height

The overgarment block is a base for casual wear designs; i.e. anoraks and duffle coats. These garments require more ease in the body so that they can be worn over trousers, skirts and sweaters.
MEASUREMENTS REQUIRED TO DRAFT THE BLOCK
(e.g. size 158cm height)
Refer to the size chart (page 129) for standard measurements.

Bust	84cm
Across back	33.4cm
Neck size	35cm
Shoulder	11.8cm
Neck to waist	36.6cm
Scye depth	19.6cm
Dart	4cm
Waist to hip	19.2cm

Body sections

Square both ways from 0.

0 – 1 Nape to waist plus 2cm; square across.
0 – 2 ½ bust plus 10cm; square down, mark point 3 on waistline.
0 – 4 2cm.
4 – 5 Scye depth plus 3.5cm; square across to 6.
4 – 7 ½ measurement 4–5; square out.
4 – 8 ¼ scye depth; square out.
5 – 9 ½ across back plus 1.5cm; square up to 10 and 11.
11–12 2cm; square out.
0 –13 ⅕ neck size plus 0.3cm; draw in neck curve.
13–14 Shoulder measurement plus 1.75cm.
2 –15 ⅕ neck size minus 0.2cm.
2 –16 ⅕ neck size plus 0.3cm; draw in neck curve.
16–17 ½ measurement 6–16 plus 2cm; square across.
6 –18 The measurement 5–9 plus 0.5cm plus ¼ dart measurement.
15–20 Dart measurement.
Join 20 to 11 with a straight line.
20–21 The measurement 13–14 minus 0.5cm.
21–22 1.5cm; join 20–22 with slight curve.
6 –23 ½ measurement 6–18; square up 1cm to 24.
Join 15 to 24 and 20 to 24.
18–25 ½ measurement 9–18 plus 0.5cm; square down.
Mark point 26 on waistline.
Draw in armscye shape as shown, to touch points: 3 cm from 9 and 2.5cm from 18.
4 –27 Finished length; square across to 28 and 29.
29–30 1cm; join 28–30 with a curved line.
1 –31 waist to hip; square across.

Note There is 0.5cm ease on the back shoulder.

Sleeve

Draft a one-piece sleeve (page 30) or two-piece sleeve (page 32) to fit armscye measurement.

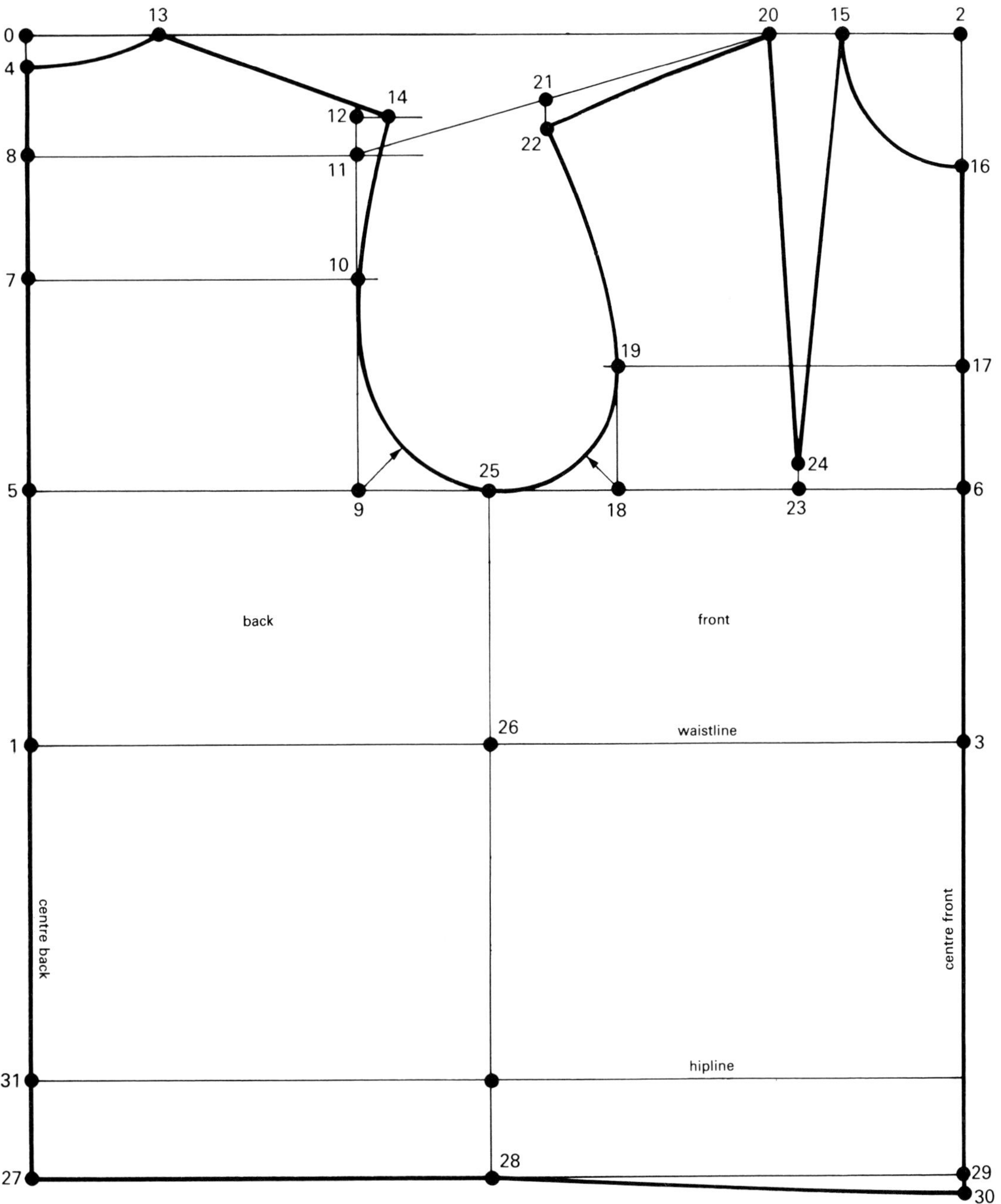
0
13
20
15
2
4
21
14
12
22
8
11
16
10
7
19
17
24
25
5
9
18
23
6
back
front
26
waistline
1
3
centre back
centre front
hipline
31
28
27
29
30

The Trouser Block

For girls, sizes 146cm–164cm height

Note 1 The bottom of the waistband of the girls' trouser block sits on the waistline.
Note 2 There is 1cm ease in the waistline of the trousers. The waistline of trousers should always be eased onto the waistband.

MEASUREMENTS REQUIRED TO DRAFT THE BLOCK
(e.g. size 158cm height)
Refer to the size charts (pages 19 and 129) for standard measurements.

Hip	89cm
Waist	67cm
Body rise	26cm
Inside leg	74cm
Trouser bottom width	21cm
Waist to hip	19.2cm

Front
Square down and across from 0.

0 – 1 Body rise; square up.
0 – 2 Waist to hip; square across.
1 – 3 Inside leg; square across.
1 – 4 ½ measurement 1–3 minus 4cm; square across.
1 – 5 1/12 hip plus 1.5cm; square up to 6 and 7.
6 – 8 ¼ hip plus 0.5cm; square up.
5 – 9 1/16 hip plus 0.5cm.
7 –10 1cm; join 10–6 and 6–9 with a curve touching a point 2.75cm from 5.
10–11 ¼ waist:
sizes 146cm–152cm height plus 1.6cm
158cm–164cm height plus 2cm.
3 –12 ½ trouser bottom width minus 0.5cm.
4 –13 The measurement 3–12 plus 1cm.
3 –14 ½ trouser bottom width minus 0.5cm.
4 –15 The measurement 3–14 plus 1cm.

Draw side seam through points 11, 8, 13, 12; curve hipline outwards 0.25cm.
Draw inside leg seam 9, 15, 14. Curve 9–15 inwards 0.75cm.
Construct a dart on the line from 0:
sizes 146cm–152cm height 7.5cm long, 1.4cm wide
158cm–164cm height 8.5cm long, 1.8cm wide.

Back

5 –16 ¼ measurement 1–5; square up to 17 on hipline, 18 on waistline.
16–19 ½ measurement 16–18.
18–20 1.5cm.
20–21 1.5cm.
21–22 ¼ waist:
sizes 146cm–152cm height plus 2.7cm
158cm–164cm height plus 3.5cm.

Join 21–22 to touch horizontal line from 0.

9 –23 ½ measurement 5–9.
23–24 0.25cm.

Join 21–19 and 19–24 with a curve touching a point 4cm from 16.

17–25 ¼ hip plus 1.25cm.
12–26 1cm.
13–27 1cm.
14–28 1cm.
15–29 1cm.

Draw in side seam through points 22, 25, 27, 26.
Curve hipline outwards 0.25cm; 25–27 inwards 0.25cm.
Draw inside leg seam 24, 29, 28. Curve 24–29 inwards 1.25cm.
Divide the line 21–22 into three parts. Mark points 30 and 31. Using the line 21–22 square down from 30 and 31.
Sizes 146cm–152cm height 30–32 10cm; 31–33 8cm
158cm–164cm height 30–32 12cm; 31–33 10cm.
Construct darts on these lines:
sizes 146cm–152cm height 1.2cm wide
158cm–164cm height 1.6cm wide.
Curve hem line down 1cm at 3.4.

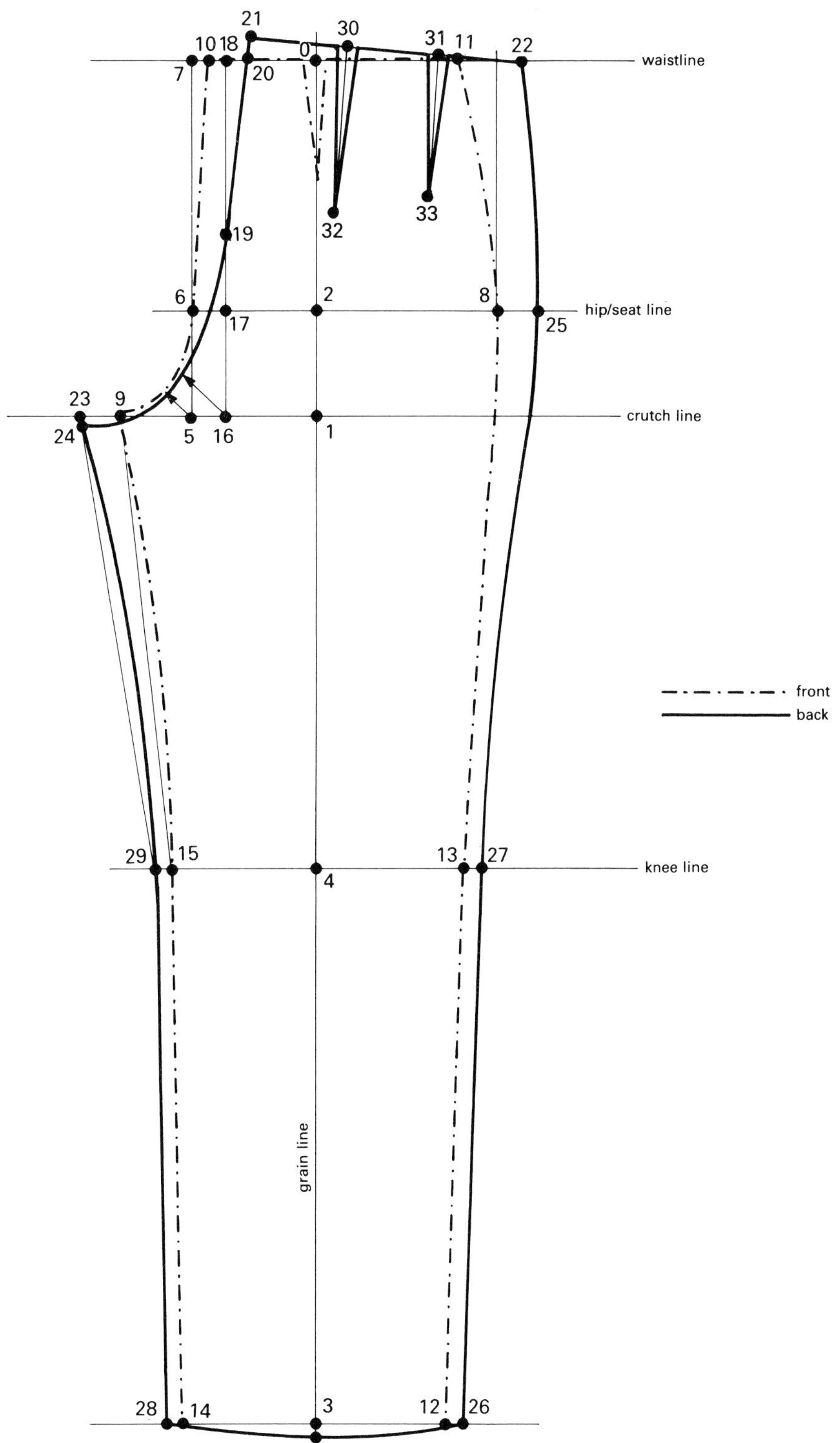
21
30
31
11
22
10
18
0
7
20
waistline
32
33
19
6
2
8
hip/seat line
17
25
23
9
crutch line
24
5
16
1
front
back
29
15
13
27
knee line
4
grain line
28
14
3
12
26

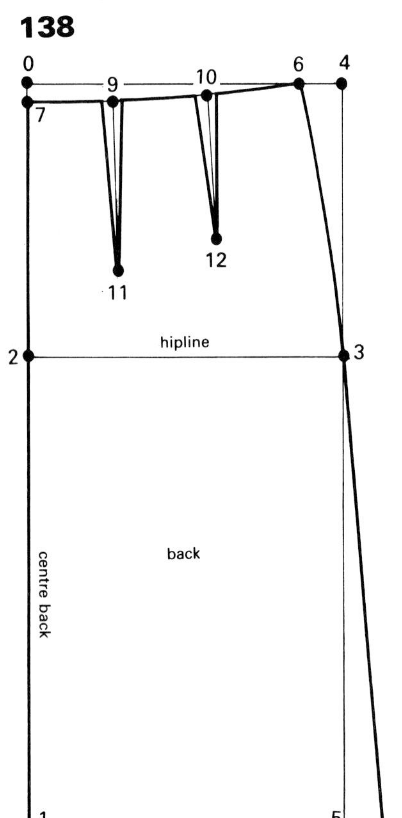

The Skirt Block

For girls, sizes 146cm–164cm height

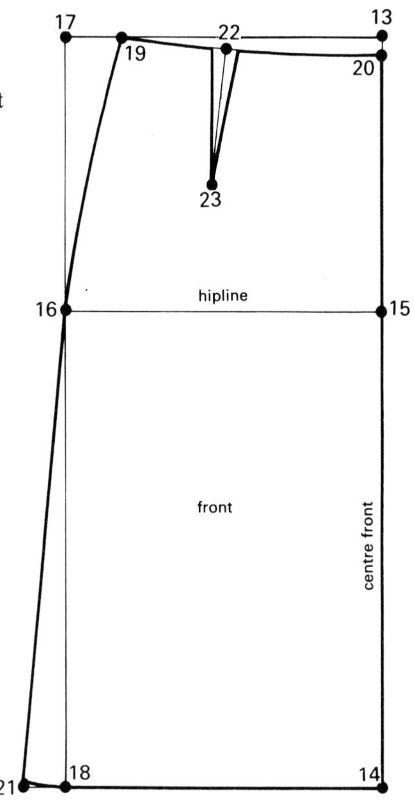

Note 1 There is 1cm casc in thc waistlinc of thc skirt. The waistline of the skirt should always be eased onto the waistband.

Note 2 The adaptation for the elasticated back waistband is shown on page 88, ref. 3.

MEASUREMENTS REQUIRED TO DRAFT THE BLOCK
(e.g. size 158cm height)
Refer to the size chart (pages 19 and 129) for standard measurements.

Waist	67cm
Hip	89cm
Waist to hip	19.2cm
Skirt length	54cm

Back
Square both ways from 0.

0 – 1 Skirt length required plus 1cm; square across.
0 – 2 Waist to hip plus 1cm; square across.
2 – 3 ¼ hip plus 1.5cm; square up to 4 and down to 5.
0 – 6 ¼ waist:
sizes 146cm–152cm height plus 2.6cm
158cm–164cm height plus 3.4cm.
0 – 7 1cm; join 6–7 with a curve.
5 – 8 3cm. Draw in side seam 6, 3, 8; curve hipline outwards 0.4cm; curve hem line 0.25cm at 8.

Dividc thc linc 6–7 into thrcc parts. Mark points 9 and 10. Square down from the line 6–7.
Sizes 146cm–152cm height 9–11 10cm; 10–12 8cm
158cm–164cm height 9–11 12cm; 10–12 10cm.
Construct darts on these lines:
sizes 146cm–152cm height 1.2cm wide
158cm–164cm height 1.6cm wide.

Front
Square up both ways from 13.

13–14 Skirt length required plus 1cm; square across.
13–15 Waist to hip plus 1cm; square across.
15–16 ¼ hip plus 1cm; square up to 17 and down to 18.
13–19 ¼ waist:
sizes 146cm–152cm height plus 1.8cm
158cm–164cm height plus 2.3cm.
13–20 1cm; join 19–20 with a curve.
18–21 3cm. Draw in side seam 19, 16, 21; curve hipline outwards 0.25cm. Curve hem line 0.25cm at 21.
19–22 ½ measurement 19–20 minus 2cm; square down from the line 19–20.
22–23 Sizes 146cm–152cm height 8cm
158cm–164cm height 9cm.

Construct the dart:
sizes 146cm–152cm height 1.5cm wide
158cm–164cm height 2cm wide.

10 DEVELOPING DESIGNS

The adaptations shown in this book are mainly classic designs. They were deliberately chosen because they are a base from which more original designs can be developed. Shapes for children's clothes are affected by fashion, and students should be encouraged to design not only different shapes, but new making-up techniques which are an integral part of the total design. A range of designs is shown on the following pages which illustrates this point. The basic block which would be required to draft the design is noted.

The basic trouser block

The basic trouser block

The easy-fitting trouser block

The easy-fitting trouser block

The easy-fitting trouser block

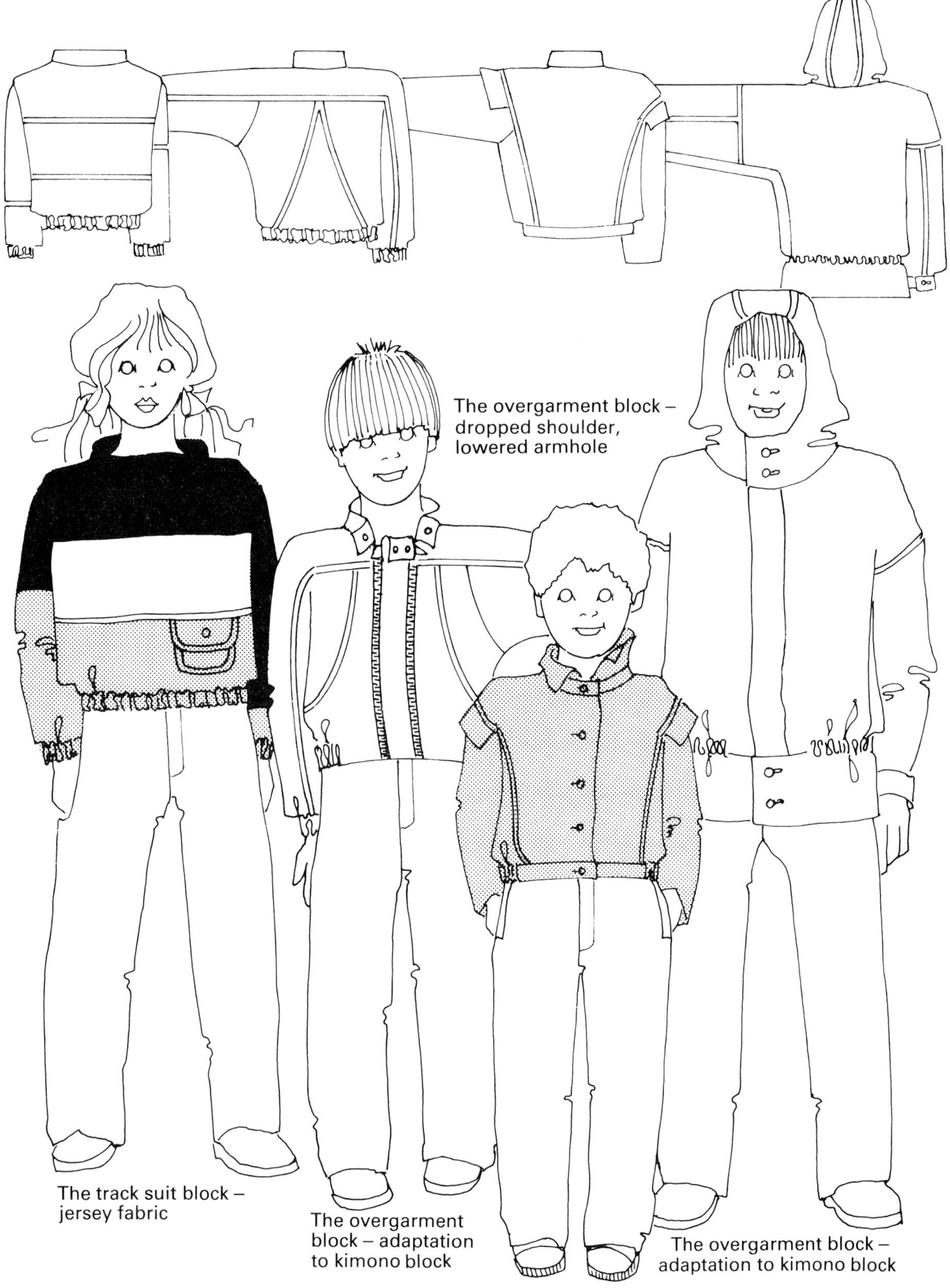

The overgarment block – dropped shoulder, lowered armhole

The track suit block – jersey fabric

The overgarment block – adaptation to kimono block

The overgarment block – adaptation to kimono block

The bodice and skirt blocks – adaptation to kimono block

The dress block

The dress block

The dress block

Bibliography

British Standards Institution (1982) *Specification for Size Designation of Children's and Infants' Wear,* BS 3728. London.

Cameron, N. (1978) 'Methods of auxological anthropometry.' In: *Human Growth, Post-natal Growth*, Volume 2, *eds* Faulkner, F. and Tanner, J. M. London: Bailliere and Tindall.

Carter, N. D. (1980) *Development of Growth and Ageing*. London: Croom Helm.

Kunick, P. (1967) *Sizing, Pattern Construction and Grading for Women's and Children's Garments.* London: Philip Kunick Ltd.

Marshall, W. A. (1970) 'Physical growth and development.' *Brennamann's Practice of Pediatrics*, Volume 1, Chapter 3. Maryland: Harper and Row Publishers Inc.

Marshall, W. A. (1977) *Human Growth and its Disorders*. London: Academic Press.

Marshall, W. A. (1978) 'Puberty.' In: *Human Growth, Post-natal Growth*, Volume 2, *eds* Faulkner, F. and Tanner, J. M. London: Bailliere and Tindall.

Rodwell, W (1970) 'Towards metric sizing.' *Clothing Institute Journal*, **XVI**, Nos 2 and 3, 1968. Supplementary notes.

Tanner, J. M. (1955) *Growth at Adolescence*. London: Blackwell Scientific Publications.

Tanner, J. M. (1960) *Human Growth*, Volume III. London: Pergamon Press.

Tanner, J. M., Whitehouse, R. H. and Takaishi, M. (1966) 'Standards from birth to maturity for height, weight, height velocity and weight velocity: British children, 1965.' *Arch. Dis. Child*, 1966, **41**, 454 and 613.